BROKEN PIECES

(and the fun things you can do with them)

A MEMOIR BY
REEDY GIBBS

Publishing Services provided by Paper Raven Books LLC
Printed in the United States of America
First Printing, 2023

Paperback ISBN 979-8-9894421-0-2
Hardback ISBN 979-8-9894421-1-9
Ebook ISBN 979-8-9894421-2-6

To whom it may concern,

In some of these chapters, I have changed a name or two, of people or places, so as not to embarrass or piss anybody off. If you do recognize a person I've written about here, but they have a different name than you, it may not be you. Or it may. But no one will ever know about your 'questionable behavior', it will remain our little secret!

Thank you for your curiosity. I hope you enjoy the journey.

"One of the fun things you can do with broken pieces is to glue them into something else, a new life against the life that had been shattered. It takes great courage and fortitude and faith in one's dream to turn one's dream into action. The writing in this memoir is superb, coming from the deepest and truest voice, with an unerring eye for detail, and the ability to create cinematic moments that jump off the page better than any movie. Reedy Gibbs is the real thing, an artist with heart, an actress with conviction, and a writer with a gift for language that will inspire any reader to find power and strength in breakage and the courage to become whole again."

— Jack Grapes, The Naked Eye

Contents

PART ONE

CHAPTER ONE

1955

Ballet Class

I WAS OUT OF BREATH AND SWEATING UP A STORM WHEN I OPENED the church door. Then the wind hit me like a bucket of ice water. And leaves were flying everywhere—burgundy-red and orange and gold, it was magical. I bet Louisville, Kentucky had the most wonderful autumns of anywhere. The air smelled like "heaven on earth" too. That's what Momma always said. We loved fall the best.

She had just picked me up from my first ballet class of the season. I never wanted them to end, would've kept dancing the whole rest of the day if it had been up to me. Ballet was the one thing I did best. I loved it more than anything, from the very first time Momma took me to one when I was only three years old.

Last spring when Momma picked me up after class, Mrs. Wooten had a talk with her. "Your daughter is a natural, Mrs. Gibbs," she said. I got to feeling funny, them talking about me like I wasn't there. So, I went and practiced some new steps, pretended I wasn't listening. "Reedy has the perfect dancer's body," Mrs. Wooten said. "She's got the grace of a true ballerina and a strong arch and a perfect point. She simply needs to apply herself more."

I heard that from my teachers at school. It never made any sense to me. I thought I applied myself just fine—whatever that meant. I hated school, just wasn't any good at it. I couldn't read fast enough for one thing, always felt like the class dummy. Every other kid would be finished with the assignment for the day, and there I'd sit not even halfway done. Another problem was, soon as I'd get home from school and try to do my homework, I'd have Packy to deal with.

Packy was my stupid big brother—except Momma told me he was a genius, so maybe stupid's the wrong word. All I knew was that he made *everything* harder for me.

Packy was the first born of all us six kids, and I was the last. I swear to goodness his favorite thing in the world to do was devil the living daylights out of me. He was old too, seventeen years older than me. Momma told me that Packy had something wrong with his brain. She called him moody, but if you had asked me, I would've said he was just plain cuckoo.

I hopped into Momma's yellow, Buick convertible, the top was down as usual even though it was pretty chilly out. "How was your first class, sweetie?" Momma was wearing her old mustard-colored coat and blue scarf, and her gray curls were all wind-blown. She told me once that she wished she could have been a dancer when she grew up. She wrote lots of sweet poems, though. Poems about God and nature and animals and us kids, all the things she loved the most.

"It was so fun, Momma!" then she went to put the top up. "Aww, Momma, do you have to put it up? It's so pretty and windy out. Can't we leave it down?"

"No, honey." She shook her head. "Wish we could, but you're all sweaty, and I do not want you gettin' sick."

I missed ballet class so much all summer, on account of there weren't any. Everybody was off doing outdoor stuff while it was warm and sunny out.

"Mrs. Wooten taught us a new step today, and boy was it hard. But guess what? She said I did it best!"

"She did?" Momma smiled, and we drove off. "What's it called?"

"Um… tour j'eta, or something like that, and she made everybody watch me do it."

"Well, for goodness' sake." Momma patted my leg. "That's wonderful, sweetheart. You'll have to show it to me when we get home."

Momma was thrilled when I took to ballet so quick and that I loved it so much too. She told me it didn't matter that I had a hard time in school because that's not what I was made for. "God made you for dancing, honey," she said. "And drawing and other artistic things. Those are your special gifts. Some people just aren't made for sitting in classrooms all day memorizing stuff out of old books."

Then I smelled something so good. It was coming from outside, so I rolled down my window a little. A man was raking leaves onto a huge pile that was already on fire. "Look Momma!" I pointed to the man. She smiled. We watched and sniffed in the gray smoke as it curled up in the air. Then she slowed the car down, and we waved to the man. And he waved back.

Momma pulled into the driveway, and the car came to a bumpy stop. "Oh, and Mom, I did a pirouette almost perfect today, didn't even get a little dizzy because now I know how to spot."

"Really?" She turned off the engine. "See now, honey." She looked at me and leaned her head to one side. "You practiced like I told you to and—" I jumped out of the car and slammed the door behind me because I didn't want to hear the rest of what she was going to say.

I ran in the house and threw my books and coat on the floor in the foyer, so I could practice my new step before I showed it to Momma. I heard a sound behind me and about jumped out of my skin. When I turned around, there was Packy, just standing there looking at me with a smirk on his face. He was always doing mean things like that. He laughed, didn't even pretend like he wasn't glad he scared me so bad. But still, I could tell he was in one of his good moods. And he looked different. His hair was combed. It usually looked like he'd been sleeping on it all day long. He smelled good too, like soap instead of BO. Then I noticed that his face was smooth, and he had on a clean shirt.

Finally, Momma came in the front door out of breath. She was kind of heavy, you know, round like an apple. She moved slow most of the time because she got tired a lot. She took off her overcoat and hung it on the hook by the front door. The coat was worn out too, just like her. It had a couple of big buttons missing.

She turned around and pointed to my coat and stuff on the floor. "Reedy, where do your things go?"

"Yeah, OK, lemme show ya first. I'll put 'em away in a minute." I ran into the living room and shoved the coffee table out of the way to make room.

Then Momma told Packy, "She's going to show me a new step she learned. Her teacher said she did it beautifully."

"No, she said I did it better than anybody else in class. Even Norma!" Norma was two years older than me and really good at ballet.

"Uh-huh," Packy said. Then they both came into the living room and sat on the couch to watch me. I wasn't used to the new cleaned-up Packy. He looked like a different person, made my stomach feel funny. He was so much taller than Momma; she looked like a little kid sitting there next to him.

"What's it called?" Packy asked. I was getting myself ready to show them. "Your new move, does it have a name?"

"Oh, yeah, um, tour… something, I don't remember the whole name." I got into position, facing away, arms straight out, right foot pointing back—I had to think hard because the step was long and complicated, with kicks and turns. Plus, Packy was making me nervous. Then I did it—it was pretty good until the end when I landed on my butt. Packy smiled one of his mean smiles.

Momma clapped. "Oh my, how pretty!" I didn't have to do things perfect for Momma to be proud of me. She loved all the pictures I made for her no matter how messy they were. She always told me I was a fine artist.

"No, wait!" I said and ran back to the other side of the room because the step took up darn near the whole living room. I did it much better the second time, landed just right. The third and fourth times were near perfect. Each one got better and better. Momma clapped every time, and Packy kept smiling. I wanted to keep going.

"Mrs. Wooten is right, honey," Momma said while she struggled to get herself up off the couch. "You are a beautiful ballerina, sweetheart." Then she stood up. "Well, I've got to get dinner started." And she walked out of the living room.

Packy got up. "That was real pretty." Then he tipped his head like he wanted me to follow him into the TV room where the old upright piano was. Daddy bought it for Packy way back before I was born. Momma told me she got it for Packy so he could take piano lessons when he was little bitty. Said he was a natural, already playing whole songs by his third lesson. His teacher could hardly believe it. Sometimes, when he wasn't in one of his dark moods, he'd make up beautiful tunes for me to dance to. They sounded like real ballet music, the kind you'd hear an orchestra play.

That day, he played his piano for a long time while I danced. Sometimes, he'd turn his head to watch me, and I'd move closer so he could see my steps. Then he'd smile and nod. It was times like that I'd remember I loved him, and he loved me. I did all the steps I knew, and even some I made up. I did new steps too, and pirouettes and leaps, and all the steps I'd forgotten the names of. Packy played and played and I started to get tired, but I kept right on dancing because I knew he was playing just for me.

But then, all of a sudden, he stopped, so I stopped dancing and looked at him. Everything got real quiet. He put his hands on his knees and looked down. I leaned over to try to see if he was looking at something. Then I got scared. He just sat there a long time. I couldn't see his face, but I was pretty sure he wasn't happy anymore. I knew better than to talk to him or go near him or even move when it happened. I always wondered why he'd change so quick like that.

Sometimes, he'd be laughing at a show on TV or at something else funny, or just be eating. Then, he'd just stop whatever he was doing, and his brow would furrow, and his eyes would go dark.

There were times when Momma would sneak a pill into Packy's coffee in the morning when he wasn't looking. They were the pills his psychiatrist had given him that he wouldn't take. And when he'd drink the coffee Momma made for him with the pill in it, he'd be happy the whole day. I couldn't figure out why he refused to take something that would make him feel better.

Slowly, Packy turned around. When he saw me, and looked startled, like he didn't remember I was even there. He stood up and stared right at me—his eyes narrowed. He looked like he was godawful mad at somebody and wanted to hurt them in the worst way. So, I backed away real slow like. Then he walked to the stairs and ran up them two at a time.

Packy's room was on the third floor. I'd never gone up there because my sister Sally, told me it was filthy and full of animals and snakes in cages, and the place smelled like dead things.

I started to shake—sat down on the carpet and scooted myself back into the corner near the front door. I pulled my knees up and held on tight. I wondered why it always happened so sudden like, and why he always ran away? I was afraid for my brother, sad, I knew he couldn't help it.

CHAPTER TWO

1955

Mary's Dolls

I just loved Mary's dolls. Mary was my neighbor who lived across the street, and her dolls always looked brand-spanking new even though they weren't. She was nice too, but I was only eight years old, and Mary was ten and really smart, so she didn't have much time to play with me. My dolls were a ratty mess, every one of them. The problem was my little nephew, Teddy. He was one-and-a-half years old, and whenever his mom, my sister Sharon, came to visit with him and I wasn't home from school yet, or even when I just wasn't paying attention, little Teddy would find my dolls and color all over their faces with crayons. The real problem was Sharon couldn't be bothered with keeping an eye on her own kid because she was already pregnant again and was always fussing about being tired. I don't know how many times I'd find little Teddy waddling around the house by himself looking for mischief to get into. And he'd always find some.

Mary's dolls looked like they'd never even been touched. Her house was perfect too. I bet everything was where it was supposed to be all the time. And it always smelled good too, like a pine tree married a bar of soap. I never told anybody this, but sometimes I wished I lived there.

This one day, Mary had invited me over to play. We were up in her room, and she pulled the big pink box out of her closet and plopped it on top of her bumpy pink bedspread. That bedspread was the softest thing I'd ever felt. It had all these tiny, cottony balls all over it that matched the pink ruffled curtains to a T. The curtains had little baby blue birds in nests sticking their tiny wide-open beaks up waiting for a worm or something.

The sun was shining through the sparkly clean windows. They were "spic and span" as Momma would say. The windows at my house were so full of smudges that when the sun shone through them, you couldn't hardly see anything outside.

Mary always let me play with her doll named Delilah because she was my favorite. Delilah had long, straight blond hair, green eyes, and pink lips. That afternoon, I dressed Delilah up in a shiny, satiny, green ball gown that had little sequins around the neck. I danced her out where the sunshine was, and she sparkled.

Then Mrs. Pfeiffer called up from downstairs. "Reedy, would you care to stay for supper?" I'd never had dinner at Mary's house before, but I'd had breakfast there a few times and loved it. Mary's mom let me put as much white sugar on my cereal as I wanted, something I could never do at home. Mrs. Pfeiffer's first name was Phoebe. Phoebe Pfeiffer. It made me giggle every time I said it.

Whenever I had breakfast at Mary's house, Mrs. Pfeiffer always had a small, glass vase full of tiny, pink tea roses on the table. She picked them fresh from the huge bush in their backyard, and they made the whole downstairs smell like one giant rose.

I yelled back down to Mrs. Pfeiffer, "Sure! I mean, yes, I'd like to stay, please… Thank you." Mary's mom was very proper.

"Alright, dear, I'll call your mother and let her know you'll be dining with us tonight."

Mary and I played for a while longer. She was good at sharing her toys. We dressed and undressed her dolls about a hundred times and pretended like they were going on dates to dances and fancy parties.

Pretty soon, something started to smell delicious, like chicken roasted in butter. It reminded me of a fancy restaurant I went to once with Mom and Dad.

A while later, Phoebe yelled back up, "Mary, you and Reedy wash up for supper." That's when I noticed the sun wasn't shining through the windows anymore, and the light was getting dim. It was getting on to dusk, and I got a bad feeling in my stomach.

I put Delilah on the pink bedspread. "I'll be right back," I told Mary. She probably thought I had to go to the bathroom, but instead, I went downstairs to talk to Mrs. Pfeiffer.

Soon as I walked in the kitchen, my mouth started watering. It smelled so good. But it didn't matter; I still had that bad feeling, and it was getting worse. Mrs. Pfeiffer was doing something at the sink, had her back to me. There was a bowl of bright green beans on the counter with a blob of butter melting over them, and a yummy-looking chicken on a great big platter with steam curling up from it.

"Mrs. Pfeiffer," I started, but got choked up. I cleared my throat. "Mrs. Pfeiffer, I think I better go home." By then, I really wanted to be at my house with Momma.

"Oh, no, dear." She didn't turn around or stop what she was doing when she said it.

"Remember you told me you wanted to stay for supper? Well, Dot said it would be just fine. So, you go get washed up now." Mrs. Pfeiffer didn't say it mean or anything, just like that was the way it was going to be, no ifs, ands, or buts. I just stood there looking at the back of her head.

Finally, she turned around, holding a bowl of hot, steamy mashed potatoes. "Oh," she said. But she looked different, like she was mad at me or I'd done something wrong. "Go on now. Get washed up, dear." She took the mashed potatoes and the bowl of green beans to the dining room.

I tried not to cry. I wanted to run away and hide. I turned around, went back upstairs, and into the bathroom. I closed the door, had to be by myself, try to figure out how not to cry. I did, though. Cry. I cried real quiet for about a minute. Then I took some deep breaths and made myself stop. I wiped away my tears and splashed water in my face. Then I heard a knock on the bathroom door.

"Reedy?" Mary said. "May I come in?"

"Sure." I dried my hands and face and tried to look happy. She opened the door and looked at me, puzzled, so I told her, "I was just washing up."

"Oh." I slipped by her and went to her room. I took more deep breaths and gathered up all the doll clothes. When Mary came back in her room, she looked around and smiled.

"Oh, thanks," she said and handed me the big pink box. "Let's put the clothes back in here." I was afraid if I said a word, I would start to cry again, so I just nodded. We lined the dolls up on her bed in all their finery, and they looked so beautiful. I loved Mary's room; it was perfect too. The furniture matched and everything.

Then Mrs. Pfeiffer called out, "Girls, come down and set the table please. Dinner is almost ready." Mary told her mom we were coming and seemed happy that I was staying. I felt bad, wished I could have been happy too, but I just wasn't.

When we went into the kitchen, I looked at the big clock over the sink where Mrs. Pfeiffer was still tending to supper. The clock read three minutes until six. I had a hunch that Mrs. Pfeiffer always served dinner at six o'clock on the dot. At my house, sometimes we didn't eat dinner until seven or even eight o'clock at night.

Mary pulled some neatly folded cloth napkins out of a drawer and put one at every place. Phoebe had already put a smooth white tablecloth on the table. It had little yellow flowers on it the same color as the napkins. Mary handed me some forks, spoons, and knives, and I put one of each on all the napkins. Then the dining room looked perfect, like a picture in a magazine. There was even classical music playing softly in the background. That's when I realized why I was scared; I didn't belong there—didn't fit in. I wasn't good enough or smart enough.

The sun must've gotten lower in the sky because it was starting to get dusky out. I looked through the living room window, through the dim light, I saw my house across the street. It looked small, sad, and messy. The front yard had a lot of dirt with overgrown patches of grass and weeds. Some bricks were missing from the front steps, and my bike was lying on its side near the porch with a broken kickstand sticking straight up. I saw that there was a tiny bit of light coming from the back of our house, probably Momma in the kitchen cooking dinner, no telling when it would be ready. I wanted to be there with Momma so bad.

The big oak tree in our front yard was the best climbing tree in the whole neighborhood. All its branches were in just the right places. I could climb so high, high enough to see the whole entire block, every single house that wasn't hidden by the big trees. Taffy, my brown-and-white cocker spaniel, was lying on the porch. He seemed to be looking right at me. Taffy was born the same day as me. His head was resting on his front paws, and he looked sad. Taffy didn't like it when I left the house without him.

"Alright, everyone," Mrs. Pfeiffer said. "Supper time!" Then she brought in that delicious-looking chicken and put it in the middle of the table. It was plump and brown on top and looked nice and juicy. By then, the whole house smelled like a fancy restaurant. Mr. Pfeiffer, and Jeff came and sat down at the table. Jeff was Mary's older brother. He was thirteen and kind of funny. He didn't talk much, though, at least not to me. Mary said he was really smart, made straight As on every single report card.

Mr. Pfeiffer came into the dining room and said, "It smells delicious, Phoebe dear," and kissed her on the cheek. Then he looked at me. "My wife makes the world's best roast chicken." He shook his head and looked at her. "I don't know how she does it. I suspect she has some kind of secret, chicken-magic recipe."

Mary laughed. "Chicken-magic, Papa, you're funny." Mrs. Pfeiffer smiled and looked at me. Then she cocked her head, and her smile went away. I think she could tell I was sad about something and wanted to know what it was. She was like that, Mrs. Pfeiffer, just seemed to know when something was troubling you. I tried to smile, but my stomach was in knots. I didn't know if I was going to be able to eat a single bite, even though it smelled so good.

"Mary," Mr. Pfeiffer said. "Would you please say grace?" Mary took my hand, and Mr. Pfeiffer took my other hand, and we all bowed our heads and closed our eyes. Soon as I closed my eyes, I felt a tear fall. I opened one eye to see if anybody saw, then opened both eyes a tiny bit and watched while Mary said grace.

"Thank You, Lord, for these and all Thy gifts, in Jesus's name, Amen." Mary's family went to church every Sunday, no matter what. If a foot of snow fell in the middle of the night, they'd still march off the next morning in galoshes and their Sunday-go-to-meeting clothes happy as ever. My family went to church every now and then. Packy never joined us, though. It was usually just Momma, Daddy and me. My sister, Sally, was fourteen, six years older than me.

She pretty much did whatever she wanted, which didn't include going to church. Scott was still living at home too, but he was almost done with high school and was sort of done with the family as well. Nobody ever knew where he was.

After her "Amen," Mary turned to me. "Wait till you taste my mom's chicken. It's my favorite." Mrs. Pfeiffer smiled while we all passed our plates to Mr. Pfeiffer, who cut up the chicken. He put some in Mary's and Jeff's plates, and Mary's mom served everything else.

Then Mr. Pfeiffer looked at me. "Would you like white meat or dark?" he asked. "Or a little of both?"

I was shaky, my throat was dry, and my voice wasn't working right. I wanted to tell him I only loved dark meat, but didn't think I could get a whole sentence out without crying. "Yes, please."

Mr. Pfeiffer leaned in. "A little of both?" I nodded. He winked, nodded his head, and put some on my plate. "Good choice," he said as he passed it to me.

I saw everybody put their napkins on their laps, so I did too. Then everybody started eating. I couldn't see my food very well because my eyes were full of tears. My mouth watered. I looked down at my plate, and, through blurry eyes, I saw white mashed potatoes with specks of black pepper and yellow puddles of melting butter running through it, bright green beans—they were never that bright green when Momma cooked them—and pieces of scrumptious-looking chicken.

Even the white meat had juices dripping out of it.

Next to everybody's big plate was a small bowl with a perfect little salad in it: lettuce, slices of tomato, and a little cabbage. I was so hungry my stomach growled. I took a bite of chicken and wiped my mouth. Mary and Mr. Pfeiffer were right. That chicken was the best I'd ever tasted. I looked around to make sure nobody was watching and wiped another tear from my eye with the pretty yellow napkin. I took another bite of chicken—I forgot about everything else for a second it was so good.

Then I got a lump in my throat and put my fork down. "Um, may I please be excused?" I looked at Mrs. Pfeiffer. "I have to go to the lady's room."

Mrs. Pfeiffer smiled. "Of course. You're excused." Mary, Freddy, and Mr. Pfeiffer were too busy eating their perfectly delicious dinner, probably didn't even know I had left the table. I walked up the stairs and felt hot tears roll down my cheeks. Soon as I got in the bathroom, I closed the door and sat down on the soft green rug and cried—I ached to be in my messy house.

At Mary's house things were perfect, in order, clean and tidy. That's not how things were at my house. Momma tried to keep the place neat, and she fussed at all us kids a lot about the messes we made. But I think there were just too many of us, and what with Packy roaming around raising all kinds of heck whenever he wanted, I think Momma just gave up. That was the thing about Mary's house. I suspected Mrs. Pfeiffer was in control all the time, and that was that. But she only had her two normal, very smart kids to keep in line.

I got up off the bathroom floor and looked in the mirror. My eyes were red and swollen. I splashed water on my face and dried it with the soft towel—it smelled like a field of flowers. I flushed the toilet, so the Pfeiffers would think I really had peed. I went out and looked down the stairs. At the bottom was the front door, and only the screen was closed. The music playing sounded like one of the ballet tunes I danced to. I walked down the stairs real slow, one step at a time. They didn't creak like ours did. My heart pounded so hard I was afraid they could hear.

When I got to the second to last step, I looked through the living room. I couldn't see Mrs. Pfeiffer, only part of Mr. Pfeiffer. So I crept down slowly, watching the dining room table, the whole time. I could hear them talking about something.

Mr. Pfeiffer was cutting up his chicken and didn't see me tiptoe to the screen door. I pushed the handle down. It was locked. I looked back to see if anybody had seen me. They were all busy eating, and Mary was talking about school stuff I didn't understand.

I unlocked the screen door, pushed it open, slipped out, and listened. I could still hear talking. By then it was almost dark out and I just turned around and ran home fast as I could. I don't know what Momma made for dinner that night, or if we even had any. But I was happy to be home. I felt safe. I ran to the kitchen and hugged tight around her big belly. She was shocked to see me. I told her what I'd done and told her I did it because I missed her so much. She could hardly believe that I snuck away in the middle of supper like that. She even laughed a little and hugged me back.

"Oh, honey," she said and wiped away my tears. "Don't you worry. I'll explain it to Phoebe." The next day, I thought about it and felt bad and like a big stupid baby. I was sorry that I'd missed out on that delicious chicken dinner too.

That was the last time I got invited to Mary's house for supper. Or for breakfast. And after that night, I was glad I didn't live at her house.

CHAPTER THREE

1955

Creepy Things

I woke up early one dark, cloudy Saturday morning. Everything was quiet, so I was pretty sure nobody else was awake. I listened good and hard to make sure. I loved being the only one awake in the house. I felt like a spy or something creeping around in the dim dead silence.

I figured Packy was still asleep. He hardly ever showed his face before noon, if he showed it at all. It seemed he liked to spend most of his time up in his nasty old attic. I couldn't even imagine what he did up there all day long. It gave me the creeps just thinking about it.

I tiptoed to the stairs and looked down into the misty blue hallway. I always knew when a storm was brewing, things looked different—gloomy, watery. I could smell it coming too, knew we were in for some dark, wet days. I heard a low rumbling in the distance.

The portraits Daddy had painted of all us kids were barely visible because the light was so dim. The pictures were hanging on the wall by the stairs. At the top was Packy, then Sharon, and Jud, then Scott and Sally, and I was at the very bottom. It was only our faces in the paintings, and we were looking off somewhere in the distance with just a sliver of a perfect-shaped, profile shadow by our faces. Daddy was a fine artist.

I looked over at the mirror next to the stairs. It was on the hall closet door. It was too dark to make out my own reflection, but I noticed something I hadn't seen before; a dark place high up in the corner—couldn't tell what it was, though. So, I went to the kitchen and got the stool—I didn't want to wake up anybody, so I did it quiet as I could. I put the little ladder by the closet door and climbed up. I stared at the thing for a minute and wondered, "What the heck?" I could hardly believe my eyes. That dark place I saw looked just like a patch of fur—it gave me a shiver. All these short hairs seemed to be growing right out of the wooden door.

I knew it had to be some of Packy's doings, but for the life of me I couldn't figure out what it was or how he did it. I knew better than to wonder for too long why he did anything, though. I was plenty used to things not making sense growing up with him around.

I reached up and poked at it—couldn't help myself. And sure enough, it was a bunch of little hairs, and each one popped right off when I touched it. It was creepy at first, but kind of fun too. I ran my finger over the whole thing and pop, pop, pop! Just like I was shaving the door.

Then a week or so later, Momma was having her Christian prayer-group ladies over and asked me to help her tidy up. I wasn't used to doing chores at our house. Neither were my brothers or sisters. Momma never made us. Oh, every now and then, she'd get a bee in her bonnet and start yelling, "Good Lord, pick up after yourselves!" or "Do some dishes!" and a bunch of other stuff. I think because our house was so full of kids, everybody running in and out at all hours of the day and night, she finally gave up. She probably thought it was easier to do whatever she could do herself and just leave the rest rather than try to get any of us in line.

Momma looked worn out when she asked me to help, and I felt sorry for her. When I said I would, she smiled, thanked me, and handed over a clean rag. I dusted the coffee table and the two end tables, and then I pulled back the curtains by the front windows so she could vacuum behind them. When I did, I was surprised to find a bottle full of something yellow with no top on it. Momma always saved juice bottles, and everything else for that matter. The pantry was packed with saved stuff.

I picked up the bottle, thinking maybe somebody had forgotten to put it back in the refrigerator, and sniffed it. Well, I tell you what, I yanked it away from my nose pretty fast, almost dropped the darn thing. I couldn't believe it; it was a full bottle of pee just sitting there big as you please.

I screamed over the vacuum cleaner noise and flagged Momma down until she shut the thing off. "Mom, look!" I held it up for her to see. "A bottle of pee!"

"What?"

"A bottle of pee! I swear Packy's nuts! He must've peed in the bottle and left it right there for anybody to find. What's wrong with him, Momma?"

She took the bottle and looked at it, horrified. "Well, for goodness' sake!" Then she marched to the bathroom, mumbling the whole time. I heard the toilet flush. "Who ever heard of such a thing?" she kept on talking to herself while she went out to the kitchen. "That would've been a fine howdy-do for one of my church ladies to discover!"

CHAPTER FOUR
1956
Packy's Attic

PACKY WENT AWAY TO COLLEGE WHEN HE WAS SEVENTEEN YEARS OLD, about the time I was being born. It didn't take him long to graduate because of him being a genius and all, and by the time he came home to live, I was three. His bedroom was up in the attic where my other two brothers, Jud and Scott, shared a different bedroom until they moved out.

After Jud graduated from high school and married Bobbi, his sweetheart, they moved into their own house. Then a few years later, Scott left for college, and Packy got the whole third floor to himself. When I was nine, I went up there for the first time ever.

The door to the attic was never locked. It was never locked, and it was never talked about. It was just understood. "Don't go up there, or else..." I knew he had all these snakes and frogs, and I didn't know what all in about a million cages. It was too scary to even think about. My sister Sally sneaked up there this one time, when Packy wasn't home, and said it was super creepy. She told me she'd never go back up again no matter what. I was surprised she went up there at all because I didn't think she even cared, didn't know she was that kind of brave, either.

She said besides it being filthy dirty and terrible scary, it smelled Godawful too. Told me she had to hold her nose the whole time. I asked her what it smelled like.

"Well," she said and squeezed her eyes real small and scrunched up her nose. "You know what *he* smells like, right?"

"Uh-huh." I did too, and it wasn't good. He usually smelled like he didn't take a bath for a whole year.

"Like that, and other rotten things." Then she thought for a minute. "Smells like dead things, mixed with snake."

Everybody in my house knew what snakes smelled like. Packy had lots of them, and a few ended up escaping into some other parts of our house, like the kitchen. One came slithering out of the place where the heat came from—the thing with all the holes. I was getting something from the pantry for Momma because she was cooking dinner, when, all of a sudden, a big old snake poked its ugly head out, and I jerked around because I noticed something moving. And there it was, head all wobbly. It frightened the living daylights out of me. Then its split red tongue licked the air, and I screamed and ran out of there so fast it about scared Momma to death.

There was this other time when one came out of the downstairs toilet. We all heard a scream, and there come Momma running out of the bathroom, hands waving over her head yelling "Packy!" at the top of her lungs. Well, you can bet everybody scurried to the bathroom to see what all the screaming was about. And there it was: one evil-looking snake head moving back and forth, rising right straight up out of the toilet bowl. Like one of those charmers was playing a flute for it.

So anyway, this one day, I was on my way down the hall to the bathroom when I saw the attic door was open a tiny bit. Since it was usually closed up tight, I got to wondering what was going on. So, I looked all around and listened hard. Everything was quiet, except for Momma banging around down in the kitchen.

I put my nose to the opening of the attic door and sniffed. Boy, was my sister right. I backed away and tried to blow that smell out my nose. It was so bad I could taste it. I pictured my brother's room full of all those slimy things crawling around in their cages stinking up the place. I looked around to make sure Packy hadn't snuck up behind me. He did that a lot, just loved to scare the pants off me every chance he got.

I went into Mom and Dad's room and looked out the front windows. Mom's yellow convertible was nowhere to be seen, so I was pretty sure Packy was gone. Sometimes he'd leave for the whole day or even longer, and nobody'd know where he'd gone, or when he'd be back, or if he was lying in some ditch bleeding to death with her convertible on top of him. Maybe that was why Momma was banging things around extra loud in the kitchen that day. She'd get furious when he'd take off in her car and leave us stranded at home. He wouldn't even tell anybody he was going. Mom'd get all ready to go shopping with her list in hand. Then she'd step out the front door only to find there was nothing to leave in. Sometimes Packy'd be gone with the car when I was supposed to go to ballet class after school. I'd get ready anyway, hoping with all my might that he'd be back in time so Momma could take me. I'd wait by the front door, and it would get later and later, and I'd get madder and madder, and he wouldn't get home until the class would've been half over. I'd cry and throw a nasty fit because ballet was the only thing I had to look forward to. It was the one thing I loved after being miserable and feeling stupid in school all day long. When Packy'd finally get home and walk through the front door, Momma'd start screaming and fussing at him. "How could you be so inconsiderate, Packy? I told you to ask me when you wanted to use my—" But he'd already be halfway up the stairs before she could get out a full sentence.

She'd complain to my dad too. "Fuzzy!" she'd yell. "Would you *please* do something about your son!" I thought that was funny because Packy was her son too.

Daddy always looked ashamed and helpless. "Honey… what do you want me to do?" he'd stammer.

One time, Momma just shook her head, folded her arms, and said to Daddy, "Well. The supermarket's closed now, so there's not going to be any dinner tonight!" Then she took off her apron and stormed off. We didn't have any either. I made peanut butter and jelly sandwiches for me and Daddy when we got hungry.

I don't know why Momma thought Daddy could have done anything about Packy, anyway. I was positive there wasn't a single person alive that could've made my brother behave like he was supposed to.

I went back to the attic door and stared at the opening for a good long moment asking myself, Did I want to do it? Did I really want to see his spooky old room? What if he caught me? I scared myself so bad I went back to my room. I imagined what he would do if he did catch me, especially if he was in one of his scary moods. Why he might lock me in a closet with some of his snakes, or grab me up with his huge hands—I still had bruises from when I tried to get him out of my room a couple days before. And I didn't bruise easy.

I caught him rummaging through my dressing table drawer where I kept my diary. I got so mad I gave him a good push, and he almost fell on his butt. That's when he took out after me. He grabbed my arm so hard I though he broke it. I kicked like crazy, though, wrestled myself free and ran downstairs screaming for Mom. Packy chased me for about a minute. Then I guess he gave up or just didn't care anymore and went off somewhere.

I went and looked at the attic door real close. It was open about an inch, and the smell was leaking out into the hallway. I held my breath and put my eye up to the opening. The sun was coming in bright through the windows from the other bedroom. It made light stripes on the dark wall shining through the railing. There were about a million teeny-tiny white specks floating in the sunlight. I stopped and listened just to make double-sure he wasn't up there.

I looked all around, put my finger on the doorknob, and pulled it open a little. But it made a loud creaking sound, so I froze. Those little white specks danced and swirled when I opened the door a crack, reminded me of dandelion seeds floating around when you blew on them.

There was just enough room, so I slipped through the opening onto the first step. I couldn't hear a thing after I stepped through the door—the quiet in there had a sound all its own. I could hardly believe I was going up to Packy's room. I got scared, and a chill ran through my body. I shivered. I wanted to go back down, but instead, I walked up the next step. The stairs were made of plain old wood, and they were filthy. Each one had a thick layer of grime with dust on top, and spiderwebs were hanging down all over the place.

I thought I heard a low buzzing, so I listened hard, tried to figure out where it was coming from. Sure enough, where the step and the wall came together, something was sort of quivering in the corner. I bent down and looked close. It was a big fat fly caught in a spiderweb, its little wings flapping so fast and it was wiggling like crazy for its poor hopeless life.

I usually hated flies and tried to swat them every chance I got, but I felt kind of sorry for this one. At least when I killed them dead with a flyswatter, it was fast. Now the poor thing was just stuck there all helpless, struggling and shaking, waiting for some big ugly spider to come gobble it down piece by piece.

Then, not even an inch away, I saw a big black spider creeping toward the fly. I jumped back. I'd never been scared of spiders or bugs much, figured they wouldn't hurt me if I didn't bother them. But this one was the hugest one I'd ever seen. My heart pounded in my chest. It was shaking too, looked like it was watching the fly. It was probably waiting for the right moment to dig into its fat, juicy meal. I got creeped out, decided if I was going to go all the way up, I better just do it.

I touched the wall to steady myself, but it was sticky, so I yanked my hand back. The wall was sort of yellow but gray, and there were splotches and drips running down it. I wondered why it was so filthy. The rest of our house wasn't always tidy, but at least it was clean enough and didn't stink. Packy's attic reminded me of a spook house, like the Haunted House at Fountain Ferry.

When I got up to the next step, I felt a sharp pain in my foot. I grabbed onto the railing and yanked my foot up. The railing was greasy, but I held tight and looked at my foot. A good-sized splinter was sticking out near my big toe, and it hurt so bad I almost started to cry.

I sat down on a step and looked at it closer. When I pulled it out, my foot felt like it was on fire. Maybe I should just go back down the stairs, forget the whole thing, I thought. But I didn't. I limped up the rest of the stairs on the side of my foot. When I got to the top, I saw another bathroom I didn't even know we had. I thought about using it because I really had to go. But then I thought about how filthy it probably was, and I just held it. I wondered why a full-grown man wanted to live like that? By then, Packy was twenty-seven years old. I knew he had real problems, but why on earth did he want to live in such squalor?

Then I heard a far-away car horn. It startled me out of my trance, reminded me that I needed to listen. I stood still—everything was quiet. But I hurried anyway. I got to the top and limped down the hall, past what used to be my other two brothers' bedroom. The door was wide open.

The room was small, had a slanted ceiling and a layer of dust on everything. The walls were pale green and didn't have any splotches on them. It had two twin beds with no sheets or pillows, just old tan covers thrown over them all haphazard like. The old windows made the trees outside look squiggly.

I walked on the side of my hurt foot fast to Packy's room. I hadn't heard the front door open or slam shut yet, so I was pretty sure Packy was still gone. I prayed he was and that I was still safe. I came to the doorway of his room. The stink was worse, smelled of chemicals and something rotten. I gagged and pinched my nose closed. It was dark; all the shades were pulled closed except for one that was ripped and hanging down. I flipped on a light switch by the door, and one small bulb lit up in the middle of the ceiling. It was dim, hardly shed any light at all. I crept in, and the floor creaked. The walls were a dirty gray, and there were spiderwebs everywhere. Great big jars were all over the place—mostly full of some cloudy greenish liquid. A few had frogs in them, gigantic dead frogs just floating. I didn't know frogs got that big. Their legs and arms, or whatever you call those things, were hanging all droopy-like. Their eyes were bluish-white and bulging. They seemed like they were watching me. Some of the other jars had big, fat, dead, curled-up snakes in them—at least I hoped they were dead.

An old bare mattress lay on the floor speckled with dark red stains, and a blanket the color of green mud was thrown across it. Two of the walls had bookshelves that went up to the ceiling. They were full of dusty books of all kinds: art books, poetry and music books, books about composers and about reptiles and lots and lots of snake books. Then I saw some wire cages on the other side of the room behind the mattress with live snakes in them. My heart beat faster.

Some of the snakes were moving around. It was so creepy. A few smaller cages had live rats in them and a kind of possum-looking thing, and one had a bunny in it. I crept a little closer. The brown bunny was small and cute, wiggling its nose and looking around.

Then I remembered that snakes eat things like bunnies, and that was probably why Packy had them. He was going to feed that bunny to some big, nasty snake. I wanted to free the poor little thing, let them go. But Packy would know it was me that did it and feed me to the snakes instead!

There was a dark, broken-down dresser by the window, and some of the drawers were hanging open with clothes spilling out. The room was so sad and scary. I felt sorry for the bunny and all the critters, but mostly, I felt sorry for my brother living up there in that awful place all by himself.

I heard a car door slam! I couldn't believe I'd forgotten to listen again. I limped to one of the grimy windows, making sure to watch where I was going. Besides all the living and dead things everywhere, there was stuff all over the floor: filthy rags, dirty clothes, even some nails and tacks. I saw something shiny in the corner. It was a brand-spanking new penny. I picked it up and put it in my pocket, hoping it would bring me good luck, maybe help me get out of there alive. I looked out the window, but could barely see out, it had so much grease and grime on it. I had to get close to see anything at all. And there it was, Momma's yellow convertible! Packy was standing next to it looking around at the other houses. It looked like he wasn't in a hurry to come inside, though, looked like he was in one of his good moods. But I knew better than to count on it. His good mood could change to hateful in a second.

Maybe he'd go for a walk, I thought. He did that sometimes. I ran to the door and almost fell down because I forgot about my foot. I had to hurry, though, so I limped as fast as I could. I got halfway down the stairs and remembered I left the light on in Packy's room! My foot was killing me, but I couldn't think about it. I limped back up, switched off the light, and hurried down the stairs.

When I got to the bottom, I looked back up and saw blood on the steps. My blood! But I had no time to fix it, to wipe it off, so I just prayed he wouldn't notice it on top of all the filth. I slipped through the opening and started to close the door. Then I remembered the loud creak it made before, so I just left it the way it was.

I heard heavy footsteps running up the stairs. I went around the corner into Mom and Dad's room and hid behind the door. I prayed he wouldn't get suspicious, wonder why his attic door wasn't closed all the way.

I squatted down, made myself as small as I could and listened. I was out of breath but tried to breathe quietly. I heard him stop at the door to his attic. He didn't make a sound for a long time. I held my breath.

I heard Momma's footsteps coming up the stairs. "You been up in my room?" Packy asked.

"You talking to me?" Mom said.

"Yeah, d'you go up?"

"No, why? I should go up there and clean—"

"No, don't! Just leave it."

"OK." I bet she was glad; that was probably the last thing she wanted to do.

Mom sounded tired as usual, like she didn't have anything left in her, like she'd run away from all of us if she could. I heard Packy go up the stairs. I tiptoed to Daddy's bathroom and made it just in time. I could breathe again. And I could pee. I closed the bathroom door, sat on the toilet, and thought about what I'd done—how I finally went up to Packy's room. I could hardly believe it. I almost got caught too. I enjoyed thinking about what I got away with, the chance I took, and nobody would ever know.

CHAPTER FIVE
1958

A Big Box of Snake

IT WAS THE MIDDLE OF SUMMER, JULY SOMETHING, AND A NICE BREEZE was blowing. The air felt good, even though it was still way too sticky out. We'd had a good soaking the day before, so it was a little cooler, almost bearable.

The sun was hitting part of the backyard dead on because it was noon. Mainly, it was baking the cement part in front of the basketball hoop on the garage. Lots of the neighborhood boys enjoyed playing on it. I couldn't understand how, though, because the net on the hoop was so old, strings all mangled and torn, hanging down like a bunch of cobwebs. I was sure no ball could make its way through that mess. Our two huge oak trees shaded the rest of the yard. Packy was twenty-eight years old with nothing better to do then stir up trouble.

He was standing in the middle of the backyard in front of a great huge box. It looked like the one our brand-new stove came in when the old one quit working. I watched out of my bedroom window wondering what the big lunatic was up to. Probably up to no good as usual, I figured. Couldn't help but watch anyway, like when you can't pull yourself away from watching a car wreck even though you know you'll be sorry you did.

Packy was leaning over the box, tending to something inside. I couldn't see what it was because his big sweaty back was in the way, so I climbed up on my bed to get a better look. I knew it had to be something creepy inside, like a giant lizard or a bunch of rat babies, or worse. I still couldn't see a thing, so I ran downstairs and out onto the back porch.

The air smelled like it did after a good rain, sweet and clean. I breathed it in deep. Billy, from across the street, was peering into the box. He was Martha and Margaret's seven-year-old brother. His mom and dad had twelve kids, and he was the youngest. Momma told me their family was Catholic, and that's what good Catholics did, litter the earth with lots of kids. All Billy's brothers and sisters thought he was just the cutest thing there ever was and always gave him whatever he wanted. I was sure that's why he was such a spoiled brat. I had to kick his butt sometimes to keep him in line.

When Billy saw what was in the box, he looked scared to death and let out a loud scream—sounded like a little girl. He ran out to the side yard, then slowly inched his way back for another look. I had to see what it was, so I went down the porch steps and out into the backyard.

Packy seemed like he was in a gentle mood, looking in on whatever it was. I called out to Billy, "Where's Martha and Margaret?" His twin sisters were a couple years younger than me, and we played a lot because they lived so close. Billy didn't even bother to answer me. He just shrugged and stared at the box. *Real polite, Billy!* I thought. Packy looked at me, then back in the box.

"What's in the box?"

He grinned at me, then said, "Why don't ya come see?" I knew that look. He was challenging me, like he had something special, a secret, and was daring me to come see it.

I hated when he toyed with me like that. I shook my head and made a face, like I couldn't have cared less. I inched close enough to see inside the box, though, and it was a gigantic snake! I gasped and jumped back. Packy laughed. Billy did too.

I was used to seeing Packy's snakes, but this one was like nothing I'd ever seen before. It would've scared the poop out of anybody. My brother loved snakes, all kinds of them. It didn't matter what variety, or how big they were, or even if they could kill you with one bite. He had plenty of them up in his attic. But I swear the one in that box was as long as the house and as big around as a football.

I stared at Packy, tried to size him up, figure out what kind of mood he was in. I walked closer while I kept my eye on him. He watched me too. I could never tell what he was thinking. Sometimes, I really wished I could. Sometimes I was glad I couldn't.

"What kind is it?"

"King snake," he said. "Full-grown." He shrugged. "He's harmless." *Harmless, my butt*, I thought. *About as harmless as you, you big nut.* I leaned in far enough so I could see the whole creepy thing. Its head was the size of a skillet, but it was kind of pretty, in a slimy, terrifying kind of way, with all its fancy markings. It looked like a purse I once saw in Bacon's Department Store.

The snake seemed to be trying to stay in one corner, the only shady spot.

All of a sudden, it moved its head up and looked right into my eyes. I froze. My heart pounded. Then it forked its long, black tongue out and waggled it around.

I heard a car pull into the driveway and knew it was my sister. Well, I can tell you, I was more than happy to get far away from Packy and his slimy friend.

We'd been expecting Sharon and her kids to come for a visit. I heard Momma holler, "Hi y'all!" She just loved my sister, thought she was real special. Sharon had the prettiest singing voice, and she could draw, and was funny too. After Sharon got herself pregnant in college, she married her boyfriend, Brud, and they moved to Winchester, Kentucky, because that's where he got a job. After that, we only got to see them every few weeks.

I ran through the house and out into the front yard, and as soon as the car stopped in the driveway, little Tisa jumped out and ran to me. "Tisa!"

My sister yelled. "Tisa! Wait 'til I stop—" I grabbed her, swung her around, and we hugged. She always smelled like cherry cough drops.

"I got her!" I put Tisa down. "Oh, my goodness, you look so pretty!" Her little pink dress had stitching and tiny red flowers with green stems and leaves embroidered all over the top part.

Tisa giggled and spun around in circles so I could see it. "It's my new dwess! See, see?" she squealed in her little magpie voice. "It gots wed flowers on it!" She almost toppled over, but I caught her, and we headed around the house to the swings in the backyard.

Tisa was four years old and got her name from her big brother Teddy, when they were both tiny. When she was born, Teddy, Momma's first grandchild, was only two years old, and when he saw his baby sister, he tried to say "sister," but it came out "Tisa," and the name stuck. After she grew up, many years later, Tisa told me she just loved coming to our house. Loved escaping the constant fighting of her mom and dad and loved going on adventures with me.

I ran into the shady, grassy part of the backyard with Tisa bouncing and laughing in my arms. I galloped around the big, old oak tree where the tire swing hung and circled around the sandbox with clumps of wet sand in it, and through the no-longer-blooming daffodils still wet from yesterday's rain.

"Teedlebug!" Packy called. "Teedlebug, come over here. I want to show you what I've got." Tisa ran to him before I could stop her. I chased after, but Packy scooped her up, pointed down at the box.

"Look. This is my friend." Tisa looked down into the big box, and her eyes got big as saucers, and her sweet smile disappeared. "Oh, don't be scared, Teedles. Isn't he pretty?"

Tisa looked back up at Packy. And that was the moment I knew my brother was going to do something terrible. I knew it, and Tisa knew it. She started to cry.

I ran up to her. "Here, sweetheart, come—" I tried to take her, but with one swipe of his huge hand, Packy swatted me away.

I fell back and landed on my butt. I got up quick, though, and yelled at him loud as I could. "PACKY! You give her to me!" He looked shocked, livid.

Then he looked at her scared little face and smiled. "Don't be afraid, Teedles. He won't hurt you," he said. "See, I'll show you. Now, just remember… don't move and he won't hurt you." He bent over with Tisa inside the box. She screamed.

"PACKY!" I yelled. "PACKY! MOM?! PACKY!" Tisa squirmed and cried. Packy shushed her, but she kept on. Then he set her down inside the box. She hung tight to his arms, but Packy pulled her off and stood up.

"NO!" I screamed.

"It's OK. Don't…" he said. Tisa froze, tears dripping all over her pretty pink dress.

"Goddamn you!" I yelled. I ran to her, but Packy blocked my way. "You take her out of there! You hear me? You take her out of there this minute! Goddamn you!" I got close and saw the snake sniff her or whatever snakes do. The creature moved real slow around her tiny body, and its big, ugly skillet-head started moving up her leg. I was jumping around like a chicken with its head cut off, trying to figure a way to get her out of there.

I screamed again. "MOM!" Tisa sobbed and squeezed her eyes shut tight. I went to reach for her again, but Packy slapped my hands away and hit the box too, by accident. The box jerked, and Tisa let out a squeal. Then the snake started to move around real fast. I was frantic, could hardly see anything for the tears in my eyes.

I ran into the house and looked everywhere for Mom. "MOM! MOM!" I yelled. "Packy put Tisa—" Just then, Mom came through the front door holding Gibbs, Sharon's littlest baby.

He was sound asleep in her arms. "Shhhh, what?" she whispered. "Don't wake the baby." But I didn't care who I woke up, didn't care about anything except rescuing Tisa from the snake.

"Mom! Packy put Tisa in the snake box!" I yelled "And she's—"

"Shhhh, honey, not now…" She pushed right past me, heading up the stairs.

"SHIT, MOM!" I screamed at the top of my lungs. I couldn't believe I said it, but it got her attention alright. She stopped halfway up the stairs just as little Gibbs started bawling. I ran out the back door, hoping she'd come after me and catch Packy red-handed.

By the time I got there, Packy was holding Tisa in his arms again, talking to her real quiet-like.

"He didn't hurt you now, did he? You're OK, see?"

Tisa just lay there over Packy's shoulder, limp and crying. I wiped the tears from my eyes and screamed, "Mom's coming out here, and she said you better stop it and give me that child!"

Packy just looked at me with a stupid grin on his face. He knew perfectly well that I was lying, that it didn't matter what I said, because Momma wouldn't do a single thing about it. I never understood it. She punished me whenever I misbehaved. He was her kid too, even if he was big and old and mean. Why didn't he ever get punished? He did far worse things than I'd ever done.

Why did he get to control everything in our house? I was always too afraid to invite anybody over because of Packy. Lord knew what he might do.

I got so mad until I was fuming—then I just ran straight at the big box and kicked it hard as I could. The snake started moving around all wild-like, and the box started gyrating like crazy, and the snake's big old head rose right up out of the box. Well, soon as Packy saw that his precious snake was upset, he just dropped Tisa, but I caught her before she hit the ground. Then I took off fast as I could. I ran around the house, little Tisa bouncing in my arms. I figured Packy would be busy consoling his stupid snake for a while.

I ran and ran, had to find a safe place where we could hide. But where? My mind was going a million miles a second. My room wasn't safe; that was for sure. Nowhere in the house or even close to it was safe from him.

Tisa whimpered, her tiny arms wrapped tight around my neck. She started shaking. "It's alright," I said quietly into her little ear. "I've got you now, sweetheart. It's OK." I ran through the neighborhood, didn't want to stop, wanted to run forever. I wanted to go far away, where there were no snakes, no big, crazy, sick brothers, or moms and dads too busy to keep the small people safe. I longed to find a place where there was no fighting, where people were happy because they knew how to love.

I ran past house after house: the Bisigs', the Hubers', the McGees', and all the houses in between. Then I saw a bunch of bushes I remembered playing in across the street behind a neighbor's backyard. I ran toward it, looking around to make sure no one followed us. We crawled into the green cave and collapsed on the ground. The ground was still soggy from the rain. But it was warm, and the grass smelled sweet. I put Tisa on my lap, and we held each other, finally safe in our quiet hiding place.

Eventually, when Tisa stopped shaking and could breathe easy, she picked some dandelions and clover blossoms. I found a stick and dug a hole in the wet dirt to put her flowers in. We decided it was a beautiful salad in some fancy restaurant. The noise from the neighborhood filtered through the leaves into our green 'house.' We heard sounds of cars passing, daddies arriving home from work, voices of kids playing, birds singing, and the scratching of squirrels burying food.

Suddenly, the flowers in our makeshift bowl moved, and we saw a worm wiggle its way through. Then it poked its little head right out of the blossoms. It surprised both of us, and we laughed. Then a ladybug and an ant came climbing over the bumpy grass.

"Look." Tisa pointed at them. "They're coming for dinner!" We played until we got hungry for real dinner, and it got to be twilight. When we could hardly see anything in our shady hideout, we walked home hand in hand, unsure of what we would find when we got there.

CHAPTER SIX
1959

After-Christmas Surprise

A couple of days after Christmas, everybody left Mom and Dad's house to go back home. The place was finally quiet for the first time in a week. Both my sisters were gone, two of my brothers, their wives, husbands, kids, cousins, and friends—the silence was nice. I should've been able to hear a pin drop, except my ears were still ringing from all the loud fun we had. I didn't know where Mom and Dad were, but figured they were probably resting and enjoying the stillness by themselves. I didn't know where Packy was, either.

He was bigger than full-grown by then. Twenty-nine years old and still living at home. He hardly ever left the house, especially when I wished he would, which was most of the time. That day he was nowhere to be found, and I was glad. I figured he was probably up in his creepy old attic with his only friends: his snakes, and frogs, and other varmints.

A few days earlier, on Christmas Eve to be exact, a foot of snow fell—a whole twelve inches. We were surprised because it usually didn't snow much in Louisville. When it did, it refused to stick. It would melt almost the second it hit the ground. The morning after a good snowstorm, I'd hurry and look out the window hoping to see a winter wonderland—praying the schools would be closed, but most of the time, there wouldn't be a speck of snow left anywhere—like it never even happened. That Christmas Eve, though, it was piling up like crazy.

The snowflakes were plump and fluffy and coming down so fast, you couldn't see anything out the windows but sparkly white. When my nieces and nephews saw those big, heavy flakes floating down from the sky, they started jumping up and down, bouncing around the house like a bunch of little basketballs. I was older, almost twelve, so I settled them down long enough to get their wraps on them. Then I put on my coat, and we all ran outside. The second we were out the door, the kids scattered, running everywhere. They threw snowballs, made snow angels, and giggled at the smoky-looking steam coming out of their mouths.

I inhaled deep, filled myself up with the clean smell of fresh, icy snow. "Smell the air, y'all!" I yelled to the kids. "Doesn't it smell delicious?" They huffed and puffed and shook their little heads 'yes.' I couldn't help but laugh.

Then I looked up at the flurry of white falling around me and opened my mouth wide. While I was looking up, I saw Packy in his attic window. I waved. He didn't. The kids saw me waving, and they started waving at him too. Packy stared at us for a long time. Then he just faded away from the window. It was spooky.

Momma said Packy couldn't help the way he was. Sometimes, he'd be friendly one minute, and we'd be having a good time. Then, suddenly, he'd change to being mean and hateful, like he'd been taken over by some kind of demon. Whenever he changed like that, he'd take his rage out on whoever was handy—that was usually me.

The kids and I played until our noses turned bright pink. We swept up big piles of snow and jumped in them, and we made snowmen—more like snow-blobs, really—and I chased them around while they threw snowballs at me.

Then Momma came out on the front porch with her arms full of cooking pots. "Hey," she yelled and shook the pots together so we'd hear her over our racket. Everybody just shut up and looked at her. "How 'bout y'all fill these pots up with snow and I'll make us some snow ice cream?"

We all cheered and ran up on the porch to get one. We filled those pots so fast because Momma made the best snow ice cream of anybody. Once, she told me her recipe, said it was our little secret because she'd never told another soul.

The kids and I played for a while longer until Momma stuck her head out and yelled, "Who wants snow ice cream?" We ran up to the house and couldn't get through the door fast enough. We tossed our wet coats and hats near the front door and huddled by the fireplace to defrost ourselves. The whole house smelled so good, like Christmas trees, roasting turkey stuffed with Momma's delicious stuffing, and cookies. Finally, Momma handed out bowls of her sweet, rich, snow ice cream. And sitting there by that burning hot fire while eating the frosty snow ice cream was about the best combination I could ever think of. We ate it fast because it was just too good to eat slow, and because nothing melted quicker than snow ice cream. We all had seconds, and some even had thirds, until it was all gone.

The kids surrounded Momma, hugging her up. Some cried for more, and some even threw full-blown fits.

Momma comforted the crying ones and pulled them in close. "Alright now." She pointed out the window. "Look, it's still snowing! Go back out and play some more." The little ones whined, but Momma said, "You've had more than enough sweets. You don't want to spoil your appetites, do you? It'll be suppertime soon. The turkey's almost done."

"I do! I wanna spoil it!" some hollered.

Others yelled, "Yeah, we do!"

"I don't care. I want more snow ice cream!"

After Momma finished laughing, she said, "Maybe I'll make more snow ice cream after y'all eat a good dinner." Then they complained at the thought of eating anything other than more snow ice cream. But Momma rounded them up just the same and hustled them over to the pile of coats by the front door. "Now get those coats on and go back outside. Why, look at all that beautiful snow. It's just waiting for y'all to come out and play in it!" By then, our coats were damp and stiff as a board, so the kids moaned and carried on about that.

But Momma finally shooed them out. "I said go on now, git!" And she told me to keep an eye on them, make sure none of them got into any mischief or ran out into the street.

Then Momma went to the bottom of the stairs and screamed up to my big sister Sally. She had to shout pretty loud to be heard over the noise: "Sally, honey would you get the sleds for the kids? I think one of 'em's broken, but there's at least three good ones in the garage behind Fuzzy's fishing gear." My Daddy just loved to fish.

"Mom," Sally screamed back. "I got a ton of homework!" Sally was home for the holidays from her first year of art college. She was never happy being saddled with keeping an eye on us kids, though. She'd use any excuse in the book, whether it was true or not, just to get out of babysitting.

Daddy never bought a Christmas tree until Christmas Eve because that's when they were cheapest. He'd buy it, and we'd rush right home and decorate it. My brothers, sisters, and cousins would sometimes arrive early enough to help. Momma would make popcorn so us kids could string it with needles and thread to hang on the tree, along with tinsel and sparkly icicles. Momma would prepare hot chocolate too, enough for whoever was there. And sometimes she'd let us have Christmas cookies too, if we'd eaten a good healthy portion at dinnertime. It was like one big party. We'd talk and joke about what we wanted for Christmas and what we'd probably get instead.

After Christmas was over and the rest of the family was gone, I felt kind of lonely, but happy too. I guess I missed everybody. I almost wished they all lived near us. Almost.

Since we always got our Christmas tree late, we liked to leave it up for a good long time after Christmas was over. It made the house look pretty and festive. Also, my family was good at putting off hard jobs, like undecorating the Christmas tree. Packing up all those ornaments and dragging the old tree out back to burn was not a fun job. You got poked even more.

It was almost the end of January, and Momma was busy cleaning the dining room table. Then she stopped and looked over at the sad, nearly dead Christmas tree. She stared at it for a good minute, shook her head, and put her hands on her hips. "Would ya look at that mess? Pine needles everywhere!" she said to no one in particular. "Why they're just waiting to stab somebody in the foot." But her feet were the only ones in jeopardy because she was the only one who ran around the house barefoot all year long. She just loved having naked feet, no matter how cold it got, and the longer we had that Christmas tree up, the dryer and sharper those darn needles got. By then, I guess she was just fed up with the whole Christmas nonsense.

I was on the couch trying to work on a book report that was due soon. "Oh, Momma, please don't let's take the tree down yet. Can't we keep it up a little bit longer?" She shook her head again and looked at me funny. "Just look at it, Momma. It's still pretty. Kinda. And it smells so good."

"Afraid not, honey. It's gotta go. It's a fire hazard now. Come on. You start taking the ornaments off, and I'll go get the boxes from the basement." I didn't even try to argue with her—once Momma made up her mind about something, there was no changing it.

We talked about all kinds of things while we worked. About funny stuff that happened when my brothers and sisters and their families were there. Like when Packy brought one of his snakes down on

Christmas morning while we were eating breakfast and how the kids screamed, and started running all over the place. Everybody was yelling at him, but Packy just laughed. We talked about the fights that broke out and who was right and who was wrong.

Meanwhile, I took all the ornaments off the tree, and got stuck by about a million pine needles while I was at it. Then we wrapped each ornament in old newspapers and put them neatly in the boxes. Our hands turned black as coal from all the newsprint by the time we were done. When the tree was finally stripped bare, we pulled it out of its holder—got showered with even more needles—and carried it out back so Daddy could burn it when he got home from the office.

Before I ran the vacuum cleaner, I had to yank out tons more pine needles that had gotten stuck deep in the carpet. Then I had to pick up the ones that fell all over the place when we lugged the thing out back. The best part was, once we got the living room all cleaned up, it looked so pretty and tidy. Then Momma went to make dinner, and I went outside to play in the new snow.

That winter, we had more snow that stuck around than I could ever remember. Just a week before we took down the tree, we had another snowstorm and I didn't have to go to school for two whole days.

An hour or so later, when it got to be twilight, I went back inside and couldn't believe my eyes; that dried-up, old Christmas tree was sitting in its stand again, all sad and lopsided. And there was Packy unwrapping ornaments one by one and hanging them back on the tree.

Momma was standing in the dining room all red-faced with her hands on her hips. "Packy, stop! Packy, please!" she yelled. "We just finished cleaning up this mess!"

Well, he didn't say a thing. I could tell he was in one of his spooky moods. It was impossible to talk to him when he was like that. His mind was somewhere else. He probably didn't even hear a word Momma was saying. She was just like some dirty little gnat flying around that he couldn't have cared less about.

"Packy!" she screamed with her fists balled up. I thought she was going to start crying she was so mad. She threw her hands up in the air and made a loud growling sound. Then she stomped back out to the kitchen, where she went about banging pots and pans louder than usual. See, Packy was way over six feet tall, and Momma was a measly five-foot-something, so she didn't stand a chance.

Packy's back was to me. I hid in the corner and stayed quiet, made sure I was ready to run in case he looked around and started after me. I couldn't tell if he even knew I was there.

He took another ornament and went around to the other side of the tree. I had to duck down so he wouldn't see me. I listened for a long time—my heart beating fast. I peeked out from behind the chair and saw him looking down at the ornament. I noticed that his hair was combed, and he was wearing a clean shirt, one I hadn't seen before. I wondered if he had taken it from Daddy's closet, wouldn't put it past him. If I hadn't known better, I would've thought he was all dressed up to go to a party or something. Only Packy didn't have any friends. Oh, Father Joe down the street was his friend. But Father Joe was kind of like Momma's prayer-group ladies, good Christian folks who loved everybody and spent time caring for the ones who needed it most, no matter how messed up they were. But Packy didn't have a single regular friend that I knew of anyway.

My brother was a pure mystery. So, I got to thinking; maybe he did have friends. Maybe he had a whole bunch of odd, genius friends like himself that nobody else knew about. And maybe they meet in some hidden, empty house somewhere out in the country. Maybe that's where he went whenever he left in Momma's car. I pictured one of those scary, falling-down places I'd seen in a book once. A place that nobody lived in, kind of like a haunted house. I imagined a bunch of greasy-haired weirdos dressed in dirty, wrinkled clothes sitting around a few half-burned candles on old rickety crates. I thought about them talking in some foreign language Packy knew by heart, sharing all kinds of intellectual stuff that most of us wouldn't know the first thing about. Or maybe even talking in their own special made-up language that nobody knew but them.

While I watched him messing with the old, dead Christmas tree, I got lost thinking about the strange people that might be his secret friends. Then I noticed him staring at me and got the feeling he wanted to be alone. So, I went outside and watched him through the living room window. The lamps on either side of the couch were turned on and the tall one near the fireplace, so I could see in pretty good. I didn't think he could see me because it was plenty dark out.

He pulled a big string of lights out of one of the boxes and looked at it for a good long time. I bet he just wanted the tree back up where it was supposed to be, like the way it was when all the family was there, having fun and laughing a lot. I got sad for him—my eyes started to burn. I hoped he did have friends, odd genius friends like himself, hidden away somewhere.

We endured living with that old, dead tree, looking more decrepit every day, for about a week. Then Packy did another one of his disappearing acts, only this time he stayed gone for a whole day and night. So, Mom and I got busy and put everything away, cleaned up the whole mess again. Then Daddy dragged it out to the fire pit, and it instantly burst into flames the second he threw a match in its direction. When Packy finally did come home, he didn't even notice anything was different.

CHAPTER SEVEN

1959

Mom and Dad

THE RAIN HAD BEEN COMING DOWN IN BUCKETS ALL NIGHT LONG AND it was still pitch-dark out, way too early to be up on a Sunday morning. But there we were, Mom, Dad, and me shivering on the front porch in our robes and slippers. We were saying goodbye to my sister Sharon and her noisy brood. She had driven down with her four kids from Lexington on Friday especially for my birthday. They had to leave at the crack of dawn to get to their church service on time on account of it taking a whole two hours to get back home from Louisville. The screaming and yelling it took to get those wild monkeys dressed in their Sunday-go-to-meeting clothes and out the door was a sight to behold. But we did it, and at last, there was some peace and quiet in the house again.

Momma made us breakfast, and we were finally sitting down to eat. I didn't know where Packy was—sleeping, probably. The only time I ever saw him awake this early was when he'd been up all night. At least that's what it looked like. I knew to steer clear of him on those mornings because he'd be creepier than ever, eyes all bloodshot and full of mischief.

I was tired from getting up so early and helping to get the kids ready to go. But I was glad to have Mom and Dad all to myself for a change.

The tall lamp by Daddy's chair in the dining room was lit, and the world outside had taken on that quiet, secret glow that happens right before the sun comes up. The room looked different, like the colors had been sucked right out. Everything was different shades of gray.

"How'd you meet Momma, Daddy?" I asked. He looked over at her while he finished chewing his bite of toast and bacon; then he looked back at me.

"At a dance, sweetie, a long time ago. Back in… 1929." He looked at Momma again. "Why, your Momma was so pretty. Prettiest girl at the whole dance. She was a sight for sore eyes, she was, couldn't take my eyes off her." Momma's round cheeks turned pink. "I remember like it was yesterday." His eyes sparkled when he said it, and he kept staring at Momma. She batted her eyelashes real fast like she was flirting with him. Then she took a bite of her whole wheat toast.

Whole wheat bread was the only kind Momma would ever buy. "All that white Wonderbread junk is terrible for your body," she'd say. "It just gums up the works, like glue." She'd shake her head whenever she talked about it. "Don't know why parents feed their kids that crap." (That was the only bad word Momma ever used, and when she did, you better believe she meant business). It didn't matter to her that everybody else in the world, and all my friends, had delicious white bread to eat. She didn't care the least little bit.

"Your Daddy was awful pushy at that dance." Mom took a sip of her hot Sanka.

Momma didn't drink real coffee much, but she loved her pretend coffee. She liked it scalding hot too. Whenever we went to a restaurant, she always asked the waiter to bring her a bowl of boiling water so she could set her cup of Sanka in it to keep it extra hot.

"Well, I didn't have a choice now, did I, hon?" Daddy said. Then he looked back at me, and his eyes got big. "She had so many boys swarming around her, darn near broke my arm trying to get to her." Momma shook her head and chuckled.

"What's the first thing he said to you, Momma?" She made a face like she was trying to remember. Then she shook her head again.

She frowned at Daddy. "Oh, it was just pitiful. He said, 'Well, hello there, beautiful!'" She made her voice deeper when she said it, trying to sound like Daddy. We laughed and laughed. "He said it about an inch from my ear too." Daddy almost spit out his half-chewed bite; he thought that was so funny.

"Oh, and she smelled so good." Then he leaned in and looked over his glasses at Momma. "She liked it too, me talking right in her ear like that. She even swooned a little."

"Oh, Fuzzy, I did not." She smiled and glared at him. But Daddy gave me a look and nodded his head, like he'd spoken the truth and she knew it, and he was done talking.

I noticed the sun coming up, and the curtain behind Daddy ruffled from a slight breeze blowing through the open window. Momma didn't care that it was a cold rainy day in February. She just had to have fresh air blowing through the house no matter what.

Daddy still had a puddle of yellow egg yolk on his plate. He liked his eggs over easy, like me. We both loved scooping up the runny, delicious yolk with our toast. He sopped it all up with his last crusty bite and closed his eyes. After he chewed for a long time, he sat back in his chair, stretched out his long legs, and crossed one foot over the other. That meant he was done eating. We always had to wait for Daddy to finish because he was the slowest eater of anybody.

"Daddy, why do you eat so slow?"

He cocked his head and looked at me. "Well." He looked away like he had to think about it for a minute. Then he wiped his mouth with his napkin. "See, I like to think about all the things that have to happen for the food to get from where it came from to when it lands on my plate." He smiled. "And about all those people who work so hard, and about your momma making everything taste so good."

Momma always said Daddy would've looked like a hobo if it wasn't for her. He just didn't care about what he looked like, no matter where he was going or who was going to be there.

He'd put on a shirt or tie with gravy stains on it, or plaid pants or ones that clashed with his shirt, and Momma would fuss at him and make him go back and change. But see, I don't think Daddy saw things the way other people did. I think he saw everything through his artist's eyes. He didn't judge people by what they wore or how they looked, but by who they were down deep inside their hearts.

One of Daddy's favorite things was going on hunting and fishing trips. Then when he'd get home, he'd paint these beautiful pictures of the lake just before sunrise, with cattails shooting out of the marshy earth, and geese and ducks flying overhead and watery reflections of the whole scene. He told me there was nothing better in the world than getting up before dawn when it was still pitch-black out, and sneaking off with his buddies.

Daddy just loved to exaggerate too, couldn't help himself. But it made Momma real mad. "Oh, Fuzzy!" she'd say. Then she'd go about correcting whatever fib he'd just told.

One time, he explained it to her. "Why, honey," he said. "I'm just trying to make the real story a little more interesting is all."

"It was shameful," Momma said. "The way your father shoved his way through to me on the dance floor like that. Then he grabbed my hand without so much as a 'may I have this dance?' and dragged me out on the floor."

"That's right I did," Daddy said. "I think the band was playing a jitterbug, remember, hon? But be honest now… I swept you off your feet," he said with a twinkle in his eye. It was funny, and Momma thought so too. "Left all those other boys wishing they were in my shoes." Momma shook her head and rolled her eyes. I thought she was going to say something, but changed her mind. "And we won the dance contest!" Dad sounded proud.

But Momma still didn't say a word. She just looked at Daddy and kept shaking her head. Then she picked up some dishes and headed out to the kitchen.

As soon as he was sure Momma couldn't hear him, Daddy lowered his voice, like he was going to tell me a secret. "She was a natural, your mother. Best dancer I ever danced with." His eyes got watery with remembering, and he stopped talking for a minute. I think his mind kind of drifted away in the memory. I bet he was thinking about their first dance. "Why, she could follow any lead I gave her. Didn't matter if it was a waltz or foxtrot or jitterbug. Never seen anything like it."

I gathered up some breakfast dishes and followed Mom into the kitchen. She was leaning over the sink with the water running.

"What'd you think of Daddy that night, Momma?" I asked. She took her time before she said anything. She poured dish soap in the water and stirred it around with her hand.

"Well, back then, your daddy was a different man, honey." I handed her the dishes I'd brought out, and she stacked them on top of the other ones next to the sink.

"I know, Momma, but what was he like?"

She breathed out heavy, like she didn't want to tell me the truth about who Daddy was back then. "Well, frankly, honey, he was obnoxious and quite full of himself. And I soon found out he was a playboy, and he drank too much."

"Oh. Then why'd you dance with him?"

She shrugged. "Well, your father didn't give me much choice in the matter. But also, that's just the way it was back then. It was different. You danced with anybody who asked you, even if you had a date with somebody else, or you didn't like the boy who asked you. It was the proper thing to do."

Later on, when it was just me and Daddy, he told me he couldn't help himself and that while they were dancing, he asked Momma out on a date. He wanted to take her to the big Valentine's dance that was coming up. Now, Momma was only nineteen at the time, a freshman in college, and Daddy was twenty-seven, so she said she turned him down flat. "No, I'm sorry," she said. "I'm busy."

Daddy told me that he then yanked her real tight in his arms and leaned his head over so she had to look him in the eyes. "Oh, come on, please?" he pleaded. "I don't know what I'll do if I can't dance with you again." He said he smiled his best puppy-dog smile. "I'll behave… I promise." Then Momma laughed in spite of herself. He said it took a little more convincing, but she finally said she'd go to the dance with him.

Now, I don't know whether it slipped Daddy's mind that he already had a date for the big Valentine's dance, being so enamored with Momma and all, or if he just didn't care. He said he couldn't remember, but on the night of the dance, he told Momma that he'd promised to pick up his friend Seaton's date, Alice. He said that he'd drive Alice to the dance because Seaton's car was on the fritz. And he told Alice the same story—that Mom was Seaton's date, and she was going to meet him at the dance. Daddy said they both bought the story. I bet Momma had her suspicions, though.

Daddy was a smart cookie. And funny. Momma told me he could charm the pants off you even if you weren't wearing any. Daddy told me that Seaton was his best friend and that the two of them had a pact: they'd lie, cheat, or do whatever was necessary for each other when it came to pretty girls.

So, when Daddy and his two dates got to the dance, he and Seaton went back and forth all night keeping up their lie. And at the end of the dance, Daddy took Alice home first.

When he walked her to her dorm, he told me he said. "I'm sorry, Alice. I wish I could come in and spend some time with you tonight, but I have to get Dot back home."

He said Alice moved in real close. "Oh, it's alright, Fuzzy," she said stroking his chest. "I wish you could too, but I understand. Seaton's lucky to have a friend like you." Then she puckered up and leaned in to give him a big kiss like always.

But Daddy said he could just feel Momma watching from the car, so he grabbed Alice's hand and gave her a nice friendly handshake. "I'm sorry, Alice. I better go. I promised Seaton I'd get Dot back early." And that was that. I could imagine poor Alice standing there, lips all ready for one of Daddy's special kisses, but instead, she had to watch him drive off with Momma.

When he got Momma back to her dorm, I bet he sweet-talked and put his own special brand of moves on her.

Daddy was the worst kind of playboy before he met Momma, according to her. He had hundreds of girlfriends, but soon as he met Momma, he told me something took hold of him, and he lost interest in all the other girls and went after Momma full throttle.

Before Daddy came along, Momma said she 'played the field.' That's what they called dating lots of boys at the same time. She'd have dates with a different boy every weekend. She considered herself a real expert at playing hard to get, thought she had a handle on how to control the boys. Thought she knew how to keep them at arm's length, always wanting more. But she met her match with Daddy.

He was used to getting what he wanted, and he wanted Momma. He swallowed her right on up, plain and simple, didn't give her time to see any other boys. They dated a whole lot for a little while until she gave in to Daddy's charms and got herself pregnant. That was the beginning of my oldest brother, Packy.

Daddy swore Momma never knew a thing about him having two dates for the Valentine's dance until well after they were married. If that's true, I bet she wasn't happy about it.

CHAPTER EIGHT
1959
Packy Attack

I was in my room working on some stupid math problems. Classes had only started a month earlier, and our teacher, Miss Sills, was already giving us too much homework. Me and some of the other kids in my class couldn't believe we got her for core, which meant we had her for the whole day. She was the worst of all the sixth-grade teachers in the school because she was just plain ornery. She had this gravelly voice, kind of sounded like a man, and she thought she was the funniest thing since Lucille Ball. She was odd looking, too—had these tight gray curls and a great big belly. She actually looked like a man wearing a woman's wig and a muumuu. I would've felt sorry for her if she hadn't been so mean to me. She didn't smile much either, except for when she was making fun of somebody—usually me. And she smelled funny—a cross between old dead flowers and horseradish.

Math was the worst. I hated it. It took me forever to figure out the problems, and Miss Sills thought I was dumber than a box of rocks. When I didn't finish my work for the day, or if I got something wrong—which was often—she'd point it out in front of the whole class, pretending like she was just joking around. I couldn't stand her, and I wasn't the only one.

The school held auditions for the play, *Peter Pan,* and Mom said I should try out for it. Even though I was scared, I did, and got the role of Wendy. It was so much fun, and I learned the lines before anybody else. After that, I started taking some acting classes and decided I loved it as much as ballet.

I was nice and comfy, sitting on my bed with the covers bunched up around me. I liked doing my homework there and got used to it since I didn't have a desk in my room. I used my big geography book as a hard surface to write on. I usually didn't get around to starting my homework until shortly before I went to sleep, but that wasn't working out too well. So, I figured I'd try doing it soon as I got home from school.

I'd been working on it for a while and feeling pretty good because most of it was done.

Then I heard Packy's loud footsteps coming down the hall. Before I knew what was happening, he burst into my room like he always did, and I stood up on my bed.

"Get out!" I screamed. Then I lost my balance and bounced around, trying to gather up all my books and homework. "Mom! Make Packy get out! I'm trying to do my homework!"

My feet got tangled up in the covers, and I fell over a couple of times. He laughed every time. I got madder and madder.

He grabbed my math book and started riffling through it. A bunch of little pieces of paper I'd been using as bookmarks flew out everywhere. "Damnit!" I yelled. I'd put them in certain places so I'd remember the parts I needed help with.

"What'cha readin'?" Packy asked. Like he cared. He held my math book down real low, just out of my reach. I tried to grab it, but he yanked it away just before I got to it. I almost fell off the bed. He thought that was hilarious. I would've punched his lights out if he hadn't been so big and tall. I climbed down off the bed, and he raised the book up high. I jumped up and grabbed it. He smirked and, with his other hand, yanked my history book from me.

"Stop it!" I screamed at the top of my lungs. I tried to punch him, but he pulled back. Then I started slapping at him, but he put his huge hand on top of my head to hold me back so I couldn't reach him. "I hate you! Give 'em back!" He smirked and tried to grab my homework papers. I held on tight, though, and they ripped in half. That's when I fell and hit my head on the table by my bed. "Ow! Goddamn you!" I screamed.

I gathered as many books and papers as I could and looked down at my wrist. It was bleeding! "Ow! You stupid! Look what you made me do!" I ran out of my room, leaned over the banister, and hollered, "Mom! Help!" Then I went back in my room, rubbing my head where I could already feel a big knot swelling. "I'm telling Mom everything, you big fat pig!" and I ran down the stairs.

The whole downstairs smelled like pork ribs boiling in sauerkraut. That was my favorite dish of all the ones Momma made. They were bubbling away in the huge aluminum pot on the stove.

Whenever she made it, I could hardly stop myself from eating too much.

Mom was at the sink washing dishes. She had her blue apron tied around her big belly. She'd been heavy ever since I could remember. I thought maybe it was because having six kids must be too many. You probably couldn't help getting fat after having so many babies.

I stomped over next to her. "I hate him, Momma. I hate him so much. Look, he pushed me down." I squeezed the cut on my wrist hard, and a big dark bubble of blood oozed out. I held it over her dishwater, so she had to look at it. "See? I'm bleeding." She didn't even give it a glance. "And I got a big bump on my head, too." I leaned over and pointed to it. "Right here. Ow! See? It's gonna be huge." She pushed my head away and brushed the gray curls off her forehead. She looked sad, like she was about to cry. And tired too. But she always looked tired. "And he tore up my homework!" I stuck my bloody cut in her face again. She looked at it for about a second and touched it. "Ow! Mom!" I yanked my arm away.

"Honey, just…" She took a deep breath and shook her head. "Just stay away from him." Then she wiped her hands on her apron and went to the stove. I followed her.

"Mom! How am I supposed to stay away from him? He was in *my* room! Why won't you ever do something?" The cookie sheet on top of the aluminum pot was so old it was practically black. Mom grabbed the potholders and took it off the pot. She must've forgotten about the big bubble of steam just waiting to explode out of the boiling ribs, because it almost hit her square in the kisser, but she backed off just in the nick of time. Then she shot me a look like it was my fault her face almost got burned off.

Mom once told me that steam made the most painful burns of all, and that I should always put lots of cold water on any kind of burn. I wondered if she was going to stick her whole face under the faucet.

The smell of the ribs boiling made my mouth water so much that I almost forgot I was mad.

Momma threw down the potholders and pushed past me. She went back to the sink and turned on the cold water.

I couldn't figure out why she never helped when Packy was tormenting me. Except that he was so much bigger and stronger than her, maybe she was as afraid of him as I was.

I was about to yell some more. But when I wiped the tears out of my eyes and looked at her, she seemed small. Her shoulders were hunched, and her head was hanging down. It looked like she was about to slide right into the soapy dishwater. I saw through the window over the sink that the afternoon light was beginning to fade into dusk. The dimming light made the curtains look dirty, and the room was losing its color.

I gave up and went back to my room. Momma was sad, and I was mad, and I couldn't see any way we would be friendly with each other.

By the time I got up there, my room was empty. I figured Packy probably got bored with me being gone and nobody else to torment. I tried to calm down so I could get back to my math problems. But then I saw my torn-up pieces of homework scattered on the floor, and I got furious again.

A few minutes later, I heard the front door open, and I ran downstairs. I was halfway down when Daddy walked in. "Hi, sweetheart." He had a big smile on his face and looked tired from working all day.

"Daddy, can you pleeeease put a lock on my door?" I pleaded. I hurried down the rest of the stairs and stood in front of him in the foyer. "Packy keeps coming in my room and grabbing my books while I'm trying to do my homework. I can't get anything done! He made me fall and cut myself too, and he tore up my homework!"

Daddy bugged his eyes out and cocked his head, like he was waiting for a hello or a hug or something. Usually, I'd run to him when he got home, and we'd do a little dance together. He'd sing, "Lump-de-dumpty-de-dumpty-dump." I was always happy when Daddy got home, but that day, I was just too mad to dance.

"Hi," I said, and he held out his arms. I gave him a quick hug. "Hi. Packy won't stay out of my room, Daddy, and he's so mean and stupid, and now my math homework, that I worked on really hard, is all torn to pieces! I can't get anything done when he keeps barging in, Daddy. And look!" I showed him the cut on my wrist. "This is where he pushed me down, and I was bleedin'!" Then I looked around and lowered my voice. "And Momma didn't do a darn thing about it."

"Oh, honey." He put down his big brown briefcase, took off his coat and hat, and put them on the chair in the living room. "I'll tell you what." He leaned in close to me. "I think I've got a lock that I can put on your door. It's in my big red toolbox. You wanna go see if you can find it? If you do, I'll put it on right now." I ran off before Daddy even finished talking. "It should be in with the screws and nails, honey," he yelled after me.

My daddy was real handsome. He had thick wavy hair that was fuzzy when he was a kid. That's how come he got his nickname, "Fuzzy." His job was president of Gibbs Inman Printing Company downtown because his daddy started the company when Daddy was just a boy. I never met either one of my grandfathers, or my grandmother on Daddy's side. They all died before I came along. That's the trouble with being born last in a big family: everybody's always dead or far away doing other things by the time you come along. All that's left are just wild stories about the fun you missed.

Daddy's workshop was in the basement and always smelled like oil and metal. He had painted the shape of each tool on the wall in neat little rows above his worktable. Then he screwed in hooks at the top of each and hung all the tools in their rightful place. It looked like they all had shadows.

I rummaged through Daddy's red toolbox and found one of those hook-type locks, the kind you hook the hook part into the hole. I kept on looking, hoping I'd find the good kind. Finally, I gave up, figured something was better than nothing. I ran back upstairs with it and said, "Is this the one you mean?"

Daddy was sitting at the dining room table reading his newspaper. Momma wouldn't even glance at a newspaper, said it was nothing but a bunch of bad news, and she had better things to think about. Daddy sat up in his chair at the head of the table and shook the newspaper to make it fold right. "Oh, good, you found it." I handed him the lock, and he blew on it and brushed off the dust.

"Daddy, don't you have one of those better ones? You know, the kind that has like a bolt thing? Like the one you put on Sally's door?"

"You mean a deadbolt? No, honey. But this one should do the trick, don't you think? Come on. We'll go put it on right now."

Then Momma yelled from the kitchen: "Reedy, let your father relax now. Don't bother him. He's been working hard all day."

Daddy looked toward the kitchen, then back at me. He winked, nodded his head, and motioned toward my room. Sometimes, Daddy and I had little secrets from Momma.

We snuck up to my room, and I watched Daddy screw the hook part onto the door, and the hole part onto the doorjamb. And just like that, the lock was on. I gave him a big hug and kiss.

"Thanks, Daddy!" I said and went in my room and locked the door. I heard him chuckle and go back downstairs. I looked around my room and felt sort of safe for the first time. I picked up the pieces of my homework, smoothed them out, and put them together like puzzle pieces. Then I got comfortable on my bed again.

A little while later, I heard Packy coming down the hall toward my room, and sure enough, he tried to open the door. But he only got it open about an inch before the lock stopped him. I froze.

I could see his eyeball through the crack. My stomach knotted up. I didn't move a muscle and hoped he would just go away. But he didn't, of course. Instead, he stared at me through the opening. I stared back. I wished the darn lock had been the good kind, so he wouldn't have been able to see me at all.

Then Mom yelled up from the kitchen, "Come to dinner, you all." Packy chuckled, and I felt blood rush to my face. I hated him so much sometimes. Then he almost unhooked the lock, but soon as I saw his big fat finger slip through the opening, I ran to the door and pressed down hard on the hook. We stared at each other through the gap. After a few seconds, he walked away, and I heard him go downstairs. And I thought I was going to be safe.

CHAPTER NINE
1960
My Thirteenth Birthday

My birthday party was on Saturday, so Mom and I baked a cake. It was white with chocolate frosting, my all-time favorite. And boy oh boy did the whole house smell delicious while it was baking in the oven and when it came out. Before the party, though, and before I even invited anybody, I had a talk with Mom because I was really worried.

"Momma, what about Packy?" She had just finished vacuuming and was fussing around the living room, straightening up. I had to talk loud so she'd hear me. Sometimes she just didn't listen. I'd say something, and she'd say something back that didn't make any sense at all.

That's when I knew she wasn't paying attention. "Mom, I hate having my party here 'cause I just know he'll ruin it like he ruins everything." I knew he would, too.

"Oh, honey, it'll be fine."

"No, it won't!" I went and stood right in front of her, so she'd stop what she was doing and listen to me for a change.

She took a big breath, turned off the vacuum, and grabbed my hands. "Honey, I already talked to him, I told him that he needed to behave himself on Saturday and leave you girls alone because it was your big day."

Like that was going to do one bit of good.

"I promise he won't be a problem." Then she went about wiping the dust off tables and things and picking up pieces of fluff off the carpet that the sweeper left behind.

But Packy was always a problem. That's just who he was. I thought for a second and realized that her telling him about my party was probably the worst thing she could've done. Now he was bound to show up and do something weird or horrible or both.

"You always say that, Momma. You always say he won't be a problem. But it's just not true. I can never invite anybody over 'cause of him."

"Sweetheart, sweetheart. Don't worry about it. I told him he can use my car on Saturday so he'll probably go to the library." She blew some curls out of her face. "Now, go invite your girlfriends." She turned me around and swatted my behind, like the matter was settled. I prayed Momma was right this time, that Packy would mind her for once in his miserable life.

I could hardly wait for my party. I had a new friend named Annette who was coming. She'd just moved into the neighborhood and lived a couple of blocks away. She seemed really smart, and I was surprised she even wanted to come. I only invited her because she asked me what I was doing for my birthday, you know, to celebrate and all. So, I told her about the party and, just to be nice, asked her if she wanted to come. And she said sure.

Jennifer, a friend from school, was coming, plus Linda, who'd been my best friend since I first started seventh grade. We had homeroom together and liked each other from the very first day we met. Martha, Margaret, and Mary from across the street were coming too. Mom and I got up super early on Saturday to tidy up the house and make some food. I was so relieved because, just like Momma promised, Packy was nowhere to be found. Mom and I made a big fruit salad, a large pot of sweet mint tea, and Benedictine sandwiches out of cream cheese, onions, and grated cucumber. I loved Benedictine, could've eaten the whole bowl of it all by myself. I was surprised because when we went shopping, Momma bought white bread to make the little sandwiches out of.

"This is your thirteenth birthday, honey, I want it to be real special." We even cut off the crusts so they'd look pretty.

Most of the girls got there almost at one o'clock on the dot, and soon as they arrived, we started yakking it up. Everybody was hungry too, so Mom brought out the food and mint tea right away, and we had the best time eating and talking. They just loved the little Benedictine finger sandwiches, thought they were adorable and yummy. I'd fancied up the serving plate with some parsley and purple grapes, so it looked like what they would serve in a restaurant.

While we chatted and ate, I heard heavy footsteps coming down the stairs—*Packy!* I thought. I knew this was going to happen. A big lump formed in my stomach.

I must've looked worried because Annette said, "What's the matter, Reedy?" She was the only one in a three-block radius who didn't know about Packy, on account of her family had just moved in.

"Oh, no, it's nothing," I said and rolled my eyes. "It's just my big brother." I hoped and prayed he'd go about his business and leave us alone. But instead, he came around the corner and just stood there in the living room looking at all of us.

By then, Packy was thirty years old. He was so big and tall that everybody just stopped talking and stared at him. He looked different. Better different. His shirt didn't have nearly as many wrinkles as usual, but one of the buttons was missing, and his bushy chest showed through. His hair was actually combed, for a change, and had a nice little part in it. For a long moment, Packy just stood there, didn't say a word. Then he reached out and handed me a shoebox with a pink ribbon wrapped around it, real haphazard. I looked into his green eyes, tried to figure out what he was up to. He seemed to be in one of his good moods, as best I could tell.

"Happy birthday," he said and smiled a little. Then he tipped his head to one side. I didn't move. I knew I was going to have to open his stupid box, but I really didn't want to in front of my friends. "Go ahead. It's not gonna bite ya." All the girls laughed. I didn't. I took the box. He stuck his hands in his pockets and watched me.

Packy had never given me, or anybody else, a serious present in his life, as far as I knew. Not for birthdays or Christmas or anything.

I was trapped, scared he was going to surprise me with God knows what, and embarrass me in front of my girlfriends. I felt the knots in my stomach twist tighter. I couldn't think of a way out. Everybody looked at me, waiting to see what was in the box. I took off the ribbon and opened it.

It was a snake. Surprise! It was brown with markings on its back, coiled up just lying there. When the girls saw what it was, they squealed and ran as far away as possible, and still be in the room. I wasn't surprised. I stayed real calm, like it was no big deal. Packy smiled. He seemed pleased, like it was our little joke.

"This is Sssammy, the Sssnake," he said. The girls laughed at a snake named Sssammy. "He's harmless, wouldn't hurt a fly. Well, he might eat a fly, but he wouldn't eat a human. Unless it's a fly-sized human."

They thought that was hilarious. Then Packy gave me a little nod, so I reached in and pulled the snake out of the box. The girls screamed and carried on about how brave I was. Why, you'd have thought I was some kind of superhero or something.

I let Sammy lay on my arm. Then he slithered slowly down toward my hand. I wasn't even a tiny bit scared. I moved my arm around like I was a real snake handler. All the girls ooooh-ed and ahhh-ed when it moved its head up and darted its black forked tongue out a few times. I felt so brave. See, I was used to being around Packy's snakes. He'd taught me the right way to pick them up and hold them.

"Oh boy," I said. "Just what I wanted for my birthday." Everybody laughed and laughed. Then they inched closer.

"Who'd like to hold Sammy?" Packy asked. Well, no one volunteered, but Annette moved in and petted it for about a second before she ran off laughing.

"Eeeew!" she screamed and gave a little shiver. The rest of the girls crowded around.

Then Jennifer asked, "What'd it feel like?"

"Did you really touch it?" Linda asked.

Annette nodded her head. "It was slimy!" She crumpled up her face. "Kind of dry, but slimy, too." The girls giggled and squirmed their bodies around. It looked like Sammy was watching her.

"I think Sam likes you," Packy said. "You looking for a new pet?" Everybody thought that was hilarious too. Annette shook her head. Then Sammy started moving down off my arm and onto the coffee table, so Packy got hold of him and put him back in the box. "You've had enough fun with the girls, Sam." He turned to my friends. "He's not used to birthday parties. Time for his nap." They thought my brother was just the funniest thing. Then everybody took a long last look at Sammy before Packy put the lid on the box—he and I smiled at each other. Then the girls said "goodbye" to Packy and his friend, and he went back upstairs. Once he was gone, Annette and Jennifer asked all kinds of questions.

"Where'd he get Sammy?" Jennifer asked. "Where do you even get a snake?"

"Yeah, and what does it eat?" Annette asked. "Mice? I think they eat live mice! Did you ever see it eat a live mouse?"

Martha, Margaret, and Mary knew Packy, sort of, so we took turns telling the other girls all about his strange zoo upstairs in his attic, about his lizards, and frogs, and rats, and about all the different kinds of snakes he had locked up in cages and that some of them were dead.

That day, things were different because Packy wasn't the freak of the neighborhood. Instead, he was a most interesting person. And I was brave and interesting too, because I lived with him. That was the best part of my birthday, Packy dressing up all nice and surprising me. Why, he acted like we had planned that birthday show together.

CHAPTER TEN
1962
Tommy & the State Fair

I WAS SO HAPPY BECAUSE I WAS FINALLY IN THE NINTH GRADE. IT WAS Friday, the end of the second week of school, and time to go home. I was pooped, sweaty, and my hair was a big, kinky mess. It usually ended up all frizzy like that because they turned the heat up to a gazillion degrees in the classrooms. I'd be sweating up a storm by the end of the day and look like I had on a big frizzy clown wig. My blouse was a sight too because when I was getting ready for school in the morning, Packy snuck up behind me and yanked it out of my hands. And it was my last clean shirt too.

"Packy!" I shouted. Then he wadded it up in a ball, and I tried to grab it back, but he twisted it tighter. "Give it to me!" I screamed. "Give me my Goddamn shirt!" He laughed and pushed me back. I fell down on my ankle real hard. "Oww! You stupid…!" He just smiled. I saw the little purple bruise on his right cheek from when I threw my hairbrush at him the day before.

He wouldn't leave me alone was why. After it bonked him in the face, I ran downstairs to Mom quick as I could because I knew if he caught me, I'd be dead for sure.

He looked a mess, even worse than usual. He was wearing the same clothes he'd been wearing since I didn't know when, and his hair was so greasy it sort of looked wet. Some buttons were missing from his dirty, smelly shirt, and his big hairy belly showed through.

The sun was shining through my window and lit up the pimples on the side of his face. Some were bright red and oozy, looked ready to burst wide open. And some were crusty, almost black, probably dried-up scabs from him picking at them all day. He was a grown man and still had pimples. I knew why too; it was because he hardly ever washed himself.

I tried to grab my shirt, but he just pushed me back. "Mom!" I screamed. "Mom! Make Packy give me my shirt!"

"Packy?" she hollered from downstairs. Her voice sounded tired already, and it wasn't even seven-thirty in the morning. "Leave your sister alone now! She's gonna to be late for school again!" Like her fussing at him was going to do a bit of good.

"You stupid!" I yelled at him. "I'm going to be late for school again." He glared at me.

"MOM!" I screamed even louder. I was so furious I was about to cry. Then I heard her heavy footsteps coming up the stairs.

"Packy, just stop!" she yelled. "Reedy's got to get ready—"

"MOM!" I couldn't help but scream again because Packy started swatting me with my own blouse. He smirked and shook his head, like it was my fault that Mom had to come all the way upstairs. As if I was the reason for all her troubles. It didn't matter, anyway. Nothing ever mattered when it came to him and his hateful moods. He knew it, and I knew it. He could do anything he wanted, any time he wanted, and there was nothing Mom or anybody else could do about it.

When Mom got to the top of the stairs, Packy dropped the shirt and left my room. I grabbed my blouse and tried to brush out the wrinkles. It was hopeless, so I hurried and got dressed quick as I could because if I was tardy one more time, I'd be in real trouble.

I got to school seconds before the last bell rang. I ran into my classroom with my blouse looking like I'd slept in it.

I was so glad it was Friday. I'd just finished fifth-period history, my last class of the day. I hated it. The teacher, Mr. Wilson, was weird, boring, and funny-looking. He talked in this monotone voice, and his hair was too short. He looked like he just fell off an army truck or something. And he waddled like a duck. Mr. Wilson could tell you a story about Disneyland and make it sound like the most boring place on earth. I got the feeling he really liked history, but when the information came from his brain out of his mouth, you'd think he was reporting on his morning bowel movements.

I was so tired and just wanted to go home. I wished I could've been invisible, what with my big clown hair and my blouse looking even worse than before.

The halls were jammed with students, everybody shouting and slamming lockers. Then I noticed Tommy in the middle of the crowd, and he was coming right straight towards me. Tommy was in the tenth grade and he was dreamy cute. I'd secretly had a crush on him for about a whole year. My heart would jump, and I'd get butterflies in my stomach every time I saw him.

I tried to tuck in my shirt and smooth my hair down at the same time. "Hi," I whispered under my breath, just in case it was me he was looking at. Tommy was smart, and funny, and handsome, and really sweet, too. I think he was friends with just about everybody in school. It seemed like he was staring right at me. He kept walking closer and closer until he came right up to my face.

"Hi," he said. I almost wet my pants. "You going to the fair today?" He talked loud enough so I could hear him over the crowd. My stomach got fluttery, and I turned around to see if maybe he was talking to somebody behind me.

The Kentucky State Fair had just started that day. The fair was a big deal. All my friends were talking about it. Was I going? Heck yeah, I was going! Then I remembered I got an F on a history quiz the week before, and maybe Momma wasn't going to let me go. She said I didn't study hard enough.

But she had to let me go. I was almost sure she'd change her mind after she found out that Tommy wanted me to go. I usually told Momma everything because sometimes she was more like a friend than a mom. She already knew I was crazy about Tommy.

Suddenly, my throat got bone dry. I could hardly talk I was so nervous. "Yeah."

"Great! You want to meet me there? Maybe by the tilt-o-whirl?"

Oh my God. Oh my God! I couldn't believe my ears. Tommy wanted to meet me at the tilt-o-whirl! I stared at his darling face. He looked so neat and clean, like he'd just stepped out of a shower, dried off, and put on freshly ironed clothes. And he smelled sweet, like soap and English Leather cologne. I probably smelled like a wet dog. He was holding his books: algebra, English, history, but no binder. Where was his binder? Was he so smart he didn't even have to keep notes or write down assignments? I tried to push the frizz out of my face, but it just plopped right back down. It was hopeless.

Tommy leaned in even closer. "Reedy? Wanna meet at the tilt-o-whirl?" I melted. "You think you can find it?"

I tried to say something, but all I could do was nod. He smiled, and there was his gold tooth, front bottom, shining like a funny little star. I knew Mom wouldn't like it; she wouldn't understand. She'd think it was tacky. I thought it was adorable and kind of mysterious.

"Yes?"

"Yeah." I looked into his beautiful, light brown eyes. "I can."

"Great, that's great." He beamed at me. "Is four-thirty good?"

"Four-thirty," was all I could get out of my mouth. But inside, I was dancing, jumping up and down and shouting. Then I thought about Mom. What if she wouldn't let me go because of that bad grade? But she had to—she just had to!

"OK," he said and touched my arm. "See you there." I got goose bumps and watched him walk away. I didn't think he even noticed how messy I was or how sweaty, or even if I smelled. I think he saw the real me. He looked back. Our eyes met, and he waved. Then he disappeared into the crowd.

I stood there and let it wash over me like the happiest dream ever. I could hardly believe it really happened. Then I got scared—what if when we met, I was too nervous to talk?

But suddenly, I didn't care. I just started walking. Even though I couldn't remember where I was supposed to go, or why.

I knew I had to go somewhere because school was out. I walked as fast as I could through the crowd and down the stairs. I rushed past all the bodies, then remembered I had to go to my locker. Where *was* my locker? What was my locker number? It took a few minutes, but I finally remembered and found it. I grabbed my coat, my purse, and a couple of books I had homework in, and then rushed through the crowded hallway and out into the parking lot.

Mom was waiting for me. "Mom!" I yelled. She rolled down her window and smiled. "Mom, guess what! Tommy—" Then I caught myself and stopped yelling. I looked around the bustling parking lot. School buses, cars, and students were everywhere. I wasn't thinking right. What if somebody had heard me yelling about Tommy? As soon as I got to the car, I opened the door and said, "Tommy wants to meet me at the fair!"

Her mouth dropped wide open. "What? You mean Tom--"

"Yes! He wants to meet me at the fair!" I hopped in and shut the door. "He just came right up to me and asked if I would meet him at the tilt-o-whirl!"

"Oh, my goodness! How did… that's so exciting!" Mom grabbed my hand and squeezed it. "What time are you supposed to meet him? And where, do you know where?"

"Yeah, at the tilt-o-whirl," I reminded her.

"Oh, yes, you said that. Can you find it? You remember where it was last year? Near that hot dog stand, right? Let's see, it was—"

I pounded on the seat. "Mom, let's go, drive!" I demanded. "I'm supposed to meet him at four-thirty. Hurry!"

"Oh, OK, my goodness!" She started the car, and we drove off.

"Is my blue skirt clean? And my blue blouse with the stripes?"

"Yes, honey, they're both clean. They're hanging in your closet, just did the *warsh* today." (That's how we said it in Louisville. Warsh, sounded like it had an extra 'r' right in the middle.)

"Oh. Whew! Thank you!" I was so relieved because I remembered practically every piece of clothing I had was dirty, and I didn't have time to be running around my room picking up shirts and sniffing them to see if one didn't stink too bad, so I could wear it again. Especially for something as special as meeting Tommy at the fair.

"Yeah, and it's freshly pressed."

I thanked her again, leaned over, and gave her a big kiss on the cheek.

We couldn't get home fast enough for me. Then I saw where I'd written Tommy's name in the layer of dust on the dashboard a few days earlier. I would never have imagined I'd have an actual date with him when I wrote it. Maybe I was becoming magical, or psychic, I thought, like one of those people who can tell you what's going to happen in the future.

Mom reached over and brushed the frizz off my forehead. "Maybe you should try to do something with your hair."

I pushed her hand away. "Yeah, Mom. I'm gonna! I'll roll it up when we get home, if we ever get there." I thought about the bad grade I got and prayed she wouldn't remember. Plus, my room was a big mess. Sometimes that got her steaming mad, and she wouldn't let me go places. I thought about Packy too, and started praying even harder that he wouldn't be home. I was doing lots of praying on that ride home.

I just couldn't be late to meet Tommy. I always hated being late, hated that my family was usually late for everything. It was mostly Momma's fault; she just couldn't seem to get herself ready on time. Sometimes we even missed airplanes and trains, getting there just as they were taking off. Daddy'd try to hurry her along, but she'd just fuss at him. "Oh, Fuzzy!" she'd say. Daddy would plead with Momma to get herself ready so we could leave in plenty of time. She'd get so mad. "Fuzzy, go wait in the car!" she'd say. And he would too.

I hurried and got my hair looking pretty OK, had to use so much hair spray it got stiff as a board, though. I made Momma leave as soon as I was ready, even though she didn't want to.

She said, "Oh, we have lots of time, honey." But I'd heard that before, too many times. So, I fussed and carried on until she gave in, and we left.

When she dropped me off, I rushed out of the car, and she yelled after me, "Have fun, sweetheart. I'll pick you up here about six-thirty!"

"OK!" I yelled back. I ran to the end of the long ticket line. I got out the money to pay the man and kept watching the huge clock hanging by the gate. It was exactly 4:26 when I finally got through. I sort of remembered where the tilt-o-whirl was from the year before, so I ran fast as I could, trying not to crash into people. It was super crowded, probably because all us kids had just gotten out of school.

I ran past the rollercoaster and saw the hot dog stand Mom reminded me about. I knew I was close, so I slowed down and looked around for Tommy, didn't want him to see me running. I hoped my hair still looked OK. I smoothed it down as best I could.

I was pretty sure I got to the tilt-o-whirl right on time. I looked around for Tommy in the crowd of people. It was loud, kids running every which way, chasing each other, screaming and laughing. I got a chill of excitement. I looked all around and saw two little boys start to fight. Then a bigger girl tried to break it up and got punched. She started raising all kinds of hell, screaming bloody murder, and then one of the boys punched the boy who punched her, and then most of the kids were crying and punching each other. It was one big, screaming mess.

Behind the ruckus, I saw a guy who looked like Tommy, but he was far away. He had brown hair and a blue shirt. I got excited. He was mostly turned away, looking off somewhere. I could only see a little bit of his face, and then a whole bunch of people passed in front of me, and when I looked again, he was gone. I searched everywhere. I even ran to where I saw him, but he was nowhere. I got worried. Had I missed him? What if it was Tommy, and when he didn't see me, he left? I walked around the area in a panic. Had he vanished into thin air? A clock hanging in the ticket booth said 4:35. Maybe he was late.

Then I thought of something horrible. What if he was playing a mean trick on me, saying he wanted to meet me, and then not show-ing up? My heart sank. I didn't think he would ever do such a thing. But maybe it was too good to be true—why would he want to go out with me? I wondered. Mom and Dad always told me I was pretty, but maybe I just wasn't good enough or smart enough for Tommy. It all started to make sense. My eyes got itchy and filled with tears. I sat down on a bench and tried not to cry. Suddenly, I felt a warm hand on my shoulder and smelled English Leather cologne.

"Hi," a voice said close to my ear. His breath was warm and smelled sweet. "Sorry I'm late. You been here long?"

He did come! The noisy crowd disappeared, and blood rushed to my face. I probably turned red as a beet. I wiped my eyes gently so as not to smudge my mascara and turned around. Tommy stood there with a huge smile on his face. Then the smile disappeared.

"Are you OK?"

"Hi! Yeah, no, I'm fine. I just, I got something in my eye, a speck of dust or something." I stood up. He came around the bench and put his arm around my waist. A chill ran through my whole body.

"It's crazy here, isn't it?" he said. "Wanna get in line? The tilt-o-whirl's my favorite ride."

"Me too! It's my favorite ride too!" And it was. It was scary, but felt safe at the same time. We walked to the end of the ticket line.

"You look nice," he said. Then a kid bumped into him, and Tommy stumbled in close to me. I looked into his eyes, but got self-conscious and looked away.

"Thanks. Yeah, I had to change because I was a mess."

We rode almost every single ride that day. I didn't mind standing in the long lines because I was with Tommy, and we just talked and talked. Then we went to see all the beautiful quilts and ate some award-winning pie. We both liked the green apple best; the crust was nice and crispy, and the apple part had just the right amount of sweet and spice. Then we went to see the animals. The baby pigs were our favorite. We got to laughing and couldn't stop; they were so funny. They bounced around and oinked all over the place. I was surprised because talking to Tommy was so easy. I even told him about Packy, and he understood.

"I'd like to meet him sometime," he said.

"No, you wouldn't!" He thought that was hilarious. It was like, all of a sudden, I had a new best friend who was handsome and nice and wanted to be with me all the time. We stayed at the fair for a long time. It was the most fun I'd ever had. Then he asked me if I'd meet him on Monday morning in front of the school. And I said. "Yes!"

of course. Mom picked me up like she said she would, and I couldn't shut up. I talked her ear off about Tommy and everything. She didn't get a single word in edgewise.

Tommy and I did meet Monday morning. In fact, we met every morning in the cafeteria for the rest of the school year.

From that day on, I couldn't wait to go to school and always got there early. I didn't think anything would ever make me love going to school, but Tommy did.

I asked him once why he wanted to go out with me in the first place, and he told me he'd had a crush on me ever since he was in the sixth grade, which meant I was in the fifth. I couldn't believe it. I couldn't believe I didn't know. I did remember him chasing me around our grammar school cafeteria one time, but I thought he was just some weird kid who liked to play funny games.

Tommy's parents were a lot like *Father Knows Best* on TV. His dad was the head of the household for sure, and his mom seemed like the perfect mom.

Tommy's family wasn't like mine, not even a little bit. They were very 'normal.' And when Tommy met Packy, he treated him with such kindness and respect, that Packy liked him right away. That year was the most wonderful because Tommy was the best thing that had ever happened to me.

CHAPTER ELEVEN

1963

Dyslexia Camp

It was early June, and I had just graduated from ninth grade. It was the most fun year ever because I got to see Tommy almost every day. He was like my best friend. We did everything together. I was sure we were going to get married someday. It felt like we were already married, really. Except for the sex part. He never even tried anything because he respected me.

Tommy and I even liked the same things and we talked about everything. I even told Tommy a lot about Packy, like how crazy he acted, and that sometimes I hated him. But Tommy understood and helped me understand a little bit better. And I wasn't worried about my grades anymore because Tommy thought I was plenty smart. Funny thing too, it seemed like everybody at Seneca liked me then because I was Tommy's girlfriend.

Right after my ninth-grade graduation, I found out something absolutely terrible—Mom had enrolled me in a six-week summer program for dyslexic students and hadn't even told me. Well, maybe she did. She said she did. Maybe I just didn't hear her—like she said it real soft or something. It was going to be at a university, an hour and forty-five-minute drive from Louisville, and it was supposed to start in less than a week!

Tommy had just gotten his driver's license, and there was no way his parents were going to let him drive that far to see me. I couldn't believe I was going to have to leave him for so long.

As soon as I found out, I screamed at her, "Mom! How could you?"

"Oh, honey, I told you about it—"

"Did not!"

"Besides, Reedy, it's only for six weeks. Come on now. You're going to make a lot of new friends, honey. It'll be fun."

"Mom, you do not understand. I'm in love with Tommy. I love him so much. I can't leave and not see him for a whole six weeks!"

I saw a tiny smile on her face, like she was laughing at me. "Sweetheart, I know you *think* you're in love—"

"Why do you hate Tommy, Mom?"

There was that smile again. "Honey, I don't hate Tommy. He's a fine boy, but you're so young." She shook her head. "You should be dating lots of boys, not going steady with—"

"You don't know anything, Mom!" I yelled. "I'm not going to that stupid program!" I burst into tears and ran up to my room and slammed the door.

Later, when Daddy got home from work, he and Mom gave me a good talking-to. He told me that Mom had spent a lot of time searching for the right program and that they had already paid for it. And that, yes, I most certainly *was* going.

Sometimes, I hated them. Mom said the program was very important because—blah, blah, blah. Whatever! Something about reprogramming my brain and helping me get better in school. I didn't care about school. I only cared about how much I was going to miss Tommy. I cried a lot, until Mom made me a promise. She promised that she'd come get me midway through the program, so that in only three weeks, I'd get to come home for the weekend and see Tommy. I was still mad, but didn't have a choice in the matter.

The summer program was on the campus of Western University in Berea, Kentucky. Us students would stay in the dormitories—which was pretty cool. They came from all over the United States and ranged in age from nine to nineteen. I didn't know much about the program except that it was designed to help us overcome our dyslexia.

I cried and gave Tommy lots of kisses when we said goodbye. Then Mom drove me to the university on Sunday, a day before the thing started. By then, I felt a little better about going because of what Mom had said about meeting new friends and living on my own. When we got there, Mom and I walked around the campus.

"Look how beautiful it is here, honey." She put her arm around me.

It was too. There were huge trees everywhere, and lots of college students picnicking, studying, or reading in small groups. It was like a giant park with huge brick buildings all around. Mom helped me organize things in my room, and then we went to the orientation together. They told us that dyslexia was far more prevalent in males than females and often more severe. I was shocked to find out that sixty-four boys were enrolled in the program and only four girls.

I liked my roommate a lot. Her name was Lynne, and she was sixteen like me. She was from Louisville too and had a mess of frizzy red hair. The other two girls in the program were way younger. Each of us had a tutor for an hour every day, and twice a week, we had this silly marching class. There were also folk dancing classes, music classes, and percussion and rhythm classes. Those were activities that dyslexics were not supposed to be good at, but I was good at all of them. It made me wonder why I was even there. What *was* wrong with me?

There were lots of cute boys in the classes, and some of them started flirting with me. I kind of liked it too and started flirting back. It made me think about what Momma had said about me dating lots of boys.

I missed Tommy so much. At first. But once I got busy with all the classes and activities, I didn't have time to think about much else.

Some of the boys had dyslexia bad. They could hardly read or carry a tune to save their lives.

A few were so uncoordinated at dancing and rhythm classes; it was a wonder they could even walk on their own. There were some older boys that were handsome and pretty normal too. Bill was one of them.

Bill and I were in the same folk dancing class, and one day when it was over and we were all leaving the room, I accidentally stumbled forward and plowed right into him. "Oh shit!" I said.

"Whoa," he said as he helped me steady myself.

"I'm sorry."

"What've you been drinking?" he said with a chuckle. That got me to laughing so hard I almost fell down.

"I was kidding, but seriously, are you drunk?"

Well, that did it. I couldn't stop laughing, had to sit down on the floor for a minute. Bill squatted down next to me. Then, after everybody else left, and we finally stopped laughing, Bill and I started talking, and he walked me back to my dorm. He was cool and funny and really easy to talk to. It turned out he was a college student. He was attending the University of Louisville and lived on campus.

There was very little time left in the schedule to do anything other than go to classes, read, and study, but Bill and I got to be pretty good friends over the next couple of weeks. He had shaggy brown hair, kind of like the Beatles, and a few freckles. He usually wore jeans or shorts, if it was really hot, and button-down shirts with loafers and no socks.

Then, on a Friday, three weeks into the program, Mom picked me up like she said she would, and we drove home. I told her about how good I was at the dancing, and everything else, and that I didn't think I had dyslexia at all. Then I told her about the friends I'd made and even about Bill.

We got home late in the afternoon, and I called Tommy.

"Hello?" The sound of his voice made me tingly.

"Hi, I'm home!"

"Hi! How was your trip?" Before I could even get a word in edge-wise, he said, "There's a hayride at my church tonight. Wanna go?"

"A hayride? Wow! Never been on one of those before. Yeah, that sounds great!"

When Tommy knocked on the door, I ran and opened it and gave him a big hug. I about knocked him over.

"Hi!" I said. Then Mom appeared from the kitchen, wiping her hands on a dishtowel.

He laughed. "Hi, Mrs. Gibbs."

"Hello, Tommy." I think she wanted to chat, but I was too excited and just wanted to be alone with Tommy.

"Mom, we gotta go or we'll be late and miss the ride." I gave her a hug and dragged Tommy out the door.

He kept on laughing. "Bye, Mrs. Gibbs," he yelled, and we got in his car.

After we got to his church and I met all his Christian buddies, we all loaded into the bed of an old truck and sat on bales of hay. The smell reminded me of cows grazing in a pasture.

The night was pretty warm, but was cooling off a tiny bit. Once the old farmer started driving, I snuggled up to Tommy. The trip was bouncy and fun. We all waved and laughed at the cars driving alongside us on the road.

Finally, after an hour or so, we pulled into a gravel driveway that led to a huge, beautiful farm.

Chickens and cows and goats ran up to the white fence while we drove up and parked. Someone had made us ham-and-cheese sand-wiches with mayonnaise and lettuce on white bread, and we got to pet some baby animals while we ate.

It was dusk when we loaded back into the truck, and Tommy and I found a nice corner between bales of hay and sat down. Once we started driving and the darkness settled in, he kissed me, and we smooched all the way back. I was in heaven.

On Sunday, while Mom drove me back to dyslexia camp, I told her about Tommy's fun church friends, the baby animals, the sandwiches, and everything. She dropped me off, and I walked back to my dorm. I thought about the night before—about being in Tommy's arms and kissing him. I got that warm, happy feeling I always got when I was around him. Then I heard a familiar voice behind me.

"You're back." It was Bill. He caught up and started walking with me. "How'd your weekend go?" I was taken off guard, got confused and embarrassed, like he knew what I was thinking about.

"Hi." I probably turned ten shades of pink. "Yeah, um, it was OK, you know… just a weekend at home with Mom and Dad." Bill didn't know anything about Tommy because the subject of my boyfriend hadn't come up.

"Good, got a question for ya. There's going to be a baseball game at the university the week after this program's over. Would you like to go?"

"Oh, um… well, that sounds like fun, but… um, you see… let me ask Mom if it would be OK." I was a mess, could hardly put a sentence together I got so nervous.

"OK, sure." I think he'd forgotten I was only sixteen. I gave him our phone number, and he said he'd call after we got back home.

The last three weeks of classes were more of the same, and I worried about what I was going to do about the whole Tommy and Bill pickle.

After the dyslexia program was over, I didn't feel any smarter. I had been pretty sure it wasn't going to make a darn bit of difference in my schoolwork.

On the last day of the program, Mom picked me up, and I told her that Bill wanted to take me to a college ballgame.

"Oh, that's exciting."

"No, Mom, you don't understand. What about Tommy?"

She shut off the engine and turned to face me. "Reedy, you're only sixteen years old. You're too young to think about choosing a husband—"

I laughed. "Mom, I'm not gonna marry anybody right now."

"I know, honey, but you should be dating lots of boys. You need the experience so that eventually, when the time comes, you can make an educated choice." For the first time, what she said sort of made sense. My problem was I kind of did want to go on a date with Bill. But I still loved Tommy and didn't want to lose him. Then Mom stopped talking. I think she could tell that I was confused. "Honey, just tell Tommy… tell him that I said you two should not go steady anymore because you're both too young."

"Oh, but Mom—"

"Reedy, you can still date Tommy. But sometimes you can have dates with other boys too."

I was nervous about the whole thing, but by the end of the week, I had all but forgotten about Bill because he hadn't called. Until he called.

"Hello?" I said.

"Hi, Reedy, it's Bill. How are you?" The second I heard his voice, my stomach knotted up. "Do you miss camp?"

I could hardly speak. I knew he was trying to be funny, so I faked a laugh.

"Oh, hi, Bill," I managed. "Yeah, I mean no… I do not." That was the beginning of the weirdest conversation ever. I stumbled over my own tongue and tried to sound normal. But I felt so guilty even talking to him on the phone. Finally, I told him I didn't think I could go to the game because I was… busy. I'm sure he didn't believe me, probably thought I made it up on the spot because I sounded like such a spaz. I was happy, though, and not at all surprised he never called again.

Finally, after school on a cloudy September day, Tommy and I were walking out to the parking lot. We had just passed the point where we could hear each other talk over the hundreds of kids yelling. A chilly breeze blew our hair every which way. It smelled like rain was coming. I hugged my coat in tight. With each step, I felt the knots in my gut turn to boulders.

"Um, Tommy, Mom says we shouldn't go steady anymore."

He stopped and looked at me. "What?" he said in a quiet voice. My heart pounded in my ears, and I thought I was going to cry.

Engines revved behind us as several school buses prepared to leave the parking lot. Students were still lining up to get on. Lots of parents in cars waited to pick up their kids. The crowds seemed much louder than usual.

"Yeah, she said we were too young and that… and that we should date other people, not just each other."

"Oh… do you want to date other guys?"

"Well, no, but Mom says I should, said we both should."

We walked along in silence. I felt horrible. I had to hold on to my tears until after we got to Mom's car and said goodbye. Then Tommy walked back to catch his school bus. I got in the car and let loose.

"What is it, honey?" I told her about my talk with Tommy.

He took it like a gentleman, and we continued to date for a while. But it was never the same.

We weren't the same. I couldn't explain it, but little things he did started to annoy me. Then one Saturday night at a dance, we both showed up with different dates. I was crushed. Why was *I* crushed? I'd brought the whole thing on myself.

On Sunday, the day after the dance, Tommy came over to the house so we could hang out. I was so angry, but I tried to hide it.

"I'm sorry about last night."

"Yeah, me too," I said real bitchy-like. He could tell I was hiding something. I just didn't know how to handle my jumble of feelings. I hardly slept that night.

The next day was Monday, and I decided that when I saw Tommy in front of our high school where we always met up, I'd be real nice, to kind of make up for how I acted the day before. But Tommy wasn't there. I was scared at first, but figured that he was either late, which he hardly ever was, or maybe he caught a cold, or something and stayed home, which almost never happened either. So, I went up to my first class and just before I walked in the door, I saw Tommy strolling down the hall with Peggy! Peggy was this really cute, short girl that was in the same grade as Tommy. Everything slowed down. He avoided looking at me, and all I could do was watch them pass while my heart broke into a million pieces. I cried a lot and blamed Mom.

CHAPTER TWELVE

1964

Lost Love

It was some time around eleven p.m. on a hot August night—
one of those nasty nights Louisville is famous for. It didn't cool down
much in the evening because of the humidity during the summertime.
Maybe three or four degrees, if you were lucky. On nights like that, I
knew there was only one way I was going to be able to fall asleep: I'd
get in bed and pray to the good Lord that once my head hit the pillow,
I'd sweat sufficient enough to soak the sheets underneath me, and the
hot air from the window fan blasting over my wet, sticky body, would
afford a little relief so I could catch a wave of tiredness and doze off.
So, to avoid the sweltering sleepless period for as long as I could, I
lingered in Mom's yellow Buick convertible with the top down.

Mom only let Daddy buy convertibles ever since he bought her
the very first one. A convertible suited Momma to a 'T' because she
just loved to feel the wind blow through her hair, and see all of God's
glorious creation without a roof blocking her view.

Mom adored everything about nature. Said it was God's most
precious gift to us humans. It made her heart ache that most people
didn't appreciate it and took the beautiful earth for granted. In the
park, where she walked almost every single day, rain, snow, or sunshine,

she'd look at the world like it was her first day on earth. You could see it on her face. Then she'd close her eyes and breathe in the sweet, fresh air, like she could taste it.

I'd just gotten back from a fun night at Becky's house with Linda and Merilyn. They were my only real friends. I could tell them anything. None of us liked school much or made good grades. Becky was going to be a junior, and the rest of us would be seniors. We'd kid around with her about being a lowly junior, but she didn't care. She was so funny; she'd just laugh and say that the rest of us were going to get old sooner.

It was Sunday and felt like it. I was glad I didn't have a thing to do the next day. I'd made Momma happy in the morning by going to church with her—the big Unitarian church downtown. Daddy always went with her because he knew what was good for him. But none of my brothers or sisters were around anymore except for Packy, and nobody could make him do anything he didn't want to do. The rest of my siblings were already off living their lives with their husbands or wives or whatever.

Truth was I never minded going to church with Momma because it was close to the Greyhound bus station, and that meant there were usually a few stray soldiers wandering around. They'd make their way over to the church and be sniffing around, looking so yummy in their uniforms, ready and willing to steal my heart for the day. Something about a man in a uniform drove me crazy. Why, I'd have given any one of them what they wanted right there in the pews if they'd so much as asked. Of course, I never told Momma that.

I had gotten in the habit of going to church with her pretty much every Sunday so she wouldn't make my life a misery by pouting all the livelong day. Although I could never figure out what the Unitarians believed in. Every time I went, I was more confused than before.

I sat in the car chuckling to myself, thinking about the fun I'd had with my girlfriends. Since the top was down, I leaned my head back and looked up through the trees at the stars and into the blackness. The moon was almost full that night. It lit up the edges of the leaves. I closed my eyes and listened to the crickets. They were particularly loud that night—making a real racket.

Then I heard the front door open, and the porch light came on. I saw Packy step out of the house. He looked around, then reached back inside and turned off the light. I slid down onto the passenger seat and prayed he hadn't seen me. The steering wheel dug into my hip, and my face got smashed down on my purse. But I didn't move a muscle.

I was pretty certain he didn't know I was hunkered down in the front seat, but since I wasn't able to see anything scrunched down like that, I couldn't be sure. I held my breath.

I heard him walk right past me down the driveway. I sat up slowly and watched him.

Packy didn't do much of anything during the daytime—as far as I knew anyway, except draw pictures on every single scrap of paper he could find. Or play the piano, and do whatever he did up in his stinky old room. But every now and then, I'd hear him sneak out of the house real late at night when I was having trouble sleeping. I could understand it. Our neighborhood was kind of a magical place when it was quiet and dark. Made you feel invisible, like you could do anything and nobody'd ever know about it.

I watched him until he disappeared behind the tall row of bushes between our house and the Potlitzers' next door. I got out of the car as quietly as I could and let the door rest easy on the latch. Then I walked smack into a swarm of mosquitoes. I waved my hands like crazy, trying to shoo them away. It was way past their feeding time, couldn't figure why they were still out looking for blood. I hated the nasty things and Louisville was loaded with them.

I tiptoed to the bushes and tried to peek through, but they were gnarly and thick, and it was too dark, so I snuck over to the end, near the sidewalk. Packy walked up to Bobby Tillman's house next to the Potlitzers'. My heart started racing.

The Tillmans were our new neighbors. They'd moved in a couple of months before, and I couldn't believe Packy was actually going close to their house. Mom had told me that the police had forbidden Packy to go anywhere near Bobby's house ever again.

See, I made friends with Bobby when he first moved into the neighborhood. He was a couple years younger than me, but I felt sorry for him because he was a shy kid and rather odd. As soon as I made friends with him, other kids started to like him. That's how Packy met him. I invited Bobby over one day, and my brother just took to him right away. I think it was because they were both odd. My brother was like that. Either he liked you or he didn't. There was no in between. And, if he didn't like you, that was it. You might as well get over it because he never changed his mind.

Packy stared up at the moon and smiled. He looked so sweet and innocent, like a little kid; his hair all messy, sticking out every which way. I was reminded of the time when I was younger and was getting ready for my dance recital. I was scared because it was only the second time I had ever danced in front of a real audience. What I didn't know until later was that Packy was coming to watch me dance. So, when I went out on stage, I saw him sitting there with Mom and Dad and the other parents. I was so surprised I could hardly believe it. Funny thing, I wasn't afraid anymore. I think I danced better that day because I was dancing for Packy.

He looked from the moon, up to the Tillmans' house, probably at Bobby's bedroom window. I got nervous and looked around to see if anybody was watching.

When Bobby and his family first moved in, I didn't think to wonder why Bobby was so odd. He was like some little mouse, scared of his own shadow. You couldn't hardly get him to say three words. I had to talk a lot, sort of carry on both sides of a conversation and say all manner of kind things. Then finally, he would come out of himself, and before I knew it, I couldn't get him to shut up.

One day, I was in the backyard, and I heard a strange sound, kind of like a loud wail. I looked all around, and finally realized it was coming from Bobby's house. I didn't think he had a cat or anything, but that's what it sounded like. It sounded like a dog was about to attack a small animal. The sound got louder and louder, and it turned out it wasn't a cat at all. They were blood-curdling screams, and it went on for a long time. It was so scary! Come to find out it was Bobby screaming his little head off because his dad was beating the living daylights out of him. You could hear it all over the neighborhood. It broke my heart. That's when Bobby's oddness started to make sense. He was living with a monster.

Mr. Tillman seemed normal enough on the outside and was even handsome when he left for work every morning in his suit and tie. But deep down, he must've been full of hate and ugly meanness.

After Packy and Bobby became friends, Mr. Tillman put the kibosh on the relationship. Then Bobby no longer spent any time with Packy. I understood Bobby's parents' concern. I mean, Packy was nearly twenty years older than Bobby. But either way, my brother got his heart broken bad. After that, Packy hardly ever came out of his room for any length of time. He didn't laugh much either, or smile like he did before. It was like living with a zombie.

That night when Packy walked up to the Tillmans' house—I held my breath. He peeked through the downstairs windows. The whole place was dark. The only reason I could see anything at all was because the moon was shining so bright, and there weren't any trees in Bobby's yard blocking its light.

Packy walked slowly up their driveway. It looked like he was waiting for something. I thought maybe he and Bobby had set up some kind of secret meeting in the middle of the night. A chill ran through my body, and I shivered. Packy disappeared around the other side of their house, and I slipped by the bushes and crept onto the Potlitzers' long front porch. My heart pounded in my ears. I tiptoed from one pillar to the next and finally sat down behind the last one, the one closest to the Tillmans' house.

I looked up at their house and noticed something dark moving on the roof. I couldn't believe it. It was Packy! He was making his way toward what must've been Bobby's bedroom window. I'd never been inside their house before, so I didn't know for sure, but Packy stopped right in front of that window. What was he thinking? I'd just heard Mom and Dad talking the day before about how Packy would go to jail if he was caught anywhere near Bobby. Of all the crazy things he'd ever done, this had to be the craziest. Did he want to go to jail? Maybe he did. Maybe he felt guilty about all the things he'd stolen, like the fancy priest's robes and chalices from the Catholic church—the one over on Bardstown Road, probably. After he converted to Catholicism, Packy started robbing the place. That's a fine how-de-do, I thought. Joining a big fancy church and then stealing from it. How could he not feel guilty?

Packy got interested in Catholicism because of Father Joe McGee. Joe was the oldest and kindest son of another large Catholic family down at the end of the block. Some years before, Joe had left home, and when he came back, he was a priest. Paul was Joe's little brother, and the youngest in the McGee family. He was the meanest bully you'd never want to meet, too. Paul was big for his age, and even though I was a few years older than him, I was just as scared as the rest of the kids in the neighborhood.

Packy hardly had any friends, and Father Joe was always kind to him, even before he became a priest. He just seemed to understand and appreciate Packy's troubled, artistic nature.

After Father Joe entered the priesthood, he and Packy got to be real close friends. Sometimes they'd talk for hours. Joe told him all about Catholicism and what it meant to him. I bet it was Father Joe's love and compassion that led Packy to Catholicism. But then a couple years later, Father Joe moved far away, and Packy took it really hard. He must've felt like he lost his best friend. Shortly after that, Bobby and his family moved into the neighborhood.

A couple of years later, I read a letter Packy wrote, by way of explanation about his stealing. In it he wrote that Jesus had spoken to him and had told him to steal the religious items because the Catholic church put too much importance on them—something about idol worship. He wrote he was just responding to Jesus's request. He said he told Jesus to let him take those articles and walk right out of the church in broad daylight without anybody seeing him, and that's how he'd know for sure that it really was Him, Jesus, speaking to him and not the devil himself.

Packy didn't just steal from the church, though. He also took expensive religious art books from bookstores, the large heavy kind worth hundreds of dollars. I looked through some of them once, and they scared the bejesus out of me. There were photographs of exquisite paintings of bearded men sitting around up in heaven, judging human souls. The men appeared to be calmly watching hordes of naked humans as they violently struggled their way through purgatory, grabbing onto anything—other people's legs, arms, hair—trying desperately not to slip through the clouds and drop to their fiery deaths into hell. Their tormented, screaming faces were twisted in agony. After I saw those pictures, I thought better about Unitarianism.

Packy stole other things, like fancy pincushions in the shape of little crowns, with golden thimbles in the middle. And round filet mignon steaks wrapped in bacon.

Those we had to eat because we couldn't very well take them back to the grocery store, and we didn't want them to go to waste. (They were delicious, too.)

I figured Packy had had just about enough of himself. He knew Momma would never ever betray him, or turn him in, or let anybody else, no matter what he did or stole. Maybe he was just tired of all his dark secrets, worn down by his own sickness.

I watched my poor brother crawl to Bobby's window and look in. Bobby must've had a nightlight on because it was the only window that wasn't pitch-black. Packy moved in real close, like he was about to go through the window. But he just sat there and watched, all hunched over.

He looked back up at the moon, like he was hoping to squeeze a miracle out of it with just his might. His face glowed in the moonlight. I felt so sorry for him. I wanted to help, wanted him to know that I understood. But I wanted him to come down from there before it was too late. I started to cry. Tears mixed with my mascara and stung my eyes. I wiped them with my shirt to stop the burn.

Packy put a hand on Bobby's window. I felt my heart break. Before I knew it, I was sobbing.

Packy's foot slipped and made a loud scraping sound on the roof. A few seconds later, a light came on in the Potlitzers' upstairs window. I heard footsteps, and their porch light came on. I ran to the other end of the porch and jumped into the shadows near the bushes. My heart pounded in my chest, and I felt a sharp pain in my knee. I lifted it up and felt around in the blackness. It was a small pointed rock. I grabbed it and threw it into the bushes.

The Potlitzers' front door opened. I couldn't see much, but then a flashlight beam shone all around the porch. I held my breath and ducked down even further. I hoped Mr. Potlitzer would go back inside and mind his own business.

I heard footsteps running down the driveway and saw a flashlight beam scour the neighborhood. I peeked out of my hiding place, and a blinding light flashed past my eyes. I ducked down and heard a loud crack, like a gunshot coming from the Tillmans' roof. I looked out and saw Mr. Potlitzer walk back up the driveway with his flashlight shining on Packy.

"Who… who is that?" he shouted. "What are you doing up there?"

Packy didn't make a sound.

"Packy?…Is that you? What the hell are you doing up there?" Packy's foot slipped on the roof tiles again. "You hold on now. Stay right where you are!"

I couldn't see what happened next, but I heard it. "Bob?" Mr. Potlitzer yelled. "Bob Tillman!" That was Bobby's father's name, the most hateful dad ever.

I crawled around the bushes into my own yard and snuck into my house. I was filthy and bleeding. I struggled to stifle my sobs.

Packy was in for it. This time he'd gone too far. I was on my way upstairs when I heard Mom and Dad talking, but I couldn't make out what they were saying. I hurried up to my room and got in bed just the way I was. I pulled the sheet up to my neck and pretended to be asleep. About a second later, I heard someone come in my room. I smelled Old Spice.

I held my breath and felt a kiss on my forehead. Then I heard my window fan come on, and seconds later, my bedroom door closed. I thought about my poor mixed-up brother and wondered if Mr. Potlitzer had called the police. Was Packy going to jail? Or would he do something stupid, like jump off the roof and hurt himself? My brain ached. My swollen eyes burned; I couldn't keep them open any longer. I drifted off to sleep as I heard sirens in the distance.

When I woke up the next morning, the house was deathly quiet. Dad was probably at work, but Mom wasn't home, and Packy wasn't either. I could've kicked myself for falling asleep the night before. I feared the worst.

Mom finally got home later in the afternoon looking like a swollen-eyed zombie. When I asked her what was wrong, she explained briefly what had happened the night before, and that Packy was in jail awaiting his arraignment. Before she went upstairs to lie down, she told me to pray that Packy get sent to a mental hospital instead of jail. I hugged Mom and told her I would. Then I went up to my room and cried my eyes out. Again.

CHAPTER THIRTEEN

1965

Mental Hospital Visit

It was still winter—another cold, gray, miserable mid-April morning when it seemed like spring would never come. It was Saturday, though, so at least I didn't have to go to school for a couple of days.

I was eighteen, a senior in high school, and had my fingers seriously crossed that a miracle would happen and I'd actually graduate—it was going to be a close call. I loved art class, though, and got a lot of As in it. Most of the rest of the subjects, like math and English, history and geography, bored me to distraction. I just couldn't memorize all those damn facts, or make them stick in my brain. Mom tried to help me sometimes, but she was usually too busy or too tired. I was pretty much on my own.

Graduation was about a month away, and I had so many stupid tests coming up that I absolutely dreaded. I had to spend some serious time studying, or trying to, if I wanted to have any chance of graduating.

I lay in bed looking out the window at the dark, cloudy sky and pretended I had nothing to do. I'd gotten used to feeling safe, knowing that nobody would come barging in my room any time they wanted to, and throw my books around, or root through every single thing I owned, no matter how personal, right in front of me.

After the roof incident, Packy had been committed to the state mental hospital.

This is what normal must feel like, I thought—no horrible surprises coming at you when you least expected them. I was sad too, thinking about Packy being locked up in that horrible place.

And I knew darn well the only way I was going to be able to avoid visiting Packy was if I could steer clear of Mom. Maybe I'd tell her I had to study all day—but no, then I'd have to study all day.

I got out of bed and landed on a pile of mostly dirty clothes. I looked around and remembered I had to get my dirty clothes together or I wouldn't have a thing to wear to school on Monday. I'd put it off as long as I could. How was I going to feed myself, get down to the basement with my arms full of dirty clothes—basically live in the same house as Mom—and avoid running into her at the same time? I figured I would just have to stay vigilant and keep my eyes and ears open at all times.

I got dressed—secretly hoping my clothes would make me invisible—then picked through everything. I gathered up the dirty ones, tiptoed to my bedroom door, cracked it open, and peeked out both ways. The coast was clear, so I snuck out into the hall and started down the stairs as quietly as I could.

Suddenly, I heard something behind me. "Morning, honey." Shit! I froze. Mom was usually cheerful in the morning before she got tired from everything she had to do. By the afternoon, she wasn't so friendly. "What time are you going to go see Packy today?"

Goddamnit! I was caught. I wanted to crawl in a hole. I looked down the stairs. Green haze hung in the air. It always looked eerie and lonely on those cold rainy mornings. I got a familiar sick feeling in the pit of my stomach.

Packy had been living at Central State Mental Hospital for about eight months. I tried to get out of going to see him whenever I could because the place was horrible and gave me the willies.

Seeing my big brother drugged, trapped, and helpless was like watching some rare, feral creature stuck in a cage with no possible way of escape. I couldn't even look him in the eye. I knew he was dying inside, and there was absolutely nothing I could do to save him. I was sad for my big brother. But he'd brought it on himself.

To be honest, I was glad he wasn't living at home anymore. Because now he couldn't do all the things he usually did to make me hate him. I knew he had problems, had his "moods," but I never understood why his genius brain couldn't get it together at least a little bit. I mean, he had an IQ of 185—what the heck?—and spoke eight languages. He was even able to teach substitute Spanish for a while. So why couldn't he, at least get an apartment, and a teaching job, and have a life of his own? In his own house? And maybe take a shower, once in a while?

Anyway, on those dark winter days when Mom would nag me to go visit him, I'd usually give in. When I did, I'd have to rack my brain, trying to think of something to talk about. I'd bring up what I was studying in school, but he didn't care about that. Why would he? I didn't. I'd tell him about my friends, or who I was dating, but he didn't want to hear any of that bologna either. After Father Joe moved away, Packy had only one friend left. Bobby. Now he had none. That night on the roof, he'd probably been trying to at least *see* Bobby one last time. His last friend—his lost love.

When Packy was at the mental hospital, he was put on heavy doses of Thorazine, and it changed him. It stole his personality. He'd watch me with what seemed like loathing in his eyes while I jabbered on like a brainless magpie.

During some visits, he'd just slouch in the chair, as if he was about to slide right onto the floor, like in one of those Tom and Jerry cartoons. Other times, he'd stare at me with dead, half-closed eyes, like he didn't know who I was and didn't care. Maybe he wasn't even listening or couldn't hear me. Sometimes he'd look out the window at nothing. But there were a few times when he was talkative or anxious. Times when he seemed about ready to leap up and start running. I thought maybe on those days he'd pretended to take his pills, but had really hidden them under his tongue and spat them out later.

One time, Mom was sweeping the kitchen floor and trying to guilt me into going to visit Packy. "Sweetheart." She stopped her cleaning. "Please, go see your brother today. He's so lonely, and he misses you."

(Yeah, right!) She leaned over to sweep all the burned bits from under the stove. "I can't sleep at night because of Packy's situation." Mom went to visit him at least every couple of days. Said she blamed herself for his being locked up and miserable.

"But Mom!" I blurted. "You didn't make him steal all that stuff from the Catholic church. He did it all by himself!" She stopped sweeping and looked at me. "You didn't tell him to break the law and sneak up on Bobby's roof either. He did it on his own, too!"

Her eyes narrowed, and she stared at me like she was seeing inside my soul, like she couldn't believe what I was saying. She shook her head and teared up. "Oh, honey, you can't understand."

She was right about that. Then she sniffled, leaned the broom against the wall, and went upstairs to her room.

And I went to visit Packy.

There were a few different ways to get to Central State Mental Hospital. I took the long route that day, trying to think about anything other than where I was going.

When I got there, Billy Joe, one of the attendants at the hospital, let me in. I knew his name because all the caretakers wore name tags. I'd seen him around a lot, taking things to the inmates or bringing them their meds. Billy Joe was in his mid-twenties with longish blond hair plastered straight back. He was sort of almost handsome, with a round face and a pinkish scar about an inch long above his right eyebrow. And Billy Joe had the most beautiful light blueish-green eyes, the kind that took your breath away. They looked like two pools of crystal-clear river water, and they perfectly matched his blueish-green hospital coat.

He opened the inner door to the main waiting room. "Hi, Billy Joe," I said. "Anybody ever call you BJ?"

He had a sweet smile, but a couple of missing teeth. The ones he still had looked like they hadn't seen a toothbrush in a while. No doubt about it, though, he had a backwoods-y kind of charm about him, and a thick hillbilly accent.

"Funny you should ask," he mumbled. "My momma used to call me BJ whenever I done somethin' good. Today's her birthday."

"Oh!" I said. "That's exciting. What're you all doing to celebrate it?" He ran his fingers through his hair.

"Um, probably go to the cemetery. She dead. I's twelve when it happened."

"Oh, I'm sorry." I started to ask how she died, but thought better of it. I couldn't bear the thought of BJ droning on about how his momma got trampled to death while she was slopping the hogs or something equally horrible. I followed him to the next set of locked doors.

They had little windows at the top, with metal wires crisscrossed inside the thick glass. "I'm so sorry."

He unlocked the door and held it open, waiting for me. "Oh, it's OK. She had it comin'." He rubbed the scar on his face. "My daddy's still in prison." I stared at him, horrified, my mouth hanging open.

Behind him was the chamber where most of the inmates hung out. The walls were clear glass so the caretakers could keep an eye on them. Faded yellow curtains were drawn, but you could see right through them into the barred courtyard outside. It was a gloomy, dismal scene.

Packy had told me that when the patients were good and the sun was out, they were allowed to go outside for an hour or so. A fly sat frozen on the curtain next to what looked like a long, faded bloodstain they had tried to wash out about a hundred times. Some inmates were lounging on old worn furniture in a dark corner, watching a small TV.

Billy Joe stood there, still holding the door open for me. He looked around, cocked his head, and gave me a puzzled look. "Miss Gibbs? You

OK? Y'are comin' in, right?" That's when I realized I'd been standing there in stunned shock from his story about how he lost his mom, for—I didn't know how long.

"Oh, sorry, OK, yeah… um, thanks," I walked on through. He winked at me when I passed by. Made me wonder if he told me that story to shock me. Like maybe he enjoyed scaring visitors with terrifying tales of his youth.

On a different visit, Packy pointed out Donny to me, a new friend he'd made. Donny was probably in his late teens and was standing too close to the TV in the inmate's enclosed main room, watching it intently. He was wearing a sweat-stained, used-to-be white T-shirt with a pack of cigarettes rolled up in the sleeve. Donny had lots of tattoos of trucks, guns and a few dead animals, with blond shaggy hair, and his hand was in a tight fist punching his other hand, like he was preparing to knock somebody's teeth out.

I sat down in the chair I usually sat in and tried to rid my mind of BJ's life story. But it was too late. A possible version of it was already playing over in my mind. I imagined poor little BJ watching his momma and daddy have a knock-down-drag-out, then Mr. BJ grabbing his trusty twenty-two and…

Just then, Packy appeared through the glass. Thank God. I refocused on the present moment.

He was being escorted through the big room by Jeff, a large, older, black attendant. Packy shuffled in like he always did—expressionless, eyes down, hunched over. The place was depressing on the best of days, when the sun was shining, but with huge dark clouds covering the sky and constant rain, it was devastating. My stomach ached.

The inmates had a kind of uniform: blue drawstring pants and plain white t-shirts. Some wandered aimlessly, some watched TV, and some played games at folding card tables.

Then there was Jake, a small man who, I was told, was dying of syphilis. He was in the final stage of the disease, and insanity had taken hold of his brain. Jake was doing what he always did—running back and forth from one end of the large room to the other, tongue hanging out, elbows bent, hands up by his chest, flopped over like some poor, little, sad puppy dog. His eyes wobbled up and down, and sometimes he'd run smack into a wall and about knock himself out. Then he'd just lie there on the floor shaking until a worker guy would come help him up.

Jeff brought my brother into the visiting room, and I got up and gave Packy a hug—like I always did. He never hugged back. Can't say as I blamed him, considering. He never did anything he was expected to do anyway; it just wasn't his way. He had no tolerance for social pleasantries. Thought small talk and all that fluff was just a bunch of pretentious bullshit.

Packy's shirt had stains on it, and the familiar smell of his body mingled with the greasy odor of unidentifiable meat being cooked. I wondered what they were having for dinner and also how often they made them take a shower. Packy looked sadder and paler than usual.

Mom told me that when Eleanor, a good Christian friend of hers, went to see Packy the week before, he asked her if she would bring him a gun on her next visit. Mom said Eleanor scolded Packy and pleaded with him not to think that way. She told him it was a mortal sin to commit suicide and tried to convince him to have faith in Jesus. He would help soothe his soul until he got released. I bet Packy just shut up. We all knew there was no arguing with born-again logic, no matter how hard you tried. Plus, what Packy was living through couldn't be soothed by anybody, not even God Himself.

Mom was always spouting off about religious stuff like that, and she knew just how to do it, too. She could talk you into just about anything if you gave her half a chance. All my brothers and sisters knew better than to argue with her when she got on her soapbox. We'd pretend to listen for a spell, then figure out a way to change the subject, or ask a question, or think of an excuse to leave the house altogether.

"How're you doing?" Damn it! What a stupid question. He didn't look at me for a long time, just stared at the floor. "Packy?" He looked up. "Are you OK?"

"Yeah," he whispered.

I'd never seen him like that before. His hand twitched, and his eyes looked dead. Maybe they gave him too many drugs by mistake. Then something Mom had told me bubbled up in my brain—I usually tried not to listen when she talked about Packy. It was too depressing, and I had problems of my own to deal with. But I remembered she had told me that Packy's psychiatrist had taken away his piano privileges a couple of weeks earlier. I was shocked! He explained to Mom that Packy wasn't responding to therapy "satisfactorily" and said that Packy was "addicted" to his music like a drug, his escape from reality, and that his addiction was blocking his way to psychiatric healing. Apparently, there was a special music room in the facility where the inmates were allowed to play a few instruments and listen to music. I imagined Packy played the piano and listened to records all the time, or at least as often as he was allowed, before he was forbidden to. I truly believed that Packy's music was his only refuge from the voices in his head and from that horrible place he was imprisoned in. The piano had always been his savior.

When Packy lived at home, sometimes he'd play the piano for hours. And sometimes I'd watch him play. He'd close his eyes and look like he was at peace.

That day, Packy's eyes looked vacant. They looked like translucent puddles of murky water, like the slimy bottom of Bear Grass Creek where we used to trap crawdads. I couldn't think of a single thing to say. My mind raced. He was my own brother. Why couldn't I think of anything to say? I wanted to run away—to be anywhere but there. He had given up. I could see it in his eyes.

I wanted to cry. To rescue him. At that moment, I loved him. Then, the memories of all the times he tormented and hurt me rushed into my mind, and I hated him. But loved him at the same time.

I felt guilty for hating him, and I hated him for making me love him. My head ached. I felt trapped. I wanted to disappear.

"You look pale," I said. He looked at me; our eyes locked. A moment passed.

"I'm alright," he said without emotion. He looked away. In that moment, I saw me through his eyes: his baby sister, too young, too silly, and ignorant to understand. I couldn't help him, and he knew it. He was done with me.

He looked down at his hands and made a smacking sound, like his mouth was bone dry. A bead of sweat slid down the side of his face, made its way down his scraggly, unshaven chin, and hung there. That place was too hot. It was always too hot. I felt sweat drip down my side.

Mom always liked our house chilly and always had windows open all year long. When it was too warm, she felt stuffy, and she couldn't stand stuffy. If somebody would dare close the window or sneak the temperature up a few degrees because they were freezing to death, she'd start screaming and tearing off her sweater.

"Who would do such a thing!? Cool, fresh air is healthy for the body!" Well, I can tell you—nobody would fess up because there was no arguing with her when she was like that. The whole family just got used to wearing many layers inside our house during the winter.

That scent of unidentifiable meat cooking wafted through the room again. The smell turned the knots in my stomach, and it started to churn. I wanted to puke. Packy rubbed the drop of sweat off his chin and wiped it on his shirt. He looked down at a small hole in his pants by the pocket and scratched and pulled at it. His eyes were half-closed, like he was in some kind of stupor. I wondered if he even remembered that somebody was sitting right in front of him.

"What're you all having for supper, Packy? Smells like some kind of beef. Do they let you know what you're having?"

He looked at me like he saw me for the first time since I got there. Then I thought I saw him smile for about a second. Maybe he was glad I was there.

"Hamburgers, maybe. They make pretty good hamburgers." I was happy I had accidentally stumbled on something he cared about: food.

"What's your favorite meal they serve?"

"Pork chops. They make pretty good chicken chow mein, too." He seemed to be coming to life a little. I saw some of his old self—the normal Packy—for lack of a better word. He seemed to be in one of his good moods, only slower, dopier. "Sometimes they can be dry, but they're pretty good."

After that, we talked a while longer about food and meals they served there. Breakfast was usually eggs, bacon, and white toast, sometimes pancakes and sausages or cereal, now and then a cheese omelet. I felt pretty good and thought he did too. It was kind of like when he used to live at home. On a good day, when nobody else was around, we'd talk for a little while.

It was OK that day. Pretty soon, we ran out of food to talk about. Then we did the usual routine. I hugged him and told him I'd come again soon, secretly hoping it wouldn't be too soon. Then I left through the big security door. I was so relieved to hear the loud clank of it shutting behind me and smell the fresh air. I was happy to be leaving, sad he had to stay but, honestly, glad he wasn't coming home.

CHAPTER FOURTEEN

1965

After High School

In the spring, after the miracle happened and I actually graduated from high school, Mom and I put our heads together to try to figure out what to do with me next. I couldn't have been happier about being finished with high school—or more surprised, really, but I'd been so distracted by all the tests, and the possibility I might not graduate at all, that I hadn't given a single thought to what I would do if I did. We knew I was not college material, but what was I good for?

Then Mom stumbled upon the Goodman School of Drama in Chicago. It was only 300 miles from Louisville—just in case, whatever—and it had an excellent reputation for training young actor wannabes. But best of all, it was in one of the coolest cities in the country—maybe even the world. The only downside was we applied too late for me to get into the regular daytime program—sticking with family tradition of being late for absolutely every fucking thing. So, I had to settle for night school. Which was fine by me because that would leave my days free to explore and immerse myself in Chicago!

Meanwhile, Packy was still living at Central State Hospital. However, things were improving. I'm sure it was all Mom's doing. I imagined her throwing a few of her special brand of fits in the presence of the powers that be, informing them that Packy was more depressed than he'd ever been, and that, in fact, he was so desperate, he had asked family members to bring him a gun. I'm sure that brought the meeting to order. Furthermore, he was losing too much weight, due to said depression, and She Was Not Happy! As I've mentioned, Mom was impossible to argue with and the best debater I'd ever known. I'm sure Mom's tearful tirade, combined with her feminine wiles, got the job done. So, I assumed that Packy was assigned a different psychiatrist who changed his meds and allowed him to spend time playing his precious piano again. When I visited him after graduation, he was like a new man. Of course, he was still not over the moon about living where he was living, but he was way less zombie-like.

On my last visit with him before I left for Chicago, he asked me, "What are you doing now that school's over?" He was cleaner and sort of looked like he was actually interested.

"Oh, nothing much. Getting ready to move to Chicago."

"Yeah, that's pretty cool. You excited?"

"Oh, hell yeah!"

He let out a chuckle. "Don't let Mom hear you talk like that."

"How're you doing? You look good."

He nodded his head. "Doing OK, yeah, feel a little better. We have a new cook. I think they got a lot of complaints. Food's pretty good now… healthier."

My visits with Packy later that summer were kind of enjoyable, even hopeful. Definitely less painful.

Before I left, I said, "I'll be thinking about you while I'm away."

"Yeah? You could write to me about what Chicago's like."

"Good, yeah, I'll do that!" I said. "And about Goodman."

Over the months that followed, while I was busy exploring that enchanted city, and learning how to act, word from home was that Packy seemed to be getting even better. In fact, he was making such good progress in his therapy sessions, and was so much more cooperative, that he was allowed to spend a couple of hours a few days a week with a small group of fellow inmates outside in the huge yard and garden area. Best of all, Packy was given a release date, which was less than a year away! Everybody in the family was happy and excited. Except me. I figured that if I came home from Chicago during summer breaks, he'd be there, and it would be just like it was before!

CHAPTER FIFTEEN
1965
Crabby

When it came to sex, I was about as green as they came. Except for a couple of times fooling around with Benny, my boyfriend, late in my senior year, I was a total virgin. And by fooling around, I do mean fooling around because nothing much happened, not for lack of trying. It was just that neither of us knew what the hell we were doing, so all it amounted to was a lot of kissing, some heavy petting, taking some of each other's clothes off—in a completely darkened room—rubbing, probing, a couple of attempts at insertion, but that was about it.

Benny graduated from Seneca High School the year before I did. He hadn't gone to college because he wanted to be an undertaker—that was a weird year. We even got engaged for about a minute.

Benny and I hung out with his best friend, Sam, quite a bit. Sam was a great guy, very gregarious and funny. Late in the summer after my graduation from Seneca, Benny told me that Sam got crabs.

"Ooooo, where? I love crabs. Maybe we can get some!"

He looked at me with his cockeyed smile. "No, not that kind… they're bugs, kind of like lice, only black."

"What? Are ya s'posed to eat 'em?"

"Eww, no!" he laughed. "They bite you," he said. "And they only bite you in the…" He looked away and blushed. "In the groin area."

"What?" A shiver ran through my body. "How do you catch 'em? Do they hurt?"

"No, they itch. You catch 'em from… when you sleep with somebody who's got 'em."

An awkward moment passed while I processed the information.

"Sam is sleeping with somebody? I didn't even know he had a girlfriend." Benny looked down at his shoes.

"Well…" He smiled a little and shrugged. "I don't think he does."

"Uh-oh. Then, where… Jesus." Benny shrugged again, and we dropped the whole thing.

In the fall, I broke up with Benny before I moved to Chicago. My new home was The Three Arts Club, a dormitory sort of place for "ladies" in the arts on the corner of Dearborn and Goethe, a couple blocks from Old Town, *the* hippest place in Chicago—or on earth, as far as I was concerned. Mom and Dad drove me up there and helped me get settled in. I felt very grown-up and excited as hell. I didn't have to worry about Packy or going to visit because he was doing better. I was happy-go-lucky.

I arrived a week before my acting classes at Goodman night school started, so I made good use of those carefree days. I explored Old Town, all the adorable little shops and restaurants, went to some mind-blowing, avant-garde theater productions in the coolest, tiny theater spaces, and got acquainted with the bus line and the "L"—that's what they called their elevated subway system. I fell in love with Lake Michigan and walked along it daily. And I loved the Art Institute and the entire Miracle Mile. Every single thing about Chicago was totally awesome. I'd always longed to live in a big city. I fell in love with the place before I even got there. I felt like it had been waiting just for me.

Finally, my night classes started at Goodman, and I quickly discovered that I loved them even more than I'd thought I would. There was body movement, vocal work—how to project your voice from your diaphragm for stage work—character study, improv, and how to break down a script. I had found my passion.

A month or so later, I began to notice that I was itchy. Down there. A lot. It was a real drag. I thought about what Benny had told me about Sam and his… condition. But how on earth could I have what Sam had? I hadn't started dating any guys in Chicago yet, let alone sleeping with any. It didn't make sense. So, I dismissed my concern, chalked it up to paranoia, and just washed more often. But as time went on, it became a real problem. I had to figure out what was going on with my lower half and was too embarrassed to go to a doctor. I didn't want Mom and Dad to find out, so I devised a plan.

First, I made sure I was going to be alone in my room at the Club for a few hours. That was easy. I didn't have a roommate at the time, and most of the girls who lived at the Club had jobs or school during the day, whereas I went to night school. Then I hung a 'Do Not Disturb' sign on my doorknob and locked myself in. I pulled the shades down and drew myself a nice hot bath in the beautiful clawfoot tub—it was the perfect shape; you could lean back and really luxuriate. While the tub filled, I pulled my hair into a ponytail, put all my dirty clothes neatly in the hamper, and spread the blue-flowered quilt over the bed. For some reason, I felt the need to tidy up.

I made sure the water was extra hot, just in case I did have them (God forbid), which I didn't think I did, because Ewww! But, if I did, hopefully I'd burn the little fuckers to death, or at least make them really uncomfortable for a while. Then I got undressed and held up my new, pretty, purple silk panties I'd been wearing that I'd just bought at Marshall Fields. I hoped I wouldn't have to throw them away because I loved them. They made me feel girly.

I stepped over the side of the tub into the hot water. I eased in slowly, a little at a time, because, man, it was hot. I inhaled the steamy moisture, felt the droplets penetrate my lungs. Finally, when I was all the way in, I leaned back, giving my body plenty of time to get used to the sweltering water. My worries seemed to melt away. I watched the steam consume the small blue bathroom. A moment later, the smell of my lavender soap took over. I closed my eyes and pictured an enormous meadow filled with wildflowers.

A slice of sun shone through the little pie-shaped window in the corner. I opened my eyes and, through the mist, watched the trees outside blow in the wind. Then I remembered what I didn't want to remember.

I tried to force myself to think about only good things: flowers, Old Town, my theater classes, anything but those disgusting parasites that might be having their way with my lower half.

I soaked in the hot bath for a good long time, even fell asleep for a bit, and drifted into a dream. I was in a strange shop filled with brightly colored flowers of all kinds. A few odd people were there, dressed in backcountry, raggedy clothes, with overly pronounced features, long hair, and beards. Some of them were playing bizarre-looking, guitar-type instruments that were huge, old, and funky. I picked up a black rose—I was going to make a bouquet. Then, suddenly, hundreds of tiny black bugs crawled down the rose onto the stems and right up my arms. I screamed and woke up. Usually, I loved taking short naps in the tub. This was not one of those times.

I washed myself well, paying special attention to *the area,* so that it was squeaky clean. I got out of the tub and dried off—I was red as a lobster. I put on some thick clean socks and did a thorough body check. Everything looked perfect, not a single sign of any unwanted critters. I sat on the bed so I could contort my body and look at certain places more closely. I squinted for the final in-depth inspection and noticed what looked like a teeny-tiny scab on the lowest part of my abdomen. It was microscopic. I picked it off and looked at it more closely.

Yep, just a tiny little scab. I knew it. I was so relieved. But I stayed focused on it just to make sure, beyond a shadow of a doubt, that I was clean. Then, I watched the teeny-tiny scab slowly creep away!

"Son of a bitch!" I yelled in a loud whisper. My mind raced. I looked at it again, and sure enough, the miniscule, nasty varmint was trying to make a getaway! I shivered and squished the tiny thing with my fingernail. Then I shot up off the bed and wiggled and hopped around the room like I was trying to escape from a swarm of yellowjackets.

"No, no, no, no!" I whispered and dropped to the floor in a heap. Then it hit me like a slap in the face; there could be only one answer, only one way I could've gotten crabs. Benny! Goddamn it! Suddenly, pictures popped into my head—Benny and Sam in bed together! Naked. Making out, rolling around, poking and sucking on things.

"Best friend, my ass!" I said to myself. "Benny, you son of a bitch!"

CHAPTER SIXTEEN

1965

Meeting Dick

WHEN DICK AND I MET, HE WAS ATTENDING NORTHWESTERN UNIversity in Evanston, Illinois, just north of Chicago. He was a serious musician, and his intense artistic nature intrigued me. He was mysterious too, seemed like a real man, a big-city guy—I got swept away. He was confident, charming, intelligent, dreamy-handsome, and so talented. And he knew how to get what he wanted. Turned out he wanted me.

Dick pursued me with a passion I'd never experienced before. With sincerity and watery eyes, he told me, "You're like nobody I've ever met—there's something pure and authentic about you, not like those superficial college chicks I'm used to dating." His flattery worked. He needed me, and I needed to be needed.

Unfortunately, we met only a couple of weeks after I had shaved my puss to get rid of the case of crabs I inherited from Benny—my lying, cheating, apparently bisexual ex-boyfriend in Louisville. I'd never even heard of the word bisexual before—you learn something new every day. I still looked like a prepubescent girl *down there*. So, instead of jumping Dick's bones on our first date—like I ached to do—I had to stall, hold him and myself back, and play the coy, innocent Kentucky girl until my pubes grew back in.

In my soon-to-be nineteen-year-old brain, I couldn't have imagined telling him the truth. I would've been mortified, convinced he would have thought I was some Southern, poor, white-trash slut who was way too familiar with STDs. I had to hide the truth, let him think I was still a virgin. I mean, I really was pretty much. If Dick had gotten even a glimpse of my lady parts all clean as a whistle like they were, he wouldn't have known what to think. Back then, in 1965, we girls were all going full bush.

My first actual, full-fledged sexual experience was with Dick. And he was almost as inexperienced as I was.

Once Dick and I were well into our romance, it finally dawned on me that every time we made love, which was often, it was quick and over before I knew what was happening. Even when we weren't going for a "quickie," for some legitimate reason—like trying to squeeze in some sweet love before running off to a movie—it seemed like we were. I mean, it was exciting and all, for about a minute and a half or three, tops. I wondered if sex was always fast and furious for everybody.

My problem was I didn't have anything to compare it with, and I didn't know how to bring it up with my friends without embarrassing myself to death. And I certainly couldn't broach the subject with Mom.

My affair with Dick began before computers and the internet, and well before I knew what was what. There were no guide books, that I knew of anyway, so I had no idea how my body worked.

I'd never even heard of an orgasm. I thought masturbation was something men did to take care of business when they didn't have a female handy. Seriously. And when I was quite young, Mom caught me touching myself and spanked me. So, I got the message loud and clear and never tried that again. Mom was always proper and modest. I never saw her without her clothes on, not even once. Now Daddy was another story. He'd come in my room to wake me up for school most mornings, buck naked with shaving cream all over his face.

I met Dick in Old Town, only a few blocks from The Three Arts Club where I was living. It was the start of Christmas break, and I was strolling around the brightly lit shopping area on Wells Street. It was one of my all-time favorite things to do, especially during the Christmas season. It was brighter and more festive than usual, with holiday lights hanging everywhere. Elves and Christmas trees were in the windows, and there were Santas on the street corners ringing big bells and shouting, "Ho, ho, ho!" It was a jolly, crisp night, with temperatures in the teens, but no amount of cold ever stopped Chicagoans from shopping, especially when it got close to Christmas. Hordes of happy people crowded in and out of all the hip little shops carrying bags and boxes, laughing and chatting, their breath making curls of clouds in the air.

I walked quickly from the shop area past all the high-rise apartments. It felt like leaving a brightly lit carnival and walking into somewhere darker and quieter. The tall streetlights reflected off the white covered everything.

It started to snow again. It was more like ice falling from the sky. I'd always heard that when the temperature was that low, it was too cold to snow. But Chicago didn't care about rules. It snowed when it damn well wanted to.

I was hurrying back to grab my suitcase from the Club. I was all packed and ready to go, fortunately, because I'd cut the time short, as usual. I hadn't even scheduled a cab to take me to O'Hare Airport to fly home for Christmas. Then a dapper young man in a black London Fog raincoat passed me going the opposite direction. Suddenly, he was alongside of me. I looked at his sweet face, but continued walking at a good clip since I had a plane to catch and was running late.

"Excuse me," Dick said in a deep, gravelly, Tom-Waits kind of voice. "Do you know where Freddie lives?" I could see that he was gorgeous, even in the dim light. And his voice alone almost made me swoon.

"What? Freddie? Freddie who?" Don't know why I asked that. I didn't know anybody named Freddie.

"Oh, I'm sorry. I thought you looked like someone I met at her place. I know she lives around here somewhere." He had short black hair and looked like he had a nice suntan or was European, Italian, or something. I'd never dated a European before—just plain old American white boys.

I was eighteen and dressed very artsy-fartsy. I was wearing my sister Sally's super-warm polar-bear coat, her red boots, and dangly silver hoop earrings. My long, brown hair hung over the coat in two low, wavy, snow-covered ponytails. The coat wasn't really polar-bear fur. That's just what we called it because that's what it looked like. It was mid-thigh length with long, off-white bushy hair, probably lamb's wool, with carved, pointy, bone buttons—I knew I looked cute as hell. I told him I didn't know any Freddie who lived around there, and we walked and chatted all the way back to The Three Arts Club—he was trying to pick me up! I told him I was flying back home for the holidays, and he offered to take me to the airport.

"Oh, no. That's OK. It's too far. I wouldn't want you to go out of your way." Yeah, I was that naïve. At least I was raised with manners. He said it was no trouble because his folks lived near O'Hare Airport, so he was going that direction, anyway.

"I used to work at the airport." He smiled; my stomach got fluttery. His eyes sparkled, and his face lit up. "I cleaned out the airplanes after flights."

"Really?" I couldn't get over how handsome he was. He was a different kind of handsome than I was used to.

"Yeah, I know a lot of people there." He dismissed it like it was no big deal. "I'll walk you right to your seat on the plane."

Wow!

When we got back to the Club, I went up to get my bags. On the way back down, I heard a heavenly jazz piano playing. I wondered if Ms. Emily, our house-mother—a real uptight bitch—had hired a professional musician to play for the evening. Every once in a while, she did cool stuff like that. But when I turned the corner and entered the huge room, Dick was sitting at the grand piano, playing. His music echoed through the halls. I stood mesmerized. His foot worked the pedals up and down, his head was bowed, and he swayed, like a real musician. His trance-like concentration brought Packy to mind. I got scared for a second.

The scent of fresh-cut roses filled the room, and I wondered—could this be my future? The place was empty but for the two of us. I put down my things and walked toward him in a daze. One white rose petal floated down and landed on the coffee table. Was my chance meeting with this beautiful man fate? A swell of euphoria welled up deep inside me as I stepped closer to him.

Dick spun around to face me. "Shit!" he said, shaking his head. His breath quickened, and he looked angry. "You scared the shit out of me!"

"Sorry, sorry." I backed up. "That was so beautiful…what you were playing."

He didn't speak for a minute. I guess I really startled him. It seemed like he was mad at me, like I'd snuck up and scared him on purpose.

Eventually, he got friendly again and drove me to the airport. He actually did walk me right to my seat on the plane, just like he said he would. I couldn't believe it. We talked on the phone a couple of times while I was in Louisville for Christmas. I couldn't wait to get back to Chicago, and as soon as I did, we started dating, hot and heavy.

CHAPTER SEVENTEEN

1967

Meet the Folks

ABOUT A MONTH AFTER DICK AND I STARTED DATING, WE DROVE DOWN to Louisville so he could meet my folks. I couldn't wait to show him off to Mom and Dad, although they already knew quite a lot about him because I wouldn't shut the fuck up about how smart he was, how handsome, and that he was a college man, as well as an amazing jazz musician.

As soon as Mom opened the door, I could see she had on her 'judgy' face. She was ready to observe, size up, and evaluate. Court was in session. I rushed in and hugged her.

"Sweetheart!" she said and squeezed me tight. Then she looked at Dick and extended her hand. "And you must be Dick."

He gave me a skeptical look, then looked at Mom's hand and gave it a good, slightly exaggerated shake. He was not impressed by formality.

"Hi, Dot," he said with a note of sarcasm. "Nice to finally meet you."

Mom shot me a look. She was not impressed by his informality. Or his mocking tone.

Uh-oh. It was going to be a long weekend.

"Yep," I said. "This is Dick!" I giggled. I was nervous. Things were already awkward.

"Yes, well, please come in, make yourself at home, Dick."

We brought in our bags and sat on the couch in the living room while Mom sat in her favorite chair: an old, well-worn, once yellow, now beige, overstuffed armchair with small faded pink flowers stitched into it. She threw her leg over the arm and made herself comfortable.

Dick looked nice. His thick, black hair was short, neatly combed, and he was wearing the same black London Fog raincoat he'd been wearing when he approached me on that snowy evening in Old Town Chicago. I wanted Mom and Dad to like him as much as I did and to be impressed with me for nabbing him.

"I've heard so much about you, Dick," Mom said. "Would you care for something to drink? Ice tea, water?"

"Water would be nice."

"Yeah, me too. I'm thirsty," I said. "I'll get it, Mom." I turned to Dick. "Water good for you, hon?" Dick nodded, and I went to the kitchen, glad to have an excuse to leave the room. I needed a minute. I filled some glasses with water while I listened to their conversation.

"Reedy tells me you're going to Northwestern University. What are you studying?"

"Yeah. I just finished my third year. I had classes in music theory, psychology, and comparative religions, which I really liked."

Shit! I had told Dick that Mom and Dad were born-again Christians, and now he was creeping into dangerous territory. Was he trying to start something? What the hell was he doing?

I threw some ice cubes in our glasses and rushed back into the living room. "Mom, I really want Dick to play something for you on the piano!"

"In a minute, honey," she said and turned back to Dick. "I bet it was interesting. Tell me a little about the comparative religions class."

So, he went off on how the class discussed the major religions of the world, and then the teacher demonstrated how they were all evolving in their own way, on their own distinct paths, and how they would eventually come to the same end. He talked about how the class had opened his mind and how he was now embracing the Eastern philosophies, in particular. And that *we* had begun studying Zen meditation at a Buddhist temple with a Japanese sensei. In the meantime, I was freaking the fuck out! Mom looked at me, her jaw tense. I'd seen that look hundreds of times—it did not bode well. I avoided her eyes.

She nodded. "Interesting, and let's see—your family's Catholic, right?" Mom's least-favorite religion was Catholicism. In a word, she hated the Catholic church. Somehow, she had gotten it in her head that Catholicism had twisted Packy's mind even more than it already was, irreparably, and was the predominant cause of his incarceration.

"Yes, my family's Catholic," Dick said.

Oh, God, I thought. *Here we go!* I took a big drink of my water.

Mom shifted in her chair. "And how do *you* find the church, Dick? See, I believe the Catholic church is deeply corrupt and flawed at its core. In fact, I'd go as far as to say—"

I put my glass down on the coffee table with a bang. They both looked at me. Then I slid my arm through Dick's. "Honey, play that piece you wrote—"

"Stop!" he said angrily. He gave me a dirty look as he pulled his arm away. "What are you doing?"

"…I just…"

Mom sat up. "Yes, let's do that. I'd love to hear you play, Dick." She stood up and reached for my hand, and we walked to the breakfast room where Packy's old piano was. "Come on Dick, join us. Let's have some music, shall we?" I looked over my shoulder at Dick a couple of times. He seemed confused, pissed off, and a bit surprised at the turn of events. It was like he had no idea what had just happened. Finally, he got up and followed us. Then he played some jazz numbers. Mom and I cheered him on. That lightened the mood considerably.

When Dad got home from work, he and Dick chatted in the living room while Mom and I filled the house with smells of dinner cooking. I never worried about Dad. He was always easy-going and friendly. And since he hated conflict, he was the ideal host, no matter who was visiting.

That evening we dined on Momma's famous pot roast with onions, potatoes, carrots, and loads of fresh parsley. Things went well for a while.

Mom asked, "Would you care for some more pot roast, Dick?"

"I would, yes. Thanks, Dot. It's very tasty."

Everybody, except Dad and me, was being weird. There was definitely an elephant in the room, and we were all pretending there wasn't.

"Thank you. Pass me his plate, honey." I passed Dick's plate to Mom, and she piled on plenty of meat and veggies. "What's your favorite dish that your mother makes, Dick?"

"Oh, she's a great cook," I chimed in. "Right, hon? She makes great spaghetti sauce and—"

"Reedy, your mom was talking to me," he said. "You mind if I answer her?"

"Oh… no, sorry."

"My mom makes the best lasagna."

"Oh, yeah, it's amazing," I said. But when I looked back at Dick, I knew it was time for me to shut the hell up. "Sorry."

Mom and Dad looked at each other. After that little exchange, I watched what and when I spoke because Dick seemed on edge.

Later, when Dick and I were alone in the guest bedroom, we talked about Mom and Dad. "Your dad's funny. Nice guy, but your mom…" He shook his head. "Jesus, she's opinionated. And that shit about the Catholic church? What the hell was that about?"

"Yeah, I know," I whispered. "See, Mom thinks when Packy converted to Catholicism, it made him get kind of crazy. Crazier. She blames the church for him being in the mental hospital."

Dick let out a chuckle. "Well, that's bullshit."

The rest of the weekend went okay, except for a couple of close calls when Christianity versus Catholicism versus Eastern philosophy conversations came dangerously close to head-butting debates. I pulled a few bait-n-switch maneuvers that thankfully worked. But basically, I just tried to keep the atmosphere pleasant and not get caught in the middle.

Before Dick and I left to go back to Chicago, Mom and I took a walk one afternoon, just the two of us. Once we were well away from the house, she said, "Honey, I don't think Dick is right for you."

"What? Why?" I asked. Not that I was surprised. Their mutual dislike for each other couldn't have been more obvious.

Mom trod gently. "I know you like him, honey, but he's very domineering and argumentative. And very closed-minded. Thinks he knows it all."

"Mom, you hardly know him. Give him a chance."

Mom was always honest, and her opinion meant a lot to me. I knew Dick was serious and intense. He was an intellectual with the sensitivity of a musician or a troubled artist. But a know-it-all? "What does Dad think?" I asked.

"Haven't you noticed how Dick tries to control you? Your dad agrees with me, sweetheart."

"Mom, I can't believe you and Dad—"

"He belittles you, honey, and doesn't care who sees it. It infuriates your dad."

I glared at her.

"Honey, I'm just telling you because I love you--"

"I know, Mom," I said, cutting her off.

"And I want more than anything for you to be happy, sweetheart, and to find a young man who appreciates how wonderful you are."

Well, I wasn't happy. I was pissed and disappointed. I thought about what she said and about Dad getting furious with Dick because of how he treated me. I thought about it a lot. I thought about conversations Dick and I had had with Mom and Dad, and with friends, and even strangers, and realized it was true.

Examples popped into my head. I felt like a fool. Mom was right. They were right about everything. I hated that they were right. So, I defended him. I lied and argued that Dick was right to criticize me. That I deserved it. And I was determined to give him another chance.

CHAPTER EIGHTEEN

1966

Regret

I RAN BACK TO DICK'S TINY BEDROOM TO ANSWER A PHONE CALL AND almost fell on my face, tripping over random shit on the floor: my overnight bag with clothes spilling out everywhere, a broken drumstick (the kind you play drums with, not the chicken-leg kind), bowls, and spoons from cereal we'd had the night before after fucking. You know, random shit. His apartment smelled like springtime, burgers, and dirty socks. The bedroom smelled like sex. I breathed it in.

Dick teased me. He held the phone out, then looked all around, pretending not to see me, and started to hang up. I screamed, "No!" and started laughing. Then he did it again. It was funny. You had to be there. We were stoned.

When I got back to the bedroom, I flopped on the bed, totally out of breath. He rolled me over and whispered, "It's your sister, Sally. She sounds upset." Then he scrunched up his face and rubbed his eye with a balled-up fist, like he was a big crybaby. He mouthed the words "Boo-hoo!" I got so tickled I thought I was going to wet my pants. He took the phone back and said, all proper-like, "Hold on a moment, please." Which only made me laugh harder.

I had to get a hold of myself because Sally did not like Dick. She thought he was way too domineering, which was ridiculous because she was Little Miss Bossy Pants herself. Also, she knew Dick and I smoked a lot of pot, but she'd never been stoned herself, so even though she was an artistic, free-thinker type, it was clear she did not approve.

I sat up, and something sharp poked into my thigh. "Ow, shit!" I whispered. I reached under my leg and pulled out a fork! Dick laughed. I didn't. What the hell was a fork doing in the bed? I threw it across the room. He ducked, still chuckling. I rubbed my wound and took the phone.

"Hi, Sally, how's it going?"

Dick checked out the wall where the fork crashed. It left a mark. He put his hands on his hips and gave me a dirty look. I stuck my tongue out at him. "Sally? Hello?"

I thought she'd hung up, so I started to hang up and call her back, hoping she wasn't mad at me for making her wait.

"Packy's dead." Her voice was loud and strong, but I couldn't read it.

I gazed at the mark on the wall and started coughing—realized I had a bad case of cottonmouth and needed a drink in the worst way.

"He committed suicide."

Everything slowed, then came to a screeching halt. I stopped breathing.

I saw something shiny under the dresser and focused. My earring! I'd looked everywhere for it. Mom gave them to me after Mamaw died. They were my favorite pair. I was crushed when I lost it. They had small diamonds in a circle and my birthstone in the middle, a round, deep purple amethyst. *Wait*, I thought about what Sally had said, her words. They ran over in my head, like a stuck song. But I couldn't make sense of them. Was she trying to be funny?

"Wait. What?" I felt a sharp pain from where the fork had stabbed me. I pulled my hand out from under my leg. Blood.

"He jumped off the water tower at Central State." Her voice sounded strange. "Reedy, he's dead."

Wait, I heard them—the words—I heard what she said. No. That's not… I heard her voice in my head—I heard the words, her words. I couldn't stop hearing them. They were unstoppable.

The words echoed in my head. "He's dead."

"He's dead."

"He's dead." The echo wouldn't stop… "Suicide."

"Suicide."

"Suicide."

They pounded, like bullets cracking my skull.

"Nooooooo!" I screamed. The phone left my hand. I heard a crash.

"No! Nooooooooo! Fuuuuuuuck!" I beat the bed. *Go back. Go back to before the words.*

"He can't—he wouldn't! He promised." My mind searched through all my memories of Packy in a split second.

No, no, he didn't. He never…

"Nooooo!" I screamed and kicked.

But he's better now. He's better. Mom said he's better in that horrible place. He's better, she told me, and soon he'll get out…

"Stop! No, no! God, no!" *He was only let out in the yard because he's better! I'll go home, and I'll see him again. He'll understand. We'll understand. The love… we shared… sometimes. I'll make it right, tell him I'm sorry, sorry I couldn't really be with him those times I came to visit—*

"He can't—nooooo!" I pounded my head and collapsed. The bed was wet under me from my tears. I screamed into the mattress and gasped for breath. I saw blood on my hand—blood inside my head—blood everywhere. My guts twisted and burned. Bile shot into my throat. I doubled over and rocked back and forth. I hated myself. I pulled my hair and clawed my face to feel my hate. Tears stung my eyes. I pounded the bed and kicked and screamed.

Dick was gentle and sympathetic after I got the news. He spoke some kind words I couldn't hear. Words I didn't remember. He stroked my hot, wet head. I screamed and sobbed. He must've picked up the phone and found out what happened. I think he tried to hold me at first. I couldn't. He waited. Then we fucked while I cried. And we fucked again, and I cried some more. It was comforting in a distracting, brief sort of way.

I thought of nothing but my brother the following sleepless night. My mind filled with images; I saw him jumping off the water tower, watched it happen in slow motion—I jerked awake. I remembered him torturing me, remembered crying, screaming, and punching him so he'd leave me alone—then I'd watch him leap to his death, and I'd wake—over and over just as I'd start to doze off.

Finally, I went and laid down on the couch, so I'd stop waking Dick with my tossing and turning. I hated myself for failing Packy, for not giving him something to live for.

PART TWO

CHAPTER NINETEEN

1966

The Funeral

Packy's funeral was a few days after he died. Fortunately, my night classes at Goodman had just ended for the year.

Dick dropped me off at the airport, and I looked like I felt—fucked up. I'd slept like shit, hadn't showered in days, and my hair was a tangled mess thrown up in a ponytail. In my zombie state, I noticed people were looking at me funny and giving me a wide berth. Most of the time, I liked flying, enjoyed meeting and chatting with fellow passengers.

While I waited to board, I thought about the mental hospital where it happened.

Central State maintained that he had accidentally fallen from the water tower. Which begged the questions: why would he climb up there in the first place? Why were mental patients allowed access to it anyway? And how did Packy's psychiatrists not see it coming?

Packy's new positive, cooperative attitude was why he'd been given permission to spend time in the gardens where the water tower was. Someone wasn't paying attention. Or could he have planned the whole thing? Maybe his good behavior was all an act, and no one saw through it.

The hospital claimed they were not responsible because it was an accident. They maintained that a staff member had seen him "slip and fall." But what really happened? The question haunted me. Could he have seen suicide as his best and most humane option—for himself and everyone else? Maybe he thought the only other possibility was moving back in with Mom and Dad when he was released from the hospital, and maybe he couldn't stand the thought of living out the rest of his days in their new, small, one-level house in the northern, sterile suburbs of Louisville.

I called Mom a few weeks earlier from Chicago. "Hello?" she said. Her voice sounded funny.

"Hi, Mom."

"Hi, honey." She wasn't her usual happy self.

"What's wrong?" I asked. It sounded like she'd been crying.

"Oh, nothing, honey. I'm fine, really. You know your dad and I sold the house. I told you, right?"

"Yeah,"

"Well, I gave Packy the news today, a little while ago… and he got furious. Don't know if I'd ever seen him so mad." She said he threw a huge fit, started screaming at her then left her in the visitor's room by herself.

Packy loved that old house; everybody did. It was three floors, five bedrooms, three baths with a full basement. It simply oozed character, charm, and mystery. None of the rest of the family wanted them to sell it. But with Packy's upcoming release, Mom was insistent. She desperately wanted him to come home to a new, clean, safe space, where he could begin life anew with daily meds, a clinically regulated schedule created specifically for his healing—with no room for snakes.

But I think Packy saw things differently. He must've seen a future where he'd be trading the hospital staff 'jailers' for Mom and Dad as his new 'jailers.' Maybe Mom's news about the house was the final nail in the coffin.

Finally, the plane began boarding. I dragged my weary body to my assigned seat and got as comfortable as I could next to the window. I always tried to get a window seat so I could watch the terrain pass underneath, get lost in the clouds, or lean against it for naps.

Then I watched with dread as the line of passengers marched past. I wanted to be alone. When the seat next to me remained vacant, I was relieved. I scooted as close as I could to the window, wadded up my jacket to use as a pillow, and instantly fell into a coma.

Then BANG! The sudden bone-shattering shock of airplane wheels on tarmac jolted me awake.

After the funeral was over, Mom and Dad were planning to drive me to Chicago so I could collect my things and move back to Louisville with them for the summer. But I couldn't imagine living in Louisville again, even for the summer.

Before I left Chicago, Dick and I talked about what was going to happen after the funeral. We talked about how much we'd miss each other over the summer and decided I should move in with him. Everybody was doing it, living with their boyfriends. It was 1966! And Dick had just rented this sweet little one-bedroom apartment near Old Town. We figured it was the next logical step. (And, best of all, I wouldn't have to move back to Louisville!)

I'd been lying to Mom and Dad and Miss Emily, the dorm mother at The Three Arts Club, for months. I had been pretending to stay at my sister Sally's apartment—she was living in Chicago at the time—when really, I was spending most of my nights at Dick's place.

When I walked into Mom and Dad's house, Sharon, Brud, and most of their kids and grandkids were there. So was Jud and Bobbi and their brood. My brother Scott was fourth in the lineup, and I realized later that Scott had been traumatized by our oldest brother's antics more than I realized. He didn't show up at all.

Scott was an extremely talented artist; he sold his paintings to art dealers all over the world. He had been going to therapy most of his life, and in the words of his therapist, "Whatever someone wishes you to do, if you don't want to, don't." And he didn't.

Sally, my closest sibling and another fine artist, was born into this world with that same philosophy already in place, so she and her family didn't show up either. No surprise, really. Sally had no use for society's rules or implied obligations. Where some people struggled with their conscience when going against what was expected of them, Sally embraced it.

From the moment I set foot on the airplane, I had massive knots in my stomach and felt like my head was about to explode. I couldn't shake the dread in the pit of my stomach about the conversation I was going to have to have with Mom and Dad.

The house was teeming with family and emotions. The weird energy blasted me in the face the minute I walked through the door. That's when I realized there was no way I was going to be able to talk to Mom and Dad—it was simply the wrong place, wrong time. But I had to eventually, and soon, because Dick expected me back in a few days. My brain ached, and my stomach was a tangled web of vipers eating me from the inside out.

Maybe if I could separate Mom and Dad from the herd, I thought, and tell them in private. Yeah, that might work. So, I tried to think it through and picture it.

"Mom, can I talk to you and Dad for a minute?" I'd whisper in her ear loud enough so she could hear me over the racket of kids screeching and multiple conversations. She'd smile, grab Daddy's hand, and we'd head for their bedroom. I sat on Dad's bed and asked them to sit because I had something to tell them.

"Mom, Dad, after the funeral, I'm going back to Chicago and move in with Dick…" Then the whole scene took off in my mind, and there was no stopping it.

Mom stands up. "What?"

Dad grabs his chest, like he's been mortally wounded. He looks at me pleadingly. "No, no, honey—"

Mom crosses her arms. "You are doing no such thing!"

I stand up meekly. "It's OK. I love him, Mom."

"We'll just see about that!" Mom storms out of the room. Next thing I know, every family member and their friends shove their way into Mom and Dad's bedroom. Above everyone talking at once, I hear, "What's going on?" Sharon says. "You're living with Dick?"

"Who's she moving in with?" Brud asks his wife.

"Are you going to have sex with him?" my fourteen-year-old nephew Teddy asks.

"Who's Dick?" his younger sister Tisa asks.

"What's sex?" their youngest brother Gibbs asks. And that would be just the beginning.

Since my family knew nothing of boundaries, the disastrous scene that had just come to life in my brain sounded about right. So, I decided I'd better wait until after the funeral when everyone else had gone.

I was more than happy to put off telling them—procrastinating was something I'd always been good at. I simply had to wait for the right moment. So, I relaxed a little and enjoyed my nutty family. I took walks with family members and friends, played badminton in the backyard with my nieces, nephews, and cousins. There was plenty of laughter, tears, and sharing of memories—the good as well as the horrific. Everyone had their own take on Packy's life and his suicide. We discussed and argued about who Packy really was and who he could have been under the right tutelage and medication.

My brother Jud, the lone straight-arrow and strictest disciplinarian in our clan, thought that Mom had been too "soft" with Packy. He said, "She should've given him the boot, kicked him out the minute he graduated from college. Then he would've had to get his life together."

My sister Sharon argued, "Oh, stop, Jud! That would've been cruel."

Then everybody else chimed in with their two cents' worth, including the nieces and nephews, and it turned into a typical Gibbs raucous celebration of disagreement and disfunction.

Then we all loaded into our different cars and left the house for the funeral. It was a nice service—with a closed casket. Most of us cried some, but there was also plenty of joking around and laughing, which was our family's peculiar way of dealing with loss and grieving—that attracted more than a few judgmental stares. We did the best we could for an unconventional family in mourning.

So finally, a few days after the funeral, a peaceful moment presented itself. Mom, Dad and I were lounging in the living room. She was comfortable and relaxed in her favorite chair, one leg bent and pulled up close to her, and the other slung over the cushy arm. She was barefoot, as usual, and her disheveled, gray hair fell in loose, wilted curls. Meanwhile, Dad slept peacefully nearby in his chair.

"Mom," I said, my guts churning. I took a deep breath and came out with it. "I'm not coming back here for the summer."

She smiled at me sweetly, head resting back on a cushion, eyes half-closed. "How's that, honey?"

She looked like I felt, exhausted and emotionally fried. The house was quiet for the first time in over a week. If I hadn't spoken, Mom might've fallen asleep right there in her favorite chair. The place was a mess from too much company overstaying their welcome. Kids' toys were scattered around. Half-full cups and glasses dripped onto the coffee table, and the dining room was a frightful sight. The table was piled with leftover food—lunch meats, condiments, vegetables, and lots of different sweets quickly melting into goo. I found myself wishing I had at least put the food away and cleaned off the table before I started spilling my guts. The house smelled like a party-house.

"Dick got an apartment, and, um… remember? I think I told you. Anyway, I moved my stuff over to his place, um… because I moved in with him."

Mom lifted her head, slowly put her feet on the carpet, and sat up. Her eyes widened. "You what?" she shrieked.

"Mom, it's no big deal. We—"

"No! Absolutely not!" she yelled and stood up. "It most certainly is a big deal! It's a huge deal!

"Fuzzy, wake up! FUZZY!"

"Huh?" Dad asked and opened his eyes.

"Go ahead, tell him!" Mom said. "Tell your father your big plans! Or should I say Dick's big plans because I know this wasn't your idea." My heart pounded in my ears. Mom frantically moved around the living room, picking up toys and glasses.

Dad sat up. "What? What'd I miss?"

Mom stared at me with her arms full. "Are you going to tell him, or should I?"

"What is it, honey?" Dad said and leaned forward in his chair.

"I want… I'm going to move to Chicago, Dad. I… I'm moving in with Dick."

Dad looked at Mom, then back at me. "What?" Mom stormed out of the room and into the kitchen. There was a loud crash of dishes. I kneeled down beside Dad. He looked at me with the saddest eyes. "What are you doing, honey?"

"Dad, I want to stay in Chicago, and Dick has an apartment, so…"

Dad shook his head and looked around the room, like he refused to accept what he was hearing. "No, honey, no, please, don't. You can't." Then he took my hands in his. "No, please, don't do this. We can… please." It looked like he was about to cry.

I felt my heart break. I was his little girl, his last baby. "Daddy, it's OK. I love Dick."

Mom came back into the living room, wiping her face with a blue dishtowel. Her eyes were red. She took my hands, pulled me up, and walked me into the hallway. She looked me square in the eyes. "Honey," she said, fighting back tears. She took a deep breath. "Reedy… go get your things together. I need to talk to your father. When you finish packing, we'll talk some more."

I went to my bedroom, closed the door, and fell on the bed. Then I buried my face in a pillow and cried as quietly as I could until I fell asleep. When I woke up, I got my things together and put my suitcase by the front door. Dad was nowhere to be seen.

Mom came out of the kitchen and said, "Reedy, you know how we feel about Dick."

"I know, Mom, but—"

"No, honey… let me finish. You know what your father and I think of Dick, but we talked about it, and if this is what you want to do, we won't try to stop you."

I was shocked.

Mom drove me to the airport, and after she dropped me off, I felt more alone and scared than I ever had. She had been my staunch supporter, my guide, the captain of my ship. She always believed in me. I felt like I was being ripped apart from the inside out. I had always trusted Mom. I was nineteen now, trying to be a woman, trying to grow up and make my own decisions. Why couldn't she see that? Or… maybe she was right.

When I got back to Chicago, Dick was happy and proud of me. I was proud of me, too. I was also disgusted with myself and heartbroken, but proud. At least I stood my ground and did what I set out to do. Or was it true that I'd only done what Dick told me to do, just like Momma said?

CHAPTER TWENTY

1967

Selling Out

When I moved in with Dick, we were living the dream—the stoner's dream, that is. We were high a lot, and when Dick was high, Dick was happy. When I was high, Packy was the last thing on my mind. I had moved on.

Our apartment was in one of those great old brownstones in the heart of Chicago's Old Town. I worked as a waitress a couple of days a week, and Dick played in nightclubs. He also supplemented our income by supplying his band members, and a few friends, with pot. Everything went great for a while. Until it didn't.

Running—can't breathe—pressure—lungs ache, legs cramp, don't stop—can't stop. Don't ever stop. Something pushing, tears my clothes. They fall away—I'm naked, filthy, freezing, try to hide—loud footsteps behind me and screeching, howling, deafening, closer, closer! Sweat stings my eyes. IT attacks! I claw deep into flesh—blood sprays, blinds me—I fall—dark shadows swirl around me. I stagger, choke—vomit fills my mouth—I spew, can't stop—try to see, to breathe, to focus. I cough, gag, spit thick, burning mucus. Stop! I'm sinking—sink deep into putrid black soup—the stench of hot breath burns my neck. IT hovers—I buck, kick, thrash, twist my boiling body. A thing just beyond reach, it's hard, ice cold. I watch through clouded eyes: a cage. I spin around. Hair slaps my face, stings, hot metal—it's closing—bars puncture my flesh, tighter, tighter—bones crush—life oozes out… wait! A scalding hand covers my mouth—breath sucks out of me, screams pierce, crack my skull. I jerk awake! My eyes strain—see only dense blackness—I scream!

"Whoa! Shhhh! Jesus Christ, Reedy!"

That voice, I knew it. A mighty hand held tight over my mouth. I bit at it. Another grabbed my legs. I slapped and kicked. I wanted to live! Wait, something in the darkness, a face—the fog faded. It was Dick. He pulled his hands away and backed up. He looked at me, wild-eyed, horrified.

"Ahh! Goddamn, woman, what the fuck! You kicked the shit out of my leg!" He looked down. "It's gonna be black and blue."

I sat up and looked around, out of breath. I struggled to come back to the present: on our mattress, on the floor, in our tiny bedroom.

"Fuck!" I yelled. My long flannel nightgown was twisted around me. I got up, wondered why I was wearing it. Then remembered it was the dead of winter, and our apartment was freezing. I was wet with sweat and tangled up. "Oh, God. Shit." I pulled and tore at the nightgown to get it off me.

"Goddamn it." He hated when I disturbed his sleep. Apparently, I slept like a baby, but only if my body was free to dance like a tornado. So many nights I'd lie awake trying not to move a muscle. My arms and legs would cramp and burn, like a thousand hot, thorny worms crawling just under my skin.

"Jesus!" he exploded. "Goddamn it, I was just falling asleep. Fuck!"

"Sorry, I'm sorry, shit!" I couldn't shake it, that dream. I tossed the covers away, got up, ripped off the nightgown and threw it anywhere. My skin was slick, sticky. I peeled my long, matted hair off my sweaty face, arms, and neck.

"Ahhh! I'll go sleep on the couch," I said under my breath. It was the third night in a row I'd woken up in the same nightmare.

"What the fuck?" Dick sat back down on the mattress and glared at me. Dick had a Neanderthal hump across his forehead, where his eyebrows were, so when he got pissed at me, which was often, he'd lower his head, furrow his big hump brow, and glare at me with what looked like pure animal hatred.

"I'm sorry," I said again. I gathered a pile of folded covers and a pillow I had stacked in the corner of our bedroom, just in case. Dick made no move to stop me.

"Jesus, what the hell, Reedy?" He rubbed his leg.

"I can't help it!" I burst into tears.

"Shhhh! Jesus Christ!" His sharp, loud whisper cut through the stillness. "You wanna wake up everybody on the fucking block?"

"Sorry." I took a breath, stormed out of the bedroom, and dumped the bedding on the couch.

The streetlight shone through our huge picture window in the living room, lighting my way in the darkness. I was still wrapped in the dream. I looked out at the quiet street and didn't care if anybody saw my naked body. A sad, stray mutt cowered slowly down the sidewalk. Then he stopped, sniffed something in the grass, looked around, lapped it up, gagged, and puked.

I turned around and marched back into the bedroom. "I am so fucking paranoid, that dream… I can't sleep or anything. I mean it. I can't, I can't—"

"Hey, just stop it!" He shot me The Look. "Settle the fuck down! How many Goddamn times do we have to go over this?"

"Oh, I don't know." My voice quivered. "Maybe until you hear what the fuck I'm saying!" The air was ice cold on my naked, sweaty body. I shivered and opened the closet door. It was pitch-dark. I felt around on the floor until I recognized the soft, furry fabric of my old green robe. I grabbed it and threw it on. It was the softest thing I owned. I would've been happy to live in it forever. I lowered my voice and moved in close to his face. "We've got a freezer full of weed and a shitload of LSD. We're gonna get busted!"

"Arrrhh, Christ almighty!" He pushed me away and sat down on our mattress on the floor. He swung his feet off, knees pointing up.

That old mattress was a hand-me-down from Dick's sister Diane. We were famous for scrounging everything and anything: old pots and pans, plates, utensils, rugs, rags, clothes, furniture, you name it. And we weren't picky. We'd take just about anything from friends, family, random strangers. We were the original make-doers, cheapskates, penny pinchers. We put a positive spin on it, called ourselves recyclers. We considered ourselves young, enlightened, starving artists, trying to survive in a cruel, unenlightened world, through our chosen art forms. At least that was the way we liked to put it, the one we hid behind. Truth was we liked doing nothing. We were lazy stoners.

"I'm only selling to Angela. That's it, just Angela!" He started to pace. I couldn't see his expression because he was facing away from the only light pouring in through the living room window. But I felt his anger like a presence. "She's a decent person, OK? A paralegal, for God's sake! One buyer, that's all. It's easy money, and we need it. You got a better idea?"

"I don't care." Tears burned my eyes. "I DON'T CARE!" I yelled. Dick shushed me again.

"I don't give a fucking rat's ass." My head felt like it was going to explode. I stormed out of the bedroom. "I'm getting the fuck out of here! Going home! I can't take it anymore!"

"Wait, wait. Look, babe, don't, just—" He put his hands on my shoulders. I jerked them off. He pointed a finger at me, and I slapped it away. Then he balled up his fists and took a deep breath.

"Look, it's just Angela. I'm just trying to—babe, come on! What the fuck!" His voice got louder. "Now you're just being stupid. I told you. The only way—the *only* way I could get busted is if they set me up." He was rationalizing. I knew it, and he knew I knew it. "That's the only way. They'd have to set me up."

I was done. The subject was closed. I pushed him away and went to sleep in the living room. Actually, sleep was the last thing I did. I stewed, I plotted, and I planned my escape, and pretended to sleep. Don't know why I pretended. Dick didn't give a shit. He was snoring within seconds.

I stared out at the beautiful old Victorian house across the street. The tall, wrought-iron streetlamps lit it up perfectly. A "Painted Lady" it was called. It was a delicious, creamy yellow with maroon and soft green trim. It had three stories with lacy woodwork, brass doorknobs, and gutters. I loved it. Many years before, someone had turned it into four apartments. I dreamed about living in it and turning it back into a single-family home.

I looked up at the small cut-glass section above our big picture window. On bright days, the sun shone through it, and tiny prisms danced all around the living room. It was magical, even on the rare occasion when I wasn't stoned.

I probably got two hours of actual sleep that night, in fits and starts. The rest of the time I spent going back over our fight, and the dream, thinking how wrong, mean, and misguided Dick was and how right I was. When I heard him snoring again, I thought seriously about kicking him in the Goddamn balls. That gave me some satisfaction. Finally, I fell asleep.

When I woke the next day, things were understandably chilly around the apartment. We didn't speak. Dick wasn't a morning person anyway, and neither was I on that particular day. He left, I'm sure, to escape the chill and probably got breakfast. I called Mom.

"Hello?" The sound of her sweet voice soothed my frazzled nerves.

"Hi, Mom." I tried to sound upbeat, but was too exhausted to pull it off.

"Reedy!" she said with sheer joy in her voice. She was always happy to hear from me, always sounded like I made her day. "How's my girl? Is everything OK?"

"Yeah, Mom, everything's fine." I lied.

"I was just thinking about you, sweetheart." Mom wrote a lot, poetry mostly, about what she loved most in the world: nature, our family, and Jesus. This poem I found in one of the two little books of her poetry that Dad had published. She wrote it when I was young.

A Poem About Reedy
how happy the pigeons are
flying about the church steeple
if she were a pigeon
oh, if my love were a pigeon
so that waking in the morning
to the sounds of cooing
she would fly about the church steeple
and coo there
happy as the pigeons about the steeple cooing

But sometimes she just wrote down her thoughts, what she was worried about, dealing with.

Once, I found some pages she wrote that looked like journaling and read like she was talking to me. She couldn't understand why I had to stay in Chicago, why I wanted to live so far away from home. It made me sad. I wondered—why did I have to live so far from home?

"Your dad and I went to the Blue Boar for dinner last night." Mom chuckled. I held the phone close to my ear. The sound of her voice lifted my spirits. I was glad she was in a chatty mood. It gave me a chance to forget about my problems.

The Blue Boar was a cafeteria-style diner in Louisville that Mom and Dad frequented quite a bit. It was good and cheap, and Daddy didn't have to leave a tip—that made him happy.

"We got so tickled talking about that Christmas we had to have our big Christmas dinner at the Blue Boar—"

"Oh yeah." Reminding me got me to laughing.

"Because your brother canceled his Christmas family feast, remember? And we didn't find out until Christmas morning when everything else was closed." The Blue Boar was not what you'd ever consider for a special occasion or celebratory anything.

"Yeah, I think Jud was finally fed up with the likes of us unruly fruitcakes making a mockery of their perfect holiday." Mom burst out laughing. She had the best laugh. It was explosive; she couldn't help herself.

Jud was the third-oldest in the family, a middle child. I believe he considered himself the only normal one, or the one and only white sheep in our family of black sheep. According to him, the rest of us were freaks, to one degree or another.

"I miss y'all, Mom."

"Oh, honey, we miss you every single day."

"I wanna come home."

"Sweetie, that would be great! When can you come?" So, she made an open-ended plane reservation for me for the next day. Dick wasn't happy about it, but he drove me to the airport anyway. It was a cool ride, to say the least. Few words were spoken.

The second I got on the plane; I felt a huge sense of relief. When we landed, Mom was there waiting for me at the gate. I had just been home for a visit the month before, but I hugged her like I hadn't seen her in a year.

It was so good to be home again. The house always had a certain smell, like someone was cooking broccoli or Brussels sprouts with an added faint scent of something sweet. I loved it.

Finally, I felt safe. I could relax. No more nightmares.

First night at Mom and Dad's, I slept like a baby. I even thought about not going back. Ever.

What would be so wrong about my living with Mom and Dad again? I could always figure out my next move from there. But that first step, the "breaking up with Dick" part—yikes. How would I do it? I knew damn well he wouldn't take it lying down. He'd blame Mom, Dad, too. Dad always played good cop to Mom's bad cop. I tried not to think about it, but couldn't help myself.

Suddenly, the whole horrible scenario played out in my head. What if I just didn't go back? What if I actually had a backbone for once in my life? What if I called Dick in a couple of days? I imagined how the phone call would go:

"Hello?" he'd answer.

"Hi," I'd say. *Stay calm*, I'd tell myself, *keep it simple. Ignore the dread in the pit of your stomach. Talk slowly, deliberately.*

"Hi, babe," he'd say. "You're calling early."

Then I'd say, trying to sound calm and collected, but failing, "Um, yeah, listen, I need—um, I'm going to stay here, for now."

"What?" he'd ask. "What are you talking about?"

"Yeah, um, I need to stay here at home," I'd say. "I think it's over. I'm—"

"What!?" he'd shout and start to get charged up.

Don't be so goddamn tentative, I'd tell myself. *Be firm!*

"Babe, what are you talking about?" he'd say. "Why are you—?"

I'd cut him off. "I'm hanging up now. Don't call me for a while."

"Wait!" he'd say.

But I would've already hung up. Whew! He'd try to call back, but Mom would already know what was going on, so we'd just let the phone ring.

That wouldn't be the end of it, though, not by a long shot. I visualized Dick driving, speeding the whole 300 miles down to Louisville, to confront me, and Mom and Dad, too. He'd knock on the front door. Dad would be at work. Mom would go answer it, unsuspecting. More than likely, she'd be wiping her hands on a tea towel—she washed dishes a lot. Mom would be shocked to see him, but probably wouldn't open the glass storm door. She'd just talk to him through it.

Finally, Dick would speak right to the point. "Where's Reedy?" he'd ask.

Mom would just stand there, eyes wide, stomach tightening, staring at him. Dick, disheveled, with a scruffy beard and darker bags under his eyes, looking like a tortured, malnourished prisoner—not having slept because of my phone call. He'd stare back at her accusingly. Then, snapping out of it, Mom would say, "What do you want, Dick? She's not here right now."

He'd notice Mom's car in the driveway and know she was lying. "Where is she?" he'd ask, a look of smug disbelief on his face. They'd stare at each other, their mutual hatred quickly turning into loathing.

"I don't know," she'd say. Then he'd reach for the doorknob, but Mom would immediately hold it in place so he couldn't open it. Then she'd lock it. "She's not here!" she'd say. She'd dig in her heels, clench her fists, and stand up straighter.

Dick would yank at the door handle a few times while looking Mom square in the eyes. Then he'd hit the door almost hard enough to break the glass.

She'd jump back in shock, her eyes narrowing. She'd grit her teeth and slam the front door in his face. She'd lock it and rush around the house, locking all the doors and windows. Maybe she'd close the drapes so he couldn't see inside, maybe even call the cops.

Mom always called Dick bullheaded. She was right—they were well-matched. But even if I did end it, I couldn't just move back in with my mommy and daddy in Louisville, Kentucky! Good Lord! Not after living in Chicago. I needed a plan. But I was getting a headache, so I forced myself to stop imagining the horrible, possible scenarios and took a nap instead.

CHAPTER TWENTY-ONE

1967

Busted

I didn't tell my folks that I'd come home because I was scared to death we were going to get busted. Or that Dick was selling drugs. Or that I was convinced the cops were going to find out—if they weren't already on to us. Or that I was terrified they already had a plan in place to raid our apartment and send us on our merry way to jail. Forever. I didn't tell Mom that I couldn't sleep and was about to go stark-raving mad. But I got the feeling that she knew something was up.

One afternoon a couple of days into my visit with Mom and Dad, I took the phone and settled into the big blue armchair in the living room. I loved sitting in it and studying Daddy's paintings hanging all around. They made me happy. I kicked off my shoes, curled up, and wrapped a throw around me. The clouds outside must've parted because the whole house went bright. I looked out the window into the backyard. The water in Mom's birdbath had a thin layer of ice on top. I thought about the summers when robins splashed in it, sprinkling the purple and yellow pansies below.

Daddy planted them around it every spring. Now the circle of dark, rich earth underneath was wet and soggy from the winter rains. I dialed the phone.

"Hello?" Dick said. He sounded sadder than usual and hoarse, almost like he'd been crying.

"Hi, babe… are you OK?"

"No, I got busted. Spent last night in jail."

"What? Oh my God!" I said a little too loud. Mom must've overheard my panicked response. She rushed in from the kitchen, smelling of sweet dish soap and wiping her hands on the fancy blue dishtowel with yellow flowers on it.

"What? What happened?" I shook my head and waved my hand.

"No, nothing," I whispered. "It's OK. It's nothing." She squinted her eyes. I smiled and waited for her to leave the room while Dick talked in my ear.

"Yeah, I'm scared. It's a fucking nightmare." Mom went back to the kitchen.

I walked as far away from her as the phone cord would allow and turned my face away from the kitchen while cupping my hand over the mouthpiece.

"Babe? You still there?"

"Yeah, sorry, Mom was… so what happened?" I wasn't surprised he got busted. I was shocked, freaked out, and maybe feeling the tiniest bit self-righteous because I told him that it was just a matter of time. I knew something was going to happen. Problem was I couldn't tell if the dread in the pit of my stomach was merely a heightened sense of paranoia I always had whenever I was stoned—which was often—or if it was a real premonition.

"It's all fucked up." He sniffled. "I was in the living room with Pete and Damion and a couple of his girls listening to that new Bill Evans album."

"Uh-huh."

"Yeah, then Pete pulled out a kilo of that great weed, so I rolled a couple of joints. Then Damion said something really funny… can't remember what… that's when I heard a banging on the door, like somebody was pounding on it with their fists. Jesus, it was loud as fuck."

"Oh shit!" I covered my mouth. "Were you already stoned?"

"Totally wiped out."

"Oh no!"

"And we all just froze and shut the fuck up. I turned off the music and asked who it was, and a man yelled, 'Federal agents and you better open this Goddamn door now!'"

"Oh, honey! Oh my God—"

"I didn't open it. And then they screamed, 'Open this motherfucking door!' And they just… kicked it in! Fuck!" Dick's voice got shaky, and he was out of breath, like he was reliving the horror.

"Oh, my God. Honey, are you alright?"

"No, no I'm not," he said. "I'm fucked up. Come home. You need to come back. Now. Today."

Shit! I had to stall. "Well… but how, how'd it happen? I mean, how'd they know you were…" I listened, tried to hear what Mom was doing in the kitchen. I heard water running and the sound of silverware clinking. "How'd they know you were selling?" I whispered into the phone. Dick didn't say anything for a few seconds.

"They set me up." *Oh my God!* I knew it. I told him. How many times did I tell him? "Yeah, it was Angela. That bitch gave me up! She got busted and fucked me to get herself a lighter sentence."

"Holy shit!"

"Yeah, and get this. Her boyfriend, you know, the one she'd been living with for like a year? He set her up to get off easier for his drug bust from the year before."

"Oh. My. God!"

"Come home, babe," he said. "It's all fucked up. I really need you right now."

"But—" I looked around. "What am I gonna tell Mom? I just got here a couple—"

"Goddamn it, come on, babe!" he said. "I… look, I can't. I think—I don't think I can…" He was about to cry. I could hear it in his voice.

"…Yeah, yeah, OK, honey, OK." I was trapped. I panicked; my mind raced. I tried to think of a way out. "I…I'll think of something to tell Mom," I told him. But I didn't want to, I didn't want to go back. My eyes burned; everything was upside down. Dick sounded destroyed, barely hanging on by a thread. I was afraid he'd do something stupid, like hurt himself. I felt guilty, scared, ashamed. What kind of person would I be if I left him there alone when he needed me so desperately? I wanted nothing more than to stay safe with Mom and Dad, but how could I? I loved him, and I was his last hope. He'd had to disengage from all of our friends. Now his only allies were me and his very traditional Italian-American, dysfunctional, unenlightened family, who wouldn't have recognized genius if it smacked them square between the eyes. In some dark, terrifying place deep inside me, I felt I had no choice. So, I went against my better judgment and promised him I'd come back and that everything was going to be fine. Then we said our tearful goodbyes and hung up.

I doubled over with fear and loathing. I wanted to die. How could I tell Mom and Dad I was leaving this soon? What would I tell them? What reason could I come up with? Why *was* I leaving so soon? I had to tell them something. They were paying for my flight, and I was supposed to stay for at least a week. I tried to think of an excuse—a good, plausible lie—but couldn't come up with one good enough. I almost never lied to Mom and Dad. I could hardly pull off lying to anyone. Always thought I'd be found out and humiliate myself. Any time I lied, or didn't tell the absolute truth, I'd get nervous and flustered, convinced it would show in my eyes, my face, my body language, and I'd be exposed for the fraud that I was.

I walked into the kitchen and said, "Mom, I need to get back."

My neck tensed, and my stomach was a mess of knots. I thought I was going to puke. She stopped doing the dishes and shut off the water. She turned around and looked at me, water dripping off her hands.

Mom was in her late 50s, and when she was happy, she was still pretty. There was an old black-and-white photograph of her hanging in Daddy's room. She was nineteen years old at the time and had a beautiful oval face, a wavy brown bob, and a cute little nose—I got Daddy's nose, among other things.

Mom had been overweight as long as I'd been around, but she had the prettiest light green eyes, and her short curls were now gray.

"But you just got here. What's the matter? Is Dick in some sort of trouble?"

"Um, no, he just needs me to come back."

"Why?" she asked. Then she reached for the dishtowel on the counter, dried her hands, and pushed the curls off her forehead—she was gearing up for battle.

She folded her arms and cocked her head to one side. "Why does he *need* you to come back right now?" she asked. I just looked at her, praying she'd stop asking questions. "I know what it is, Reedy." She shook her head. The knots in the pit of my stomach squeezed tighter. "Dick can't stand for you to be with your family because we love you. He's trying to steal you away from everyone you love and anyone who loves you. He wants to isolate you, so he can have you all to himself. He can't stand it when you're happy. Can't you see that?"

"Mom, please, you don't understand."

"Yes, I do!" She unfolded her arms and made her hands into fists. "Honey, why do you let him order you around like this?"

"He's not. I've just got to get back!" I was caught. "Mom, he got busted and spent last night in jail!" I couldn't help telling her. But I tried to show her that I was strong, that I wasn't a child anymore.

Mom stood there wide-eyed. "He went to jail for dope? Dick's selling drugs?"

I struggled to control myself, but I was losing it. I always lost when I fought with Mom. "Dick really needs me now." I was out of breath, and in spite of my efforts, tears streamed down my face. I swiped them off, and we gazed at each other for what felt like an eternity. She stared into my soul. I'd never seen that look before. She shook her head and started to say something. Then she just stopped. Tears filled her eyes, and she turned and went back to washing dishes.

I looked out the splash-covered window over the sink. The sun was getting low in the sky, hitting Reverend Slider's house across the street. His windows were spotless, and the sunlight made them sparkle. Mom turned around again.

"Reedy," she whispered. "Please, please don't do this. Don't—"

"I have to," I cried uncontrollably. "I'm sorry, Momma. I have to go."

She stared at me for a moment. Then she dried her hands and walked away, leaving the dishes the way they were, half done. I went back to the living room, sat on the couch, and buried my head in a pillow. Mom had gone back to her bedroom and closed the door.

I broke Momma's heart that day and hated myself for it. She gave up. I imagined she saw right through me. Saw me for what I was—a scared, pigheaded child pretending I wasn't. I thought I was standing up for myself, doing something brave—cutting the apron strings. When, really, I was scared shitless. I felt like I was being torn apart by two people I loved.

I made a reservation to fly back to Chicago the next day.

The following morning, Mom drove me to the airport. Very few words were spoken.

When she dropped me off, I unloaded my suitcase and went around to her side of the car. She wouldn't look at me, so I kissed her cheek.

"Thank you, Momma." My lips quivered, and my heart ached. "I'm sorry... I love you."

She didn't get out of the car or turn her head, but her stern expression softened.

"I know you do…" Then, finally she turned to me. "I love you, too," she said. Her voice sounded far away, detached, devoid of hope. I felt her disappointment like a stab to the heart. I turned and walked into the airport, choking back sobs. I went to the ticket counter and took care of business. I wanted to believe I was doing the right thing, that my actions were those of an adult or at least someone trying to behave like one.

As soon as the plane landed in Chicago, I was nauseous with panic. Dick was waiting for me at the gate. When I saw him, I was shocked. He looked like a homeless person—and smelled like one. He was wearing the same jeans and shirt he'd had on the day I left. He was emaciated, disheveled, and his eyes were bloodshot and swollen. He almost collapsed in my arms. He had thrown on his old London Fog raincoat—the same one he was wearing on the day we met. He hugged me for a long time. He was not the confident, handsome, overbearing man I knew. He didn't say a word. He just held me tight, like I was the answer to his prayers.

"Oh, baby, it's gonna be OK." Me to the rescue! I was going to make it all better. We sat down on seats near the gate.

"They don't know what's going to happen to me. Uncle Frank says there's no way of knowing at this point." He held my hand tight. "He said he's going to do whatever he can, but—"

"Who?" I asked. "Which one is Uncle Frank?" I'd heard of him, probably even met him once or twice, but Dick had lots of uncles and cousins in his big Italian family, and I couldn't keep them all straight.

"Mom's uncle, the retired police captain," he said. "Why couldn't you come back yesterday?"

"Well," I said. "By the time I called to make a reservation, the flight was already full," I lied. "And Mom thought I should wait," I immediately regretted mentioning anything about Mom. "She wanted me to stay the night so I could explain it all to Dad when he got home from work."

"What'd you do?" he said. "Did you tell them I got busted?"

"Yeah." Why can't I ever keep my big mouth shut?

"Why? Goddamn it!" He threw my hand away and jumped up. People in the airport turned and looked at us. I was mortified. "Why would you do that? Shit!" He sat back down and put his head in his hands. "Son of a bitch!"

"Sorry. I'm sorry, babe. You're right," I said and lowered my voice. "But they had to know why I was leaving so soon. I had to tell them something—"

"Christ!" He looked around on the floor like he was searching for something to punch. I knew he was exhausted and in pain. He needed me, and I had betrayed him by telling my folks.

"Oh, God, I just couldn't think. Shit." I reached over and rubbed his back. I could feel his heart racing. "You think your Uncle Frank will be able to make a difference? Does he have enough clout to get you off?" I felt terrible. I thought about all I'd gone through to get back to him, and all I managed to do was add to his grief.

My parents were a sore subject with Dick practically from the beginning. He and Mom fought like cats and dogs. Dad was nice to everybody, but Dick still thought they were in collusion to split us up. He was right.

As soon as they found out about Dick's drug bust, their opinion of him hit a new low. He was now the devil incarnate, nothing more than a common drug pusher that stole their baby daughter away and was leading her down the road to total ruin. It was bad enough that he introduced me to sex (so they thought). Now this.

Dick and I sat in O'Hare Airport talking for a good half hour. "Yeah, so Pete pulled out a kilo of that great weed," he explained. "Ya know, that shit from Colombia?" He shook his head. "Goddamn, it smelled amazing!" He smiled for a second. "So, I pinched off some and rolled a few joints, and we smoked 'em." He smiled. "Then Damion... man, he's fucking hysterical, always talking shit. We couldn't stop laughing. Then..." Then he recounted the ugly part of the evening; the door bursting open, everybody freaking out, and finally, Dick being hauled off in handcuffs.

Hordes of travelers rushed past us looking to find and catch their flights. We finally left because it got too noisy and crowded. While we walked back to the car, Dick told me we were going to have to live with Toni and Art, his mom and dad, possibly for a few months while Uncle Frank fought for Dick in the courts to assure that he'd get probation instead of jail time.

As soon as I heard about staying at his folks' house, my heart sank. Dick's parents lived in a suburb on Chicago's northwest side where all the houses were 'made of ticky-tacky and they all looked just the same.'

When I first met Art and Toni, shortly after Dick and I started dating, I was a big hit. But when I moved in with him, I got the distinct impression their opinion of me plummeted to rock bottom. They seemed to see me as some kind of Jezebel who had seduced their son and was dragging him down with me. But it was the '60s. We were Bohemians, into free love and all that crap. Art and Toni were as straight as they came, beyond old school. They tolerated me and were cordial enough, but underneath their façade was a total lack of respect that was never talked about. So now that Dick had been arrested for being a drug dealer, we were moving in with them. Oh, happy day!

We cleared out of our apartment the next day and moved in with Art and Toni. Most of our stuff was hand-me-down shit anyway, so we offered it to the landlord for the next tenant to use.

It was a dark gloomy day in Chicago, befitting our mood, and Dick and I got everything accomplished in almost total silence.

Our first night at Dick's parents' house, when Art got home from work, he sat us down and gave us a good talking-to. Toni was nowhere to be found. I figured she'd probably been instructed to steer clear and let "the boss" take care of the dirty work. Art looked as uncomfortable as we felt. He was flushed and clumsy in his body. He touched his face a lot and shuffled back and forth, pulling on the sleeves of his suit coat.

"Now, you two listen to me," he said. His eyes darted around the room.

Dick looked depressed and ashamed, like a dog that was about to get whipped for his unacceptable behavior. We were sitting on the couch as Art paced around in front of us. Occasionally, he'd stop, glance down at us with his most threatening look. "While you're living in my house, there will be *absolutely* no drugs of any kind. And you better not let me catch you calling any of those dope-fiend friends of yours. Do you understand?"

We both nodded. "I understand," Dick said.

"Your Uncle Frank will be watching you, and I will too, I'm gonna report everything to him. Yeah... um, me and your mother, we're going to tell Frank everything, you know... I will not lie for you, Dick."

"I know, Dad."

"You two are going to have to behave like good, law-abiding citizens."

Good Lord, was he ever going to shut the fuck up?

Then he looked down at me. "You'll be sleeping in the back bedroom, Reedy. Dick, you'll be staying in the basement. Your mother set up a bedroom area for you." Dick and I looked at each other. We weren't surprised, really, even though they knew we'd been living together for several months.

In so many words, Art told us we had to change our evil ways, mind our P's and Q's, and behave respectfully, like good little Catholic robots. Those Zen Buddhist-struggling-artist-bohemian-drug-addled-hippie days were gone. Forever.

Art never understood his eldest son. Dick said he stopped trying years before. The way I saw it, Art was a bully. He loved being king of the castle, the benevolent benefactor and hero of all his subjects. Loved bossing everyone and anyone around, when he could get away with it.

"And if you don't behave…" Art wagged his finger at us. "Well, you could be in a lot more trouble, Mister. I mean a *lot* more trouble." He stopped, eyes darting back and forth between us. "You understand?" Art folded his arms across his chest and stared at Dick. "You could go to jail for a long time."

"I know, Dad—" Art stepped closer and cut him off.

"I hope you do!" he said. "You better hear me now, boy."

This was 1967. Sex, Drugs, and Rock n' Roll, Baby! We were now at the mercy of Dick's super-straight, ignorant, unsympathetic parents. Dick's freedom depended on them. After Art's big lecture, Dick moped around the house, terrified for days.

Art and Toni made good on their word. They monitored our every move. We cut ties with all our musician and actor stoner buddies because they were "bad influences." Toni had to know where her son was at every moment. We knew we were going to have to put on a flawless performance until the trial was over.

My role was clear, and I got into it. I was to keep Dick's spirits up as best I could. I had to flirt, charm, and sing Dick's praises to his dad whenever I could and to help Toni with the housework and cooking. I played to her sympathies, not that she accepted my help very often. I was Dick's savior, his comfort and confidant. I felt needed. Miserable, but needed.

It was a couple of hard months for both of us, but especially for Dick. Fortunately, his parents had an old piano in their basement that was a Godsend for him. He played it every day to escape thinking about his terrifying situation. He'd play for hours, or until somebody would request he stop.

"Hey, Dick, do you have to play so loud?" his brother or other family member would yell down from upstairs. "We can't hear *Bonanza*." Or whatever crap they were watching.

Toni was more sympathetic toward Dick than her husband. She'd make special trips to the Italian market for the cured meats, cheeses, and olives that he loved. She'd make him his favorite foods, like her homemade meatballs and pasta he enjoyed so much. She smothered them in her delicious homemade "gravy" (that's what real Italians call spaghetti sauce). Her efforts were the only way she knew of showing her love and support.

Occasionally, when nobody else was home, Dick and I would sneak in quick moments of intimacy. (The urgency suited him.) But when his parents were both home, we acted like we were reforming, day by day.

Dick was given ten years' probation, and after the trial, we immediately moved to Louisville. We wanted to get as far away from Chicago and his family as we could, but one of the stipulations of his parole was that he had to live near family, for the purpose of keeping us in line. Dick's Uncle Frank negotiated with the court, and they allowed us to move close to my family—even though they were not yet part of his family because we weren't married. Still, Dick wasn't thrilled because he had no love for my folks, but he was out of options. I was secretly happy, though, and spent as much time as I could with Mom and Dad.

CHAPTER TWENTY-TWO
1968
Shakespeare in the Park

As soon as we landed in Louisville, Dick and I hit the ground running. We found an apartment a couple days after we arrived on St. James Court, and moved right in. St. James Court was a beautiful tree-lined street adjacent to Central Park, with one gorgeous, classic, old home after another, many of which had been converted into apartments.

Dick went to every nightclub in town to drum up music jobs, and before I knew it, he'd gotten a gig playing on weekends at a classy joint downtown. Meanwhile, I started looking for acting work. As luck would have it, an open-air theater called Shakespeare in Central Park was just a short walk from our new home.

The theater was started and run by a man named Doug, a real piece of work. The first time I met Doug, I went to his studio apartment to audition for the company. He was in his fifties, I guessed, and was very casually dressed in a robe hanging open over ragged jeans and a sweatshirt. He sat in an old, worn-out lounge chair with a notebook and a fat gray cat on his lap. The second I walked into Doug's tiny two-room apartment, the scent almost knocked me over. It smelled to high heaven of uncleaned kitty litter times a million. I could hardly breathe. I couldn't help but wonder if he ever cleaned the damn box. Ever.

The apartment was unbelievably dirty, too. Piles of stuff and clothes were strewn everywhere, and he didn't seem to care what anyone else thought—it was the way he liked it, and the world be damned. I rose above it all and gave a great audition.

"Tell me a little about yourself," Doug said, with a theatrical gesture, twirling his hands in circles. He wasn't a bad-looking man. He did have a good-sized paunch, though, and slicked-back, gray, unwashed hair.

"Well," I resisted the urge to gag. "I'm originally from Louisville, but spent the last couple of years in Chicago. I studied at the Goodman Drama School, then landed the role of Alice in *Through the Looking Glass* at a small theater in Old Town."

"Interesting." He jotted something down on his notepad.

"And my boyfriend, Dick, was one of the musicians with the company. He's really talented, Doug. He plays vibraharp, keyboard, and all kinds of drums." I stopped and acted like I'd just realized something. "Oh, you probably need musicians for your productions, right?"

"We do," he said. "I'd very much like to hear Dick play."

"Of course." I played it cool, but was secretly delighted.

Then Doug handed me a monologue from *Romeo and Juliet* and I read it for him. He rooted through some papers and gave me a couple more scenes from the other plays he was planning to produce over the summer, and we read them together.

"Very good." He crossed his arms and stared at me for a long moment. "I do believe I've found my Juliet."

I did not see that coming. "Really?" I gushed, despite myself.

A couple days later, Dick met Doug at the stage with his vibraharp in tow. After a very short audition, Doug hired him on the spot. I've got to say, as disorganized as Doug appeared to be, he ran a pretty terrific company and was seriously resourceful. He was a heck of a sweet guy, too. Odd, but sweet.

Doug's portrayal of Macbeth, however, wasn't the best. In fact, it was downright dreadful. But that's the thing about starting your own theater company—you get to play whatever role you want.

I was beside myself. I could hardly believe I was going to be performing with an actual theater company again. The reality of it hit me when we started rehearsing four different plays day in and day out. What with memorizing all the lines and the blocking, I wondered if I hadn't bitten off more than I could chew. It was so much work, but I loved it. It was a dream come true. And the reviews were excellent.

Toward the end of the season, after we'd performed our final performance of *Romeo and Juliet*, we took our bows to lots of applause. All us actors and Dick, who played music for the production, were exhausted, happy, and jacked up. It always took a few hours to get rid of the adrenaline and calm down so we could sleep. I was pretty pooped and a little sad.

I must admit that I was relieved the production of *Romeo and Juliet* was over because I wasn't wild about the actor who played Romeo. Neal was English and perfectly nice, really, as well as a fine actor, but he was rather awkward on his feet, and his kisses were slobbery.

So, since I was playing Juliet, I had to do double duty: act like I was madly in love with my Romeo and, at the same time, act like I wasn't the least bit disgusted every time we had to kiss.

Hazard of the trade.

Most of the actors came over to our place after the play to party and unwind. Ron, who played my father, was the first one there. He was in his 50s, stood about 5'4", and wore heel lifts in his clunky boots to make himself taller. They made him walk funny. He kind of loped. Ron also dyed his hair very dark and grew it long on one side, then swirled it on top of his balding head in a curly mess. He topped it off with black shoe polish to cover the naked, fleshy bits. But as Father Capulet, Juliet's dad, Ron was truly dynamic. He had a real flair for the classics, Shakespeare, in particular, and used his strong booming voice to bring his characters to life. There's something very special about doing a play. The entire cast becomes like one close-knit family during the length of the production, complete with its oddball cliques, and family drama.

Almost the entire company was present, all lounging around our living room with its high ceilings, grand carved fireplace, and dark oak woodwork. We were rewarding ourselves with a well-deserved unleashing of pent-up anxiety after a job well done, by the sharing of pot and booze. All of it flowed freely; we were feeling no pain.

There was plenty to satisfy our munchies too. I'd put out some homemade dip and chips and cut up fruit and veggies. The other cast members brought pizzas, cookies, ice cream, you name it. We reminisced and laughed about all the stupid mistakes, screwed-up lines, and missed entrances through the entire run of the play, and how brilliantly we improvised to cover up our messes, or how we didn't.

The party was a total blast. But it got late, and we had two shows the next day, a matinee of A *Midsummer Night's Dream* and an evening performance of *A Winter's Tale*. So, a few hours into the party, everyone started to leave. Except for Ron, who was well into a conversation with Dick about psychology and metaphysics. They were going deep, God versus Nietzsche and existentialism, and blah-blah-blah. Their stoned debate was peppered with hysterical laughter, each topping the other with 'profound' insight. It grew from fate versus coincidence to conventional religion with all its dogma, versus Zen philosophy, and all things in between. They were stoned, buzzed, and both enthralled by their own brilliance. Dick loved intellectual conversations.

I started clearing the paper plates and cups. I had no intention of really cleaning. I was way too wasted for that. I just wanted Ron to see me tidying up in hopes that he would take the hint and make a quick exit. I reached between the two of them to get a couple of plates and a plastic glass half-full of melted ice cream, but Ron was facing Dick and didn't see me. So, he swung his arm around flamboyantly, one of his grand Shakespearian gestures, mid-conversation, and knocked everything out of my hands. The plates and glass went flying and hit the wall by the window. The glass of melty ice cream exploded everywhere, finally ending up in a creamy, gooey mess on the floor. We all burst out laughing. I fell on the floor and rolled around. I was laughing so hard. Finally, Ron pulled himself together and put his hand out to help me up. I grabbed on.

"You've got to warn a person, you know, darling! Don't just sneak up and attack like that." This only made matters worse. Still holding on to his hand, I fell back down in a new fit of laughter, and Ron tumbled on top of me.

"Ow!" I yelled. We rolled around until we were laughed out. Dick just watched and laughed.

"Are you OK?"

"Ow! No!" Ron frantically tidied his hair to keep it in place and tried to sit up.

Dick helped us both to our feet.

"Thank you, Richard, my good man. You are a gentleman and a scholar."

We had moved to Louisville in the spring, a few months earlier. At the time, Dick decided to introduce himself to any new friends and theater family by his formal name, Richard. He wanted to change his image and thought the name Dick no longer suited him. He thought it was beneath him. (I thought it suited him just fine.) We'd been living together for a couple of years by then, and although I did love him and was very attached, one might even say addicted, I had also become extremely aware of our incompatibilities. (I liked to be happy, stay focused on the positive, and count my blessings, whereas he enjoyed brooding and dwelling on the negative. I liked to get along with people, and he liked to argue and debate. You know, basic incompatibilities like that.)

"Are you OK, darling?" Ron asked me. He awkwardly got on his feet. The heel lifts made it difficult. Then he turned to look at the splattered, mucus-y mess everywhere. "Oh my dear! Would you look at that. Let me help clean up."

"No, no, no," I said through coughs and snorts of laughter, with barely enough breath to be heard.

"Don't worry your pretty little head about it. I'll get it."

I went and extracted the glass and plates from the puddles, scooping up as much of the slop as I could. I held my hand under to catch the drips and started for the kitchen.

"Well." Ron brushed off his pants. "Try that nonsense again, and I'll throw even more shit all over the place!" I started laughing again, had to lean against a wall until I could get my balance.

"Don't... you just sit down there and behave yourself!"

Ron chuckled and did as he was told.

I made it out to the kitchen, only spilling a few drops. When I got there and disposed of the goo, I realized how wiped out I was. It was a happy exhaustion, though, because the party had been a huge success. Best party all summer. My cheeks and stomach ached from so much laughing, and I could barely keep my eyes open. I puttered around the kitchen for a bit, putting the few sad leftover veggies in the fridge. I chuckled to myself, then broke into full-out laughter again just remembering Ron trying to save his comb-over when he fell.

I got a wad of paper towel, wet it, and went back into the living room. I was at least going to mop up some of the sticky stuff before I hit the hay. When I got there, Ron and Dick both looked at me.

"What?" They both continued to stare at me accusingly. I couldn't imagine why. Thought it must've been part of the joke. "What?" I made a face and continued to wipe up the splatters off the walls and floor.

"Richard informed me that you refuse to marry him." I stopped and turned around to look at him. I stood there, half a leftover smile on my face. I looked at Dick.

We had been through a lot in the two years we'd lived together. First of all, my brother's suicide, then Dick's arrest for selling pot and LSD, the hell of living with his family after the bust, and then his subsequent trial. We depended on each other. Nevertheless, I was beginning to believe that Mom and Dad were right. Dick and I were absolutely not meant to spend our lives together. But I had yet to muster the courage to leave the relationship. The prospect of living on my own scared me to death.

"You do realize, don't you," Ron continued in his best Shakespearian tone, "no one will ever love you like this man does." He looked at me with authority. "Look at me, darling… I wanted to go after you myself." (As if!) "I would have too, but I saw how much Richard adores you. I have never seen anything like it."

Ron was one of a kind. When Mom and Dad came to see *Romeo and Juliet*, Mom insisted I introduce her to Ron. Turned out she was bowled over by his performance. Finally, I realized she was starstruck. She'd practically swoon when he spoke. Mom invited Ron to have dinner with the family several times, and it was obvious to me that Ron was well aware of her crush and egged her on every chance he got. Dad must've known, but behaved like he was oblivious.

Ron's past was one big mystery. At first, we all thought he might be gay because he was so flamboyant, using grand gestures when he expressed himself, on as well as off the stage. But soon after we met, he spoke of a marriage, a divorce, and a daughter from long ago.

Another time, he told us he'd never been married and had no kids. "That I know of anyway," he said. He told other cast members he'd been married three or four times and had a few kids, then others that he hadn't married because he never found the right girl. It was a game of cups with Ron. Keep 'em guessing. He was so used to telling his tales, I doubt he knew the actual truth about his own past anymore.

I looked at Ron, then at Dick, and back at Ron. "I—I'm just not ready yet…" I stammered. I wiped up more of the puddles and quickly headed back to the kitchen.

"Wait." Ron's voice had an authoritative paternal tone. It was an ambush. I couldn't believe Ron was ganging up on me with Dick. Couldn't believe he'd joined in Dick's manipulation. How could he? I was much closer to Ron than Dick was. I trusted him. I felt cornered and betrayed.

"You've been saying that for almost a year," Dick said loudly. I hurried back the long hallway to the kitchen wracking my soggy, mostly asleep brain. I toyed with the idea of slipping out the back door and never looking back, but it was the middle of the night. Everybody was asleep. And I was still super buzzed.

I looked out through the screen door. It was black. Pitch-black except for the streetlight in the alley. It shone down on the asphalt. A small critter ran across, then turned around and scampered back. I couldn't tell if it was a squirrel or a young skunk or even a rat. It dropped something it had in its mouth and ran back to pick it up. Then it just sat there in the middle of the alley. Was it eating that something?

A car whizzed through, scared the bejesus out of me. Tires screeched, water splashing as it sped through the puddles left from the rain we'd had a couple days before. My heart raced.

I looked out to see if the squirrel, or whatever it was, was still there. I turned on the porch light, but it was only a 40-watt bulb, which didn't shed much light on anything. I opened the screen door and went out on the porch so I could get a better look. I squinted, tried to make out if the little animal was still there. I went down the steps slowly.

The backyard was a jungle of weeds and tall, unkempt bushes. You couldn't get through the walkway without getting tangled up in the overgrowth. Our landlord saw no reason to hire a gardener. "It's yours," he'd said. "You can do whatever you want with it. Lawn mower is in the garage." The lawn mower was old and greasy as shit. None of us tenants wanted to touch it, let alone use it.

I saw something, a lump, maybe where the animal had been. It moved or rolled over, and I heard a faint kind of skittering sound, such a weird noise, never heard anything like it. I wondered if it was the sound of something dying.

It was still nasty hot and humid outside. A chill ran through me. I looked into the yard on both sides and tried to see if anything was lurking there. I took a few more steps and heard a low whine coming from the alley. The lump stopped moving. Wild rustling stirred the bushes behind me, and I heard a low growling. I freaked. Pot always made me paranoid as fuck, and I never could handle the dark. My inebriated brain created wild, razor-sharp toothed monsters just waiting to pounce and tear me to pieces.

I ran back inside, locked both the screen and the door, and watched out the window for a few minutes.

Suddenly, sparks exploded out of the street light in the alley, and pitch blackness consumed the world outside.

I heard Ron and Dick's voices talking softly in the living room and remembered what was going on. My chest filled with crap. I felt like an animal of prey without any means of escape. I couldn't make out what they were saying, but I imagined.

Finally, I went back in. "Look," I said, "I'm pooped. I've got to go to bed."

"Reedy." Dick shook his head. "If… if you won't marry me, I'm leaving. I'm gonna move out."

Ron stood up. With his heel lifts, he was almost as tall as I was. He looked at Dick, then back at me with an intense stare.

"Darling." Ron called everyone 'darling.' "Richard's love for you is the real thing." He made a grand gesture toward Dick. "So real, so deep. You could look the world over and never find love so true."

Such bullshit. Jesus Christ, he sounded like he was reciting a monologue for an audition or a Shakespearian sonnet or something. I couldn't think; the last bit of energy drained out of me. My vision got blurry, and I felt faint. It was too much.

And that was it. That was the moment I gave in and gave up on myself. I don't remember what happened after that. What Ron or Dick said, what I said, what I did. What I didn't do. I don't even remember Ron leaving. I just remember the mood lightened. So, I guessed I sold my soul.

Cheap. But at least then I could sleep.

One morning, a couple of months later, after I'd exhausted the feeble, bogus excuses I could come up with—I had my period. I was sick. I should've washed my hair, but it took too long to dry—we went down to the Justice of the Peace Office in New Albany, Indiana and tied the knot. It was January, cloudy, and dark. No special day. No fanfare. We both wore jeans, sweatshirts, and our coats. When we got back to our apartment, I was down and didn't even try to hide it. I sat on the edge of the bed and contemplated what I'd done. Dick came and sat down next to me. We stayed there in silence for a long moment.

Finally, Dick broke the silence. "Honey," he said softly. "Don't worry. If it doesn't work out, we can always get a divorce." Man, I felt like such a heel. Dick bullied me into marrying him. I didn't have to. He didn't hold a gun to my head. Why didn't I just let him leave me? I could've. But I was supposed to be the nice girl. Momma always said I was the one who wouldn't hurt a fly. The girl who'd do whatever it took to make everybody happy. But instead, I betrayed myself and crushed the man I supposedly loved.

I muttered something like, "Yeah, I know. It's OK." That was the best I could come up with.

My stomach churned. I thought I was going to hurl. He was right. "Divorce." That word gave me hope. I could stay in the marriage for a while. Until I got my shit together.

Then we got on with our lives.

CHAPTER TWENTY-THREE

1970

Off to California

Eventually, I got used to the idea of being married. So did Mom and Dad when I finally told them. They didn't take the news well. I just tried not to think about it. Shortly after we tied the knot, Shakespeare in the Park ended for the season, and I joined Doug's troupe of traveling actors. We were a ragtag bunch that toured high schools all over Kentucky. We performed scenes from Shakespeare, Molière, Oscar Wilde, and other classical playwrights.

We caravanned to whatever school in whatever town with our portable stage in tow. After lugging it into the gymnasium and setting it up, we'd have maybe an hour to change into our costumes and slap on some makeup. Then it was showtime! The kids seemed to enjoy the shows. I believed the creative ones saw us as wild, eccentric gypsies peddling our offerings from school to school. (That's how I saw us, too.)

After the shows, we'd change back into our street clothes, mingle, and chat with the teenagers briefly, fold up the stage, pack it in the truck, and head on our merry way to the nearest, cheapest, dumpiest motel for the night. Sometimes we'd be away for two or three weeks at a time. Dick stayed home to play his jazz gigs a few nights a week, and I'd call him from a pay phone when I could.

A couple of weeks after the tour ended, I got together with a few of my fellow actor friends, who, like me, were going stir-crazy after having lost our creative outlet, and wrote a musical. It wasn't your ordinary musical, though. *This Is my Beloved* was an intense look inside a tortured relationship between a woman and her lover. By opening night, it had become "a dark, mystical theater experience" according to one reviewer. There were Martha Graham-style dance sequences lit by strobes and other colorful flashes of light with dramatic twists and turns.

Dick composed the "chilling avant-garde music" for the piece, which he performed live, and I was the lead. I then asked Lena, a talented friend of mine, if she would play my dancing alter ego/shadow, and she agreed.

Ron, the actor who played my dad in *Romeo and Juliet*—the "friend" who colluded to get me married off, read the narrative in his deep, dramatic voice while sitting on stage left. It was wild and glorious, and we found the perfect venue for it: a dark, strangely intimate, yet cavernous abandoned theater in a questionable part of town, not far from Louisville's stockyards.

The nauseating, unsettling death smells emanating from the slaughterhouse added to the ominous feel as the audience entered the space. The production ran Fridays, Saturdays, and Sundays for a month. It was ahead of its time, but was very well received, despite its location.

Soon after the new year, Dick and I noticed that several of our artistic friends were moving away. The consensus was that Louisville was dead-ends-ville for us creative types. We so wanted to join the exodus, but were stuck because we hadn't saved enough money to make a major move. So, I got a job at a local restaurant a few days a week, and Dick continued to hustle nightclub gigs. We were determined to get the 'hell out of Dodge' as soon as we possibly could.

Then on a Sunday night, we got a phone call from George, Dick's drummer buddy from Chicago. His wife Jocelyn was my best friend, and they had moved to San Francisco a few months earlier. Shortly after they got settled, we went for a visit, and Dick and I fell head over heels in love with California and ached to find a way to join the party.

I was washing dishes when the phone rang.

Dick had been working on our bills. The dining room table was covered with them, when he answered the phone.

"Hello? Hi, George," he said.

"Honey," I yelled from the kitchen. "Let me talk to Jocelyn before you hang up." I dried my hands and sat next to Dick, waiting my turn. Suddenly, he stood up.

"Fuck yeah!" he shouted.

"What?" I whispered. Dick shushed me with a wave of his hand. Then his eyes got wide, and his mouth hung open.

"Yes!" he yelled. "Really? Are you kidding me? When? Yes! It doesn't matter. We'll do it! Absolutely yes!" Then he turned to me. "A friend of George's is booked, so he can't do this gig, and they're offering it to me on George's recommendation."

"Oh, great. Wait, what gig?"

"Musical director of the California Shakespeare Festival for the summer."

"What? Are you serious?" Dick put the phone back to his ear, but not before I heard George's laughter coming through the receiver. I didn't hear much else of their conversation because I was too busy jumping up and down for joy. It was nothing short of a miracle.

Dick hung up and grabbed me by the shoulders. "Reedy, we have to be there by Friday."

"Oh, my God!" I giggled. "How—"

"I don't know how, but we're going to do it."

"What about your parole?"

"Yeah, I'll call my uncle. He'll take care of it." And he did. Thank God it got handled! Then we hustled our asses like we never had before. First, we made our one-way flight reservations. Then I apologized to the restaurant where I worked when I told them I had to quit, effective immediately, and why. We sold our old car, gave away most of our furniture, and took the rest back to Goodwill. Anything of personal value we stored at Mom and Dad's. Then we informed our landlord we were vacating the apartment. It was one crazy week, and we made it out there in the nick of time.

The California Shakespeare Festival performed in a large theater in the heart of Los Gatos, a small, adorable California town. The business manager had secured a rental for us atop a big hill overlooking the town. As soon as we arrived, we bought a used Vespa motorbike to get us to and from the theater.

Rehearsals started immediately, and every play had already been cast, unfortunately for me. But I was delighted just to be there, and I got to be part of the background players. The company had some real heavy hitters in it, like David Ogden Stiers, whose portrayal of King Lear was nothing short of brilliant. I took full advantage of the opportunity to study the pros at work. Even better, George and Jocelyn lived only a couple of hours away, so Dick and I got to see our dear friends often.

Toward the end of the festival, which was going to close at the end of August, I realized we hadn't a clue what we were going to do next. But midway through the summer, we had heard rumors of a yoga commune hidden away in the mountains a few hours north called Ananda. So, Dick decided to check it out.

CHAPTER TWENTY-FOUR
1970
Ananda

In August, when the Shakespeare Festival season ended, Dick and I left Los Gatos and drove to Ananda on our Vespa. Ananda was the "amazing commune" we'd been hearing about. It was nestled in the lower Sierra Nevada mountains in Northern California, and Dick had gone there to check it out the month before. When he got back, he told me it was all about spirituality and yoga, and that everything people had said about the place was true.

"It's like a paradise," he told me. "You have to see it to believe it. It's one huge chunk of land with this beautiful organic garden. And the people, God, all these enlightened people live there—it's fucking mind-blowing!" So, since we didn't have any other ideas, we moved there.

We only brought a couple of small backpacks with enough clothes and essentials for a week. But before we left Los Gatos, we packed up Dick's precious vibraharp and the rest of our belongings—which wasn't much—and mailed them to ourselves at Ananda.

Supposedly, it was a three-hour drive, but it took us four-and-a-half hours. With those crazy mountain roads weaving all over the place, it was a hell of a long ride on our little motorbike. And believe me, my butt was good and sore by the time we got there.

When we arrived at the commune, and turned into the dirt driveway, our scooter kicked up a shitload of dust. But once the cloud settled, and we stopped coughing, there it was, spread out before our tired, bloodshot eyes: Ananda, in all its storybook beauty.

At first glance, it did look like heaven on earth. It had it all—rolling hills, beautiful lush organic gardens, an actual babbling brook, and lots of young, interesting yogis and hippies. And it was free! (Free was our favorite). The hills were peppered with tents on wooden platforms for newcomers, and many small A-frame cabins for residents. It was spectacular, just like Dick said. And the air was the freshest I'd ever breathed. It was nature personified, off-the-grid, spiritual—absolutely everything Dick talked about and longed for.

Secretly, in my heart, it wasn't what I wanted at all, not even close. Deep down, I longed to live in a big city near other struggling actors. I wanted to study acting, audition for plays, rehearse, perform, and go to afterparties. That's what I wanted. But Dick would've been miserable living that life. He'd be happy at the commune—or at least happier. So, I gave in, for the time being, for Dick's dream. Also, I had no idea how to make my dream happen, so I kept my mouth shut and hated myself for always wanting things I couldn't have. I was a follower. I figured, what the hell? I could do this paradise thing for a while. Maybe yoga would teach me how to be strong, and meditation would help me find myself. Anyway, I figured I was only twenty-three. I could squander a few years, try this enlightenment thing for a while, see where it took me.

One of the first things we noticed when we arrived at the commune was a big, old, white farmhouse surrounded by huge oak trees. We soon found out that Ananda was actually two places: the commune and the retreat. The commune, or farm, where we stayed for about a year, was four miles from the retreat.

As we dismounted our ride, lots of happy hippies gathered around to greet us. We were road-weary and delighted to be standing anywhere on solid ground. The weather was perfect, with a temperature in the 70s. The sky overhead was a clear blue, and there was a slight, cool breeze blowing. Some of the women wore long skirts or dresses made of East Indian-print fabric, and most of the men were in yoga clothes. Everyone was beaming from ear to ear and welcomed us with open arms and big toothy grins.

We felt at home the moment we arrived, and the residents filled us in on Ananda's philosophy.

Their ultimate goal was to reach Nirvana, or enlightenment, through prayer, chanting, yoga, daily meditation, selflessness, and charitable works. Eventually, they said, they also wished to become self-sufficient by producing everything they'd needed to survive, and to grow all their own organic food. They also wanted to be an example to the world, to prove that it was possible for people to live peacefully with love and compassion while nurturing Mother Earth, instead of abusing and raping Her.

Several of the residents met in the kitchen most afternoons, after picking loads of fresh vegetables from the garden, to prepare and eat dinner together.

That first evening, some of our new friends walked us up the hill and introduced us to the tent that would be our home for a little while. After we settled in, we made the long, downhill trek to join them for dinner.

Most of the residents were in their twenties, like us, but a few were in their thirties and forties and a few even older. The dinner was like nothing I'd ever tasted before. The large garden was a glorious work of art. It was like a painting, perfect with every imaginable color represented. Yellow and green squashes peeked out from under huge, shiny leaves. Small orange pumpkins lined several rows. Big, bright red tomatoes hung from six-foot-tall vines. Stalks of green beans had climbed even higher. There was chard, kale, mustard greens, and weird vegetables I'd never heard of, like kohlrabi. Small, curly herbs circled the entire garden, providing the perfect border.

After gathering fresh vegetables from the garden, Wendy and Sabastian, a wonderful couple who had just had a baby daughter, brought them to the kitchen where I got to chat with the residents and assist in the preparation. The meal was bursting with flavor, each dish more delicious than the last. They made a zucchini dish with fresh tomatoes over brown rice covered in a rich, tangy herb sauce. We didn't miss meat being part of the meal one bit. We never even thought about it. The entire dinner was out of sight! I felt healthier and happier having eaten it.

By the time we got back to our tent, Dick and I were in a state of euphoric exhaustion. The sun had already set, and the light was quickly disappearing, so with a flashlight in hand, we laid out our sleeping bags, got ready for bed, and lay there as darkness enveloped us.

We both knew better than to leave any food inside the tent because it would attract wild animals. But we'd forgotten to put our bag of leftover snacks, nuts, fruits, and chips, in the big farmhouse for the night. And by the time we remembered, we were too pooped to hike down the hill and back up again. So, I folded the top of the bag of goodies as tightly as I could and left it outside the tent on the deck, in the hopes that we wouldn't be disturbed by marauding varmints. I knew it wasn't the best plan, but I was too tired to give a damn.

Later, sometime in the middle of the night, I was awakened by scratchy footsteps scrambling up the wooden step of our tent platform. I sat up and froze in place, as whatever it was attacked and ravaged the paper bag and its contents. I heard grunting and gobbling noises as they devoured the snacks. Then came a louder racket, a stumbling or fighting around the deck and an unworldly howling, modulating up and down like some sort of alien police siren. Never in my life had I heard anything remotely like it. I was convinced we were going to be eaten by some huge, ferocious, bear-like monster from another planet. I slowly lay back down, zipped my sleeping bag all the way up, and pulled it over my head. I figured if I was going to be eaten alive, I was going to make it damn hard for them to get my wrapper off. Maybe they'd tire out, maybe even give up, or, at least, I'd prolong the inevitable. My heart pounded in my ears. I opened my eyes as wide as I could, but the tent was full of blackness. I slowed my breathing. I was petrified, but wanted to make sure that whatever it was didn't become aware that there was fresh live meat inside the tent. The loud ruckus continued.

In my panic, I'd neglected to alert Dick, who somehow, amazingly enough, slept through the entire event. His fatigue must've overridden his usual insomnia. I decided not to wake him. I figured better he slept through his inevitable, violent demise than be awake and aware, like I was obviously going to be, as the unknown creature ate my fear-frozen body, chunk by bloody chunk.

I had no idea how long the whole episode lasted. At the time, I would've guessed about three days, but it was probably more like a half hour or forty-five minutes. Or maybe five.

I didn't get much sleep that night. Once I heard the monsters depart, I was too scared to fall asleep. I stayed awake shaking and listening intensely for the next batch of vicious beasts to come and finish the job. So, my first night in paradise? Not so great. Although I learned my lesson—never ever leave food anywhere near where you're going to sleep. Turned out, according to some of the residents, it was probably a bunch of raccoons. Apparently, they hunt for food in groups, and they make that ungodly, eerie sound when they happen upon a feast.

It was easy to fit in at Ananda and to forget about everything else. There were group meditations, working in the garden, cooking, scheduled Sunday services, and so many new friends to get to know.

And the whole community pitched in to build additional little cabins and domes because the secret was out: Ananda was growing by leaps and bounds!

Some of the residents were serious about their "spiritual path" and kept more to the austere, Hindu monastic lifestyle, while others smoked a shitload of weed, dabbled in and experimented with tasty mind-altering hallucinogens, and went skinny-dipping in the Yuba River Guess which group we fell into?

Swami Kriyananda, the guru and owner of the more than 300 acres that the commune and retreat consisted of, was a middle-aged, white Romanian devotee of Swami Yogananda. Everyone said how spiritual and enlightened he was and how being in his Godlike presence was a true gift. They said he was going to be returning from a speaking tour soon. Dick and I couldn't wait to meet him.

Sunday morning was absolutely gorgeous, and a bunch of us drove to the retreat for the service. Although the distance was only about four miles, it took us over a half hour to get there because once we turned off the main highway, the gravel and dirt roads had never been maintained. They were a disaster. But once we got to the retreat, we parked and walked along a beautiful forested trail alive with wildlife scampering, birds singing, and the sweet smell of pine wafting through the pristine air. It was going to be a great day.

We came to the ashram, a simple geodesic dome. Upon entering the temple, I felt like I was swimming into a warm welcoming womb. A deep peace overcame my entire body and mind. Plump meditation cushions were spread out in a huge circle around the room with an altar against one side. On it were a line of pictures of swamis and gurus: Jesus, Yogananda, Satchitananda, and several others, some I didn't recognize.

Swami Kriyananda sat on a zafu, a thick Zen meditation pillow, on a small, slightly raised platform, with his legs crossed in full Lotus and his hands in a traditional Hindu mudra on his lap. His eyes were closed, his head slightly tipped to one side, and he had a sweet smile on his face. We all settled in and sat in meditation for a while until I heard the sound of a gong being struck. Then Kriyananda spoke.

"Good morning." His gentle voice reverberated throughout the temple dome with a totally calming effect. When he spoke, his hands moved into a prayer position in front of his chest. He grinned and looked around the room, meeting everyone's eyes. I got chills. "What a blessing it is to see all your beautiful faces." He spoke slowly and deliberately about living life on the spiritual path. About treating everyone with kindness, love and compassion and about developing inner strength through meditation, chanting and prayer. I was moved to tears.

After the service, crowds of followers and retreaters surrounded Swamiji and praised him for his inspiring sermon. Many questions and comments came on top of one another.

"Swamiji, you so inspired me."

"What is it like to be enlightened?"

"I attended one of your lectures, and you had such an impact on my life."

That continued for some time.

Finally, Jyotesh, who was a long-time resident of Ananda, introduced us. "Swamiji," he said. "I'd like you to meet Reedy and Richard. They just arrived a few days ago."

Kriyananda had a short, scraggly, salt-and-pepper beard and long, thin graying hair that hung limp over his shoulders. He wore ochre robes (like a monk), and had long sandalwood prayer beads around his neck. Swamiji nodded at Dick, then took my hand and looked me straight in the eye.

"Hello." His gentle voice brought a chill up my spine when he spoke. "So nice to meet you both. Welcome to Ananda." He glanced at Dick and then focused back on me. "I hope you will stay with us for a long time."

I was wearing my new favorite dress; it was only the second time I had worn it. It was lavender, ankle-length, loose-knit, with long flowing sleeves and a low scoop neckline. I loved the way I looked in it. I never wore a bra, as was the fashion at the time, I had no need for one anyway.

The way the dress hung on my body revealed my shape, and almost through to what was underneath. My wavy, brown hair hung down to my waist.

The retreat was very different. Large pines, cedars, and firs dominated the landscape. At first it seemed almost untouched by man. Then naturally worn dirt pathways appeared and snaked their way through the trees to the geodesic kitchen and temple domes, as well as the A-frame cabins, which were nicely tucked into the woodsy environment.

The day was sunny and gorgeous. I felt high, like I was stoned, and completely in tune with the universe. A soft, warm breeze rustled the trees and blew through my hair.

"Great service," Dick said. "It sure is beautiful here."

"Yes, thank you," Swamiji said. "We love it." Everyone surrounding him smiled in agreement.

"We're thrilled to be here," I said. "It's such an honor to meet you. Your sermon was so powerful."

"How nice that you came to join us." He cocked his head, nodded, and looked me up and down. Then he took a piece of my hair that dangled down my front, put it back over my shoulder, and gazed deep into my eyes. "I will call you Rani."

I was surprised. I knew he'd given a lot of his devotees Hindu names, but I didn't think it was on their first meeting. I found out *Rani* meant queen in Hindi.

There was something about his vibe, something intimate, bordering on creepy, like when he touched my hair, and when he looked at me. I dismissed it and admonished myself for being arrogant, thinking I'd foolishly been mistaken. After all, what did I know? I had never been in the presence of one so enlightened before. Maybe I just misinterpreted the moment.

Later on, when Dick and I were alone, I brought it up. "You know, when Kriyananda spoke to me, it was like, like I felt peaceful inside, got chills, you know? It was far out."

"Yeah, he's pretty cool."

"But you know something else? Remember when he just stared at me and moved my hair off my breast?" Dick looked at me, puzzled. "Oh, I don't know. I just…"

"What?"

"Oh, I'm probably… I don't know." Wasn't sure if I should say anything about the weird feeling I got. I was sort of ashamed for even thinking it.

"What?"

"I don't know. I just got the feeling—I felt a kind of sexual vibe from him, you know?"

Dick looked at me like I was crazy. "No." He shook his head and chuckled. "I don't think so. Swamis are celibate. He knows we're married anyway." And we dropped the subject.

The following week, Swamiji was driving his van to Sacramento—a four-hour drive—to give a talk at a college. Several of his followers, including Dr. Jeffrey, his naturopath, were going with him. I really wanted to go too, but Dick wasn't interested. So, I went without him. On the way there, we chatted about reincarnation, the different spiritual paths, and life in general. I loved getting to know our new friends. I was learning more and more about life, yoga, the Hindu diet, our inner God, and all things spiritual.

Swamiji's talk went beautifully. Afterwards, all the students gathered around him for autographs and questions. When we were finally able to head back home, it was well after eleven o'clock. But we were all jacked up and ravenous, so we went out for some food despite the late hour.

Everybody ordered their vegetarian dishes, and then it was Swamiji's turn to order.

"What can I get you, sir?" the waitress asked. It was an extensive menu, and Swamiji had been looking at it for quite some time.

"Yes," he said slowly in his calm voice. "Hmmm, I think I'll have… French fries and a strawberry milkshake." Most of us laughed at his childish choice of a meal.

"You know," came a voice from the other end of the table. "If I were your doctor, I'd tell you that's the worst combination of foods you could eat." It was Dr. Jeffrey, Swamiji's doctor.

We all laughed, including Swamiji, but he didn't change his order.

Once we got back on the road, it was well after one in the morning, and the rest of the folks found cozy places to hunker down in the back of the van and fell asleep. It had been set up to be comfortable for sleeping with mattresses, cushions, and blankets. I sat up front while Swamiji drove. When it got quiet, I began to feel self-conscious being alone with a real guru.

"I'm glad you came with us tonight. Did you enjoy yourself?"

"I did! I loved hearing you speak. You inspire me." He smiled and nodded, but kept watching the road. It got quieter. I tried to think of something else to say or to ask, but it was so late and I could hardly keep my eyes open. Kriyananda stopped the van at a stoplight, and the quiet got uncomfortable. I racked my brain, but my mind was blank.

All of a sudden, without a word or an ounce of finesse, Swamiji reached over, cupped his hand over my breast, and just looked at it. I sat frozen. First, I thought I was crazy, like I had entered an alternate reality. I struggled to snap out of it, to make sense of what was happening. It was the middle of the night. Was I dreaming? Hallucinating? Was this some kind of spiritual initiation?

Was I supposed to do something in return, like grab his balls? Maybe it was a test? Was Swamiji testing me? Or did I misunderstand his move? Finally, I came back to reality and simply moved his hand off my breast. I scooted close to the window and looked out at the dark night. The torn vinyl upholstery poked into my arm like a cheese grater.

Neither of us said anything. I was no longer sleepy—my mind was going a million miles a second, and we still had hours to drive. I was trapped. Mortified. I participated very little in any attempts at conversation after that and couldn't remember any of it when I got home. As soon as we got back to Ananda, before Kriyananda came to a full stop, I said good night, jumped out of the van, and hightailed it through the pitch-black night up to our tent. Dick woke up and shone the flashlight on me when I came into the tent.

"Hey!" I said and blocked my eyes from the light. "Kriyananda felt me up," I whispered.

"What?" Dick sat up. "He did what?"

"Shhh! He felt me up. At a stoplight." I sat down close to Dick because the canvas walls of the tent held no secrets in, and sound carried perfectly throughout the hills. "I couldn't believe it! Totally blew my mind."

"What the fuck! What'd you do?"

"At first, I didn't know what to do. But I moved his Goddamn hand, that's what I did. I suspected it was coming, though. Remember when he did that thing? Remember? It was when we first met him, and I told you he moved my hair and kind of touched my boob?"

"Oh shit!"

"Yeah, we gotta get out of here!"

"Shit, shit, shit! I can't fucking believe it."

"Yeah, we should just leave, right?"

Dick thought for a moment. "No."

"No?"

"No. First of all, you need to stay away from him."

"Excuse me? You think we should stay here after what he did? Really?"

"Look, Kriyananda is going to assume you told me."

"Yeah."

"We like it here, right? And he's gonna be on his best behavior because he'll assume that I know. We're not paying anything to stay here, so let's take advantage of him."

I felt a little funny about it, but his plan made sense, and I didn't have any other ideas about where we should go, so we did. We stayed put. I did avoid Kriyananda unless there were plenty of other people around, and I was never ever alone with the man.

Later, I talked to Chandra, my new best friend at the commune, and she told me she'd heard other stories about his lascivious behavior. Come to find out our Swami was a lecherous old bastard who had little to no respect for boundaries. His clumsy attempts at putting the make on his female devotees were ongoing. I heard that he fumbled often, but sometimes, he was successful and actually scored home runs. I could never understand how someone so enlightened could be so gross and disgusting at the same time.

Kriyananda had paid for the land, all the bills, and repairs, etcetera, and, it seemed, asked little else of his flock. Maybe he thought he had a right to sample some of the newly ripened fruit he was subsidizing, married or not. I mean, what the hell? It was 1970. Love was free, right? There were no rules, right? Everything and everybody was fair game.

I came to love living at Ananda, and after a couple of weeks of staying in the tent, Dick and I were given our own small wooden A-frame tucked away in the woods.

I avoided Kriyananda like the plague, and Dick said he gave the man some very harsh, silent stares. Dick could be scary as shit with just a look.

CHAPTER TWENTY-FIVE

1971

Five-Hour Meditation

It was Friday, June-something. I drove into Grass Valley to spend a few nights at Ananda's new 'city' house. Dick and I were living at Ananda's Retreat, at the time, and Kriyananda had a special Sunday five-hour meditation planned in honor of the summer solstice. All of Ananda was abuzz about it. Dick was going to be part of the service. He had a whole music section planned where he was to play his vibraharp, while Kriyananda gave his talk, before the meditation service began. I wanted nothing to do with it.

I'm sorry, but let's be real—meditation is hard. I mean it's good, but, in my opinion, you *can* get too much of a good thing. A half hour of meditation was plenty, maybe an hour if you wanted to look like Mr. Awesome. But beyond that, I mean, come on, what are you trying to prove, right?

I could think of plenty of things I'd much rather be doing to celebrate the solstice. Like spending a few days in town, or going on a shopping spree, or going to a party, or going to a movie or a play, for a few examples. I supposed Dick was more spiritual, more disciplined than I was—and more pretentious.

My little trip into Grass Valley was well-timed, though, because Dick and I hadn't been seeing eye to eye as of late, and I needed a break. We'd mostly been arguing about the five-hour meditation. He thought I "needed" it. Said I'd been "tense and bitchy." He could be a real high-and-mighty, know-it-all jackass sometimes, and I'd had it with his bullshit.

Kriyananda had rented the house in Grass Valley a few months before, for those of us in the community who either worked in town and didn't want to make that dangerous drive to and from Ananda every day, or those who preferred spending part of our week in civilization.

Once we had all pitched in to fix the old 'city' house up, it turned into one big yogi flop house. The place was great and was conveniently located within walking distance from almost everything you'd want or need: a grocery store, a laundromat, a thrift store. There was even a YMCA close by.

On Monday evening, the day after the Sunday service, my friend Chandra rode back out to Ananda with me. She confided she had secretly been avoiding that insanely long meditation as well. She had told Kriyananda she had a family matter she had to attend to. We laughed about it all the way home, and made it back to Ananda just in time for dinner. Chandra was not only a good friend; she was also another one of us young women who Kriyananda had put the moves on. With Chandra, however, he had achieved his goal—a surprise attack, as it were, where the 'act' was over in lightning-fast time, as was his way apparently.

The dinner dome was packed with friends and retreaters, and smelled like miso, hints of soy sauce, and fresh bread. I got in line and looked around for Dick.

Everyone was chatting merrily about how hard the meditation had been and how they had to push through, but reached new levels of consciousness. They raved about feeling profoundly enlightened and "seeing the world in a whole new light!" Egos were flying high that day. It was a bit nauseating, frankly, but I played along.

I congratulated them and said shit like, "Oh, I can tell. Your aura is so much brighter!"

I explained my absence with, "Yeah, I hated to miss it, but I was just getting over a cold."

Retreaters from all over the state and beyond were there, none of which I knew. Then I caught a glimpse of Dick snaking his way through the crowd with a plate of food in hand.

"Hi," he yelled. Because it was loud as fuck.

"Hi," I yelled back. "How was it?" He looked different, happier maybe? I couldn't put my finger on it. Maybe it had been all that meditating. Or maybe it was because we hadn't seen each other in a few days. I know I was happier.

He nodded, pointed to an area across the room, and mouthed the words, "I'll be over there." I nodded, and off he went with his dinner.

After chatting with a few more friends in line about their 'awesome' meditation experiences, I finally got my food and joined Dick at the table. "So, how was it?"

He shrugged. "Good." That was so like him. Stoic. Man of few words.

"Come on, how was it? Did it seem endless?"

"Yeah, at first, but then it got easier." Then we ate for a while listening to the clamor.

"I'm going to get some more rice." Dick took his plate and walked off into the crowd.

I did some people-watching while I finished eating. Then I noticed Dick was at the bread table, and I wished I'd asked him to bring me more bread. It was a sweet, rich homemade rye with crispy onions on top, delicious.

Before he left the bread table, he bent over and said something to a slightly heavyset, long-haired blond girl sitting at a nearby table. She bent her head back dramatically, then tipped it to one side, looked straight into his eyes with a soft smile on her face, and said something back to him. It was not your ordinary exchange. Her look was intimate—the way she surrendered to his gaze. There was more to this encounter than met the eye. I watched her while Dick found his way back to our table. She never took her eyes off him. I realized she was fairly tall when she stood up to get another helping of food.

As soon as Dick sat down, I stared at him for a few seconds while he scarfed down more bread.

"What?" He made an annoyed questioning gesture with his hands.

I continued to stare.

"What the fuck?"

"Who's that blond you were talking to?"

"Oh, for Christ's sake! What's wrong with you?" He continued to eat, like he had said enough. I dropped it until we got back to our A-frame.

"Well, who is she?" I asked as soon as we walked in the door.

"Who? Oh, Jesus!" He exploded. "What the hell are you talking about? Why are you being paranoid?" I doubted myself for a split second. "I think her name's Macy, or Nancy. I don't know. She's just another one of the retreaters who participated in the meditation."

"I saw the way she looked at you, Dick. I don't think she's just another one of the retreaters—"

"Let it go. Fuck!"

"Fine! But I saw that look she gave you." I did not let it go. And, once again, we went to bed not speaking.

A few weeks later, after we'd started speaking again and were on pretty friendly terms for a change, we decided to spend the night at Ananda's city house in Grass Valley. I had a shitload of laundry to do in town, and Dick needed to buy some tools, so we made a day of it.

It was early on a Saturday evening, and we were finishing the last of our supper at the dining room table. The house was quiet, mostly empty except for a couple of friends watching TV in the living room.

I looked at Dick playfully. "Hey." I tipped my head to one side. "Have you ever been unfaithful to me?" I asked. I'd been saving that little morsel ever since I saw Chunky McBlondie give him "the look."

"What? What are you talking about?"

"Oh, I don't know." I shrugged. "Just wondering. No big deal." Dick blew out his mouth, frowned, and took his last bite of rice with peanut sauce. "I'll tell you if you tell me," I said. He scowled, then looked suspicious and shook his head. "Aren't you a little curious?"

"Jesus." He took a drink of water.

"I'm just saying. It's no big deal."

Dick glared at me. Then I looked up, and we stared at each other. I smiled. "You first." I could tell he was getting nervous. Curiosity and guilt are a dangerous combination.

"Well… I have, but only a few times."

Fuck! My mind went berserk, but I tried like hell to maintain a laissez-faire look on my face. Meanwhile, my guts exploded.

"Uh-huh. Was that blond one of 'em?" He stared at me. "Was she the last one?" Dick gave a slight nod. "I knew it," I said, holding tight to my rage. Then I stood up. "You fucking son of a bitch." I burst into tears. Dick's eyes widened as he stared at me in shock.

Behind him, a ray of dusky light shone through the kitchen window. The place was a mess. Dirty dishes were stacked on the counter by the sink, and the floor was covered with crumbs and blobs of sticky goo.

I felt betrayed and humiliated. The feeling of dread in the pit of my stomach intensified. I ran out the front door sobbing.

Dick ran after me. "Wait! Reedy, stop!"

My eyes burned like hot pokers; I could hardly see. "You fucker!"

"I'm sorry! Stop! Honey, please!" I ran out into the busy street, secretly looking both ways trying to avoid cars. I wanted him to be terrified, to suffer—but I didn't want to die. I just wanted him to hate himself as much as I did.

A few tires screeched and swerved to avoid me. I ran from street to street, Dick closing in on me.

"Please! Wait! God, please, honey! I'm sorry!" Finally, in the middle of a dark parking lot, he caught up and grabbed me.

I slapped him over and over again. "Stop! Take your fucking hands off me! I hate you!" He held tight and wrestled me to the sidewalk. I struggled and pounded on him as hard as I could until I collapsed on the pavement.

"Oh, baby," he said through sobs. "I'm sorry… I'm so sorry…"

See? That's what can come of too much meditation.

CHAPTER TWENTY-SIX

1971

Kitchen Duty

DICK AND I LIVED AT ANANDA'S FARM FOR ABOUT A YEAR BEFORE WE moved to Ananda's Meditation Retreat. He taught several yoga classes each week to the visiting retreaters, so it was more convenient. Unfortunately, we were fighting a lot. And when we weren't fighting, it was because we weren't speaking. So, I volunteered to be one of the cooks for the yoga retreat. I needed something to keep me busy—a creative distraction that did not include Dick. I teamed up with two fellow Anandites, Mary, an interesting woman in her fifties, and Denise, a pretty, mild-mannered, funny woman in her twenties. We trained ourselves, studied, and shared recipes, experimented, and became really good cooks. We made all kinds of different breads, pastries, and vegetarian dishes. While we prepared the food, kneaded bread, brainstormed, and cooked, we talked. About everything.

I was bending over, looking deep inside one of the refrigerators for more powdered milk. I was in the middle of making several loaves of whole wheat bread and had a giant bowl of bubbling yeast on the counter. I found a mystery bag of something and looked inside to see what it was.

"Hey," I said. "We've still got a ton of this dill weed from the garden."

"Oh God, is that still in there?" Denise was chopping more veggies for the salad. "Shit, I forgot all about it. It's got to be dead by now."

"Yeah, it was way in the back," I said and sniffed it. "Whoa! Nope, I think it's good. Still smells powerful. Well, maybe a little funky too." I took a second sniff.

"Bring it here," Mary said. "I'll pick through it." Mary was working on a rice dish that smelled amazing. I pulled the dill out of the huge bag, and the kitchen exploded with the smell of dill pickles.

"Oh my God! Smell that," I said.

The kitchen was a good-sized geodesic dome. It had two large refrigerators along the walls, two stoves in the center, two deep double sinks, also in the center, and plenty of counter space.

We stored different flours, including whole wheat, rye, buckwheat, and white, as well as grains, spices, raisins, and other dried fruit and nuts, in gallon jars lined up on the counters along the walls. Big bundles of fresh herbs from the garden hung drying around the room. Between the herbs and our cooking, our kitchen always smelled delicious. It was well laid out with plenty of room for the three of us to navigate easily.

"Hey, I got a great idea!" I said. "Why don't we put some dill in the rice?"

"No, no," Mary said. "The rice has a really good taste. Here, try some." She filled a large wooden spoon with the rice dish and stuck it in my face. I took a bite.

"Oh Mary," I said. "That's fucking fantastic!" Mary smiled. "You have outdone yourself!" All three of us were instinctual cooks; we seldom stuck to recipes. I grabbed the spoon from her and licked it clean. Then the spoon slipped through my fingers and fell on the floor. "Shit!" I blurted.

The spoon bounced, and a few grains of rice scattered everywhere. I tried to pick it up, but got tangled in my long skirt and ended up on the floor. Mary and Denise tried not to laugh, but did.

"What the hell just happened?" Denise said and helped me up. "You OK? Is it your naptime?"

"Damn it!" I said. "Thanks, I think it *is* my naptime! I slept for shit last night!"

"Oh, no, is that man still blaming you for his sleep problems?" Mary asked and went back to working on her rice dish.

"Oh, yeah, he hardly sleeps as it is. Then I go into my nightly tossing and turning bullshit."

"What the hell's his problem?" Denise chimed in. "It's not like you're doing it on purpose."

"I know. Tell me about it. Hey, how about we put some dill weed in the bread?"

"Oooo, interesting! And chop up some of those shallots too!" Denise said. "We've got a million of 'em!" Cooking with the girls was a fun form of therapy when we'd share our problems. We supported each other and stumbled upon some really great recipes.

One day, six months or so after I'd joined the cooking crew, the girls and I had, as usual, prepared and served lunch to all the happy retreaters. The main course was curried brown rice with zucchini, broccoli, tomatoes, and scads of other lightly steamed veggies, as well as spices from our garden. We served it along with a beautiful, healthy salad dressed with our homemade soy, lemon, and garlic dressing. We also served that same special dill-onion-whole wheat bread, which we stumbled upon when I discovered that funky dillweed in the fridge. That original recipe had become a real favorite. We were exhausted, quite pleased with ourselves, and very hungry. I got myself a plate full of food and sat down at a nearby empty table on the big deck in a nice shady spot.

One of Denise, Mary, and my favorite things to do was watch the crowd's reaction as they'd devoured our dishes. We usually were showered with compliments after meals. Every now and then, we'd produce something less than spectacular, but most of our dishes were received with well-deserved praise.

After the girls finished eating, they took their plates back to the kitchen to start cleanup. I was always the slowest eater, so I watched the retreaters while I finished up. The guests wore ochre robes, saris, or other East Indian religious garb, while some were dressed more casually. Many of the retreaters had long flowing hair, or no hair at all, monk style. I overheard some excited chatter about Dick's upcoming yoga class. Everyone loved his classes. He was a pretty great yoga instructor, with his long, black hair and beard, and his deep authoritative voice. He was extremely limber and flexible too. He had it all.

While I was sitting there, I noticed a handsome stranger checking me out. He was sitting amidst a very talkative group, just staring at me, his head cocked to one side. I smiled and thought maybe he knew I'd had a hand in creating the delicious lunch he'd just consumed and was impressed.

He smiled back. Then he came over and sat down next to me. Funny thing, though, he didn't say a word. So, neither did I. It felt weird at first, but we just stared deep into each other's eyes for the longest time. I was swept away, felt like I was stoned, but I wasn't. He looked at me with a sweet, pure desire. It'd been a long time since any man had looked at me that way.

He touched my face. "Where did you come from?" he asked as though he was inquiring about some heavenly, mystical apparition. I opened my mouth to say something, but no words came out.

He smiled. "What's your name?" His voice was soft and deep, and he had the sweetest cherry-colored lips. My mind went blank for a second. I forgot everything—who I was, where I was, that I was married. It was such a strange connection, felt cosmic. I got embarrassed, wanted to turn away, check to see if anybody was watching us. But I couldn't bring myself to stop gazing into his eyes. I was mesmerized, wanted to crawl inside him, to taste him. His strawberry blond curls hung down to his shoulders. He had pale, perfect skin, and rosy apple cheeks. His eyes were hazel, the color of a mountain lake. He smelled like pine, clean and woodsy. Suddenly, I felt like I'd known him all my life. Like I'd just been waiting for him to show up.

"I…" He laughed. Finally, I forced out a feeble, "Reedy." I cleared my throat and said my name again. "Reedy."

He cocked his head. "Reedy," he repeated softly. A smile took over his entire face, revealing his perfect white teeth. "Reedy," he said again. My name sounded like music when he spoke it.

"What's yours?" That moment—his smile, his expression, his aura, his everything—gave me goosebumps all over.

"Rodney." We were wearing almost the same outfit, cut-off jeans and a blue T-shirt. Only mine had a gold OM symbol on the front of it.

For some dumb reason, I'd chosen to wear my ankle-high, black hiking boots. Don't know why. I wasn't planning on doing any hiking. I fussed at myself for wearing them. I'd bought them cheap, on sale at a kid's shoe store. They were great for hiking, but they were ugly as shit and made my feet look gigantic.

"Where'd you come from?" I asked.

He laughed.

He had a wonderful sense of humor and an infectious laugh. I was so happy. There was plenty of noise and chatter going on around us, yet we communicated in whispers.

"I've been looking for you," he said and took my hand. My face got hot. It must've turned ten shades of red. That's when I should've told him I was married, right? But, here's the thing—I didn't. Then he got up and nodded his head toward the woods. I knew if I followed him, I'd be heading for trouble. I hadn't even taken my tray back to the kitchen like I was supposed to. I craved this adventure, wherever it took me. So I followed him. The girls would be waiting for me to help clean up. But I followed him anyway. They knew all about my troubled marriage, so I figured they'd understand. We walked past the community dome, where lots of people were still talking and eating.

In my peripheral vision, I saw friends watching us, probably wondering who this guy was and why he was leading me off into the woods. And did he know I was married? And where the heck was Dick anyway? Gradually, the voices faded.

We walked down the dirt road, holding hands and talking about how we must've been together in a past life because we had such a strong, undeniably cosmic connection. He had just gotten to the retreat, came from Alberta, Canada where he was getting his master's degree in religious studies. He came to Ananda for a spiritual retreat. He asked me if I lived there.

"Yeah, I made the lunch you just ate."

"You did?" He was surprised and delighted.

"Uh-huh, I'm one of the cooks."

"Really?"

I nodded.

"Far out!" Then he stopped and turned to me. "That meal was outta sight!" He looked at me like I was some kind of genius. "What's your secret with that rice dish? It was amazing!"

"Oh, that was Mary's creation. It had all kinds of organic veggies from our garden and lots of spices, again from our garden. And a shitload of butter."

He laughed. "And where'd you buy that bread? It was incredible! I've got to buy a loaf."

"Made it… from scratch. Denise and I made up the recipe."

"You did? Wow! Man, I wanted more, but when I went back, it was already gone!"

I felt giddy, like I was high. We walked for a while in silence soaking up the beautiful day and each other. He asked me if I liked living at Ananda. I said I really liked it, but had been thinking about moving to

San Francisco to study acting. I told him about living in Chicago and going to Goodman School of Drama, and about the plays I'd done. He seemed impressed. Even though we'd just met, I felt I could tell him anything and he'd actually be interested.

Finally, I forced out, "Um… Rodney, I'm married, but it's not working out." A huge, dry ball of tension scraped and tore at my stomach. "I've been thinking about leaving." I hadn't really thought about leaving Dick until that moment when I heard the words come out of my mouth. He took my hand in understanding.

We got to a clearing in the woods where a platform had just been built. They were going to put another small A-frame up for the retreaters. We climbed onto the platform and looked around at the forest. We listened to the quiet, and the wind rustling through the trees. The spicy smell of Bear Clover filled the air. Bear Clover, also known as Mountain-Misery, was a tough, oily ground cover that was everywhere. When it rained, or people walked on it, the heavenly aroma took over. The Native Americans called it kitkitdizze, and it smelled like strong, exotic incense. A squirrel climbed down one of the trees and watched us. Then it walked over to a small acorn, but didn't pick it up. Instead, the little guy just lay down next to it and watched us.

"This place is mind-blowing," Rodney said. I sat down on the platform. He sat in front of me, wrapped his arms around my legs, and leaned in. His beautiful eyes held me transfixed, and a million more butterflies took off in my stomach. I couldn't remember the last time anyone looked at me that way. It seemed like he could see the innermost part of my being. He ran his hand over and down my long, wavy hair. A shiver ran through my body.

"It sounds like you're going through a hard time." His eyes wandered over my face. He seemed full of awe. "Such a bummer. I knew it when I first saw you… I'm so sorry." He looked at my mouth. Then he touched it and moved in slowly. He looked deep into my eyes, and our lips touched. Our eyes remained open when he kissed me. And he was so gentle. His kiss sent me soaring. I felt like I'd never been kissed before. My body was on fire.

I hadn't realized how hungry I was for something that tasted like love. How desperate I was to accept anything that felt even close. I ached, longing for a man to pay sweet attention to me. To treat me like I was interesting and beautiful. I wrapped my arms around him, our lips pressed together. Then his tongue slipped into my mouth, and my tongue met his. Our kiss went deep and deeper until we were lying down, and he was almost on top of me. I didn't want it to end.

In the distance, I heard a girl's voice yelling and footsteps running. "Reedy? Reedy?"

I sat up and looked toward the dirt road. I recognized the voice. It was Denise. She was getting closer, but was still out of sight.

We sat up. "Yeah?" I said, loud enough for her to hear me.

"Oh good! Dick's here. He's been looking for you." Finally, Denise appeared. She had stopped and was bent over, her hands on her knees trying to catch her breath.

"Shit! Thanks, Denise." Then she waved and walked back the way she had come. I was mortified. Rodney looked at me like he understood. He kissed my hand, and we got up and hurried back without saying a word. When we arrived at the dome, he looked at me with love and compassion, then disappeared into the crowd. I went to find Dick. I felt horrible and wonderful and full of guilt. I tried not to cry. I wanted to run away and disappear.

Our truck was parked at the juncture where two dirt roads connected. He looked down at me from the driver's side.

"Where were you?" Dick was angry. "I looked all over. What the hell were you doing?"

"I know. I'm sorry." I walked to the truck. I'm sure my face was bright red. My heart pounded in my ears. I couldn't bring myself to look at him. My stomach stung, raw with acid and fear.

"Where were you?"

"I was… let's just go." I got in the truck and slammed the door. I looked out the window. I felt his eye burning into me, watching me. We sat there for a moment with the motor running. Then he peeled out, gravel flying. We drove to where we always parked and walked to the tiny A-frame we'd been living in. He shut off the engine, and we sat in silence.

Finally, I told him a *version* of what happened. Told him I'd been unhappy for a long time. Told him I met a guy, and we took a walk, and talked. Dick didn't react like I thought he would. I thought he'd erupt, scream, and curse. That's what he usually would've done, and it's what I expected him to do. Instead, he didn't do or say anything. I could hear him breathing. He was quiet for a long time.

"Maybe you need something to take care of." A moment passed. "Maybe we should have a baby." We looked at each other. Another moment passed. He smiled. He smiled!

What's going on? I wondered. *Wait… is he right? Do I need a baby? Do I want a baby?* Suddenly, Rodney and all that kissing and staring in each other's eyes, feeling the strong cosmic connection and the sexual tension. Suddenly, it was gone from my mind. I got away with it! I was relieved. Dick would never know what really happened. Then I thought—he didn't want to know.

Could a baby be the answer to my loneliness? To our problems? Would it give meaning to my sad, pathetic life? Would it make me whole? Maybe that's what was missing. Maybe having a baby would make Dick happy too. Maybe it would fix everything. Was this why people had babies?

CHAPTER TWENTY-SEVEN

1971

Fire

It was the middle of July on a windy summer night, probably around one or two in the morning. Dick and I were fast asleep in the loft of our small A-frame at Ananda's Retreat. Suddenly, in the pitch blackness, Dick woke to the sound of distant screams and a loud crackling noise.

"What the hell?" Ananda was usually silent at night as no major roads were close by.

"What?" I said, coming out of a dream. "What's wrong?" I sniffed the air. "What's that smell?"

"Shhhh!" he snapped. "Listen…" I did. I heard voices. They got louder, closer, and we could hear a lot of coughing. It sounded like they were right outside the door.

Then I started coughing. "Something's burning…" I said. Suddenly, there was a loud banging, and the door flew open. Thick curls of smoke filled the flashlight beams as they scoured the room. I shielded my eyes from the light.

"Dick!" screamed the voices. "Reedy! Wake up!" Smoke filled the room, and we started coughing. Dick grabbed the flashlight we kept by the mattress, and we climbed down the ladder from the loft. Crowds of people ran past, coming from all directions.

Flashlight beams darted everywhere in the black night. I grabbed the flashlight we kept by the Coleman stove, and we followed the crowd. The wind was wild. Then we saw it: flames high up in the trees. We ran faster. The trees weren't on fire; the temple dome was engulfed in flames. The fire was raging, consuming it.

Dumbstruck, we shone our flashlights all around. Everyone was freaking out, running all over the place, filling anything they could with water from the outdoor spigots, then running back to the fire and throwing it at the flames.

Dick stopped and stared at the burning temple. "Oh my God! My vibraharp is in there!" He rushed toward the fire.

"Dick, wait!" I screamed. "Wait!" I ran after him, but the flames were too big, too hot. It was like running into a furnace, and I couldn't see anything through the thick, black smoke.

Dick stopped and fell on his knees, coughing. He loved his music; his instrument was his best friend, his life's blood, his reason to live.

Then someone grabbed me. "Reedy?" I recognized the voice. "Is that you?!" I turned and hugged Denise.

"Was anybody in there?" I screamed.

"Don't think so!" she yelled.

It was mass pandemonium. Everyone was crying and throwing paltry pails of water on the out-of-control flames. It continued for hours. By dawn, the temple was burned down to the ground. We all sat around gazing stupidly at the smoldering embers—all that was left of our beloved temple. I saw a weird shape amidst the rubble: Dick's vibraharp. It had melted into what looked like a small deformed animal with strange protrusions sticking out. We were exhausted, filthy, and in shock.

They never found out what started the fire, but fortunately, no other buildings were burned. We did lose a couple of trees, and quite a few manzanita bushes, but by some miracle, there were no injuries, or loss of life. Dick, however, was devastated by losing his vibraharp.

Within a few weeks, though, we heard some good news: Kriyananda had insured everything and Dick's vibraharp was covered and valued at $1,500. So, while Dick still mourned his loss, we then had the opportunity to think about starting a whole new life somewhere else. We were more than ready to leave Ananda. It was well past time.

That's when we happened to meet Gary Snyder, the Pulitzer Prize-winning poet whose land was adjacent to Ananda Retreat. Gary was a real character and a genuinely great guy. He, his wife Masa, and their two kids became friends. We also found out about a local family who was selling twenty acres just down the hill from Gary's. The Coughlins had lived in the area for generations and owned many acres of wooded land. But I wanted to move to the big city.

"Look," Dick said. "Living in San Francisco is too expensive; the rents are ridiculous. I just lost my vibraharp. How am I supposed to make money without my instrument? But if we can get that land for cheap, we could build a little house and live out here rent-free."

"Hmm," I said. "But how the hell can we afford to build a house?"

"Yeah, I've been thinking about that." His face lit up. "Remember that rock quarry over by Highway 49?" I nodded. "We'll build a house out of rock. We can collect them ourselves."

"Wait, doesn't that rock belong to somebody?" I asked. "Like a company or something?"

"Probably not, it was probably abandoned years ago. Never see anybody working there, do ya? It's free building material." Dick watched as I thought it over. "How about we go check out the land before we decide?"

We did go to see the property, and it was amazing: twenty acres of forested land which included a piece of a large meadow with a creek running through it. We walked the entire parcel and came across the perfect site for a rock house.

Since we had no phone, and the Coughlins' place was close, we decided we'd just go and knock on their door. Their big farmhouse, which was built sometime in the 1800s, was right off old Highway 49. It was just past the gravel road leading back to Ananda's Retreat, Gary's beautiful Japanese farmhouse, and the parcel of land we were interested in buying.

A short, round woman, in her forties, or maybe older, cracked open the door slightly and peered out.

"Yeah?" She was wearing a flowered blouse that hung out over her long pants. Her close-cropped hair was the color of straw.

"Hi, you must be Mary," Dick said. Mary was the youngest of the remaining Coughlin family. She lived with her two uncles, Francy and Jimmy. They turned out to be kind country folk, and we worked out an arrangement. We agreed to pay them $1,000 an acre, with our insurance settlement of $1,500 as a down payment. We also agreed to keep the banks out of it, because the Coughlins were perfectly happy to carry the loan themselves. We had ourselves a deal—we were land owners!

The house we built was a real beauty. Dick did the actual building, and I did lots of the other jobs, such as rock finishing work, cleanup, fetching water and tools, shopping for supplies and food, organizing and cooking in our homemade, open-air kitchen, just to name a few. We built the house out of good-sized, heavy stones that we hauled out of canyons and ravines with our bare hands—we were young, invincible. We could do anything! It turned out to be as backbreaking and exhausting as it sounds, but it was worth it. The house was a sight to behold.

We cleared the house site of trees, bushes, and whatever, had the foundation dug and filled it with concrete. Then Dick found Marcel, a professional stonemason who lived in Nevada City. Marcel helped us design and build the big rock fireplace structure in the center of the house. The fireplace faced the living room, and we added an indoor grill on the kitchen side. They shared the same chimney, and the entire structure was both beautiful and functional.

Hiring Marcel was Dick's clever way of killing two birds with one stone. The fireplace and grill got built in less than two weeks' time, and Dick closely observed Marcel's techniques. That was all Dick needed to build the rest of the house.

He had a shitload of drawbacks as a husband, according to me, which made him holy hell to live with, again, according to me. But he got things done and was a great protector—on the off chance that someone other than himself ever attacked me. He was able to pick up new abilities quickly and with very little effort.

After the rock structure in the middle of the house was built, Dick and I, and a handful of helpful, young yogi groupies, got to work on building the actual house.

Dick got quite a following from his yoga classes. He had real spiritual-celebrity status going on—he was good, charismatic, super-limber, seldom smiled, had an austere, mysterious vibe happening like he was some big, enlightened yogi. And he was very handsome, with his delicious, dark Italian skin, full black beard, and hair tied back in a ponytail. The whole package made him quite popular among the ladies and yogi wannabes.

Dick was brilliant in many ways. He could do just about anything. He'd become consumed with whatever it was and throw himself into it 1,000 percent.

But, despite his many positive qualities, Dick and I were not compatible. For one thing, he was a neat freak, obsessed with having the house clean—all the time. Which we both considered my responsibility because he was working to bring in the money. It didn't help the situation that we had interior rock walls, which made it impossible to keep a dust-free environment.

Much to Dick's dismay, I'd never been the least bit interested in housekeeping. And it was becoming increasingly clear that we hadn't thought through the house design properly. We'd neglected to look at the bigger picture. The rocks we scavenged to build the house were not smooth, round river rocks. They were large, craggy stones with millions of tiny crevices, perfect homes for creepy, crawly things as well as for catching and holding on to dirt and grime. Our beautiful rock house was unique, and rustic, and extremely chilly year-round.

Before the rock house was completed and airtight, we ran out of warm weather, and I got pregnant. Then Dick had an idea. He'd met a kind, older hippie woman named Rena while he worked in town. She and Dick hit it off right away, so he asked her if we could rent a room in her house while I gestated. Rena had no family, had never married, and lived alone in her large, old, two-story home in Nevada City. She graciously agreed, but would only accept rent money occasionally. She was a wildly eccentric character who adored cats. In fact, she had nineteen stashed in cages in the basement. She was absolutely devoted to them. Every evening, like clockwork, she would fill a gigantic black skillet with Purina cat chow, cover it with garlic powder, to discourage the fleas—and pour boiling water over it. That aroma would fill the entire house. And every evening, little pregnant me would try not to puke.

CHAPTER TWENTY-EIGHT

1972

Giving Birth

A DARK FIGURE EMERGED FROM THE SHADOWS AND SWUNG A LONG, shiny sickle, slicing deep into my abdomen. My guts unfurled, splaying everywhere. I jumped awake in searing pain and looked around the small bedroom in Rena's house.

I grabbed my huge belly, gasped, and curled into a fetal position. Fuck! A contraction! *This is it*, I thought. *I'm in labor.* The cramps were paralyzing. In a painful, sleepy fog, I started the Lamaze breathing.

The actual contraction was very different from the Braxton Hicks practice contractions my body had experienced randomly throughout my pregnancy. Those didn't hurt at all; my uterus would get rock-hard for about a minute. But the real contraction? Oh yeah, it was serious. It meant business. It meant soon I'd be having my baby!

Funny thing, despite the terror of facing my impending labor, I had the added fear of knowing full well that I was clueless. I knew exactly zero about being a mother—despite the book I'd read. Mostly.

Now my pregnancy was soon to be over, and I was sad. I loved being pregnant—everything about it. After all, the only thing I really had to do was take care of myself, and that was, hands down, my favorite job. The few things I wasn't crazy about were morning sickness and occasional swollen ankles and feet—although that did have a positive side. It was an excellent excuse to relax and put my feet up—doctor's orders. There was also the mysterious itchy rash I got on my feet and calves a couple of weeks before I gave birth. Other than those side effects, my pregnancy was a lovely walk in the park.

I told my doctor about the itchy rash. "It's awful," I said. "It usually starts in the middle of the night, and I can't stop scratching it until I'm raw and exhausted. I lose a lot of sleep."

He looked at me unimpressed for a few seconds, then said, "Yeah, well, it's no big deal, it'll go away as soon as your pregnancy is over. You'll be fine." And it did, and I was, but fat lot of good his "professional opinion" did for me.

I was nervous about Dick, too. Afraid he'd revert to the way he was before—morose and moody. During my pregnancy, he was happy, and we got along much better. He wasn't his usual brooding self, often seething with anger or discontentment. He was kind and considerate and much less argumentative. It seemed he didn't let things bother him like usual. Almost like he was a different person—one I liked much better.

Another thing I really liked about being pregnant was not having to suck my stomach in all the time. Finally, I could relax and let it all hang out—I don't care what any woman tells you. We're always sucking it in even when it looks like we're not. Unless, of course, we're not.

I loved the tiny movements, too. The kicks and punches from inside, my baby reminding me that *it* was alive and well and getting stronger every day. The little thing checking out his or her brand-new arms and legs. And, yep, they were all there and working just fine, thank you.

During the last couple of months of my pregnancy, when I was big as a barn, people treated me differently. It was almost like they didn't even see *me* anymore. They only saw my gigantic mystery bump.

"Oh, my goodness!" said a woman with long, braided salt-and-pepper hair. She was pushing a loaded shopping cart in the middle of a busy grocery store. She stopped next to me, reached out, and touched my protrusion. "You're huge!" she said with a laugh. "You must be due any day now, dear." I guessed her to be in her late forties. She was wearing sandals and a sleeveless Indian-print dress down to her ankles. About half of the residents in Nevada City were hippie types no matter how old they were. You could tell just by looking at them.

"Yeah, I know," I said. "I am huge. I'm—"

"What do you think you're having?" she interrupted. Then she leaned in. "You know, with my four, I was dead wrong every single time. Each one of mine was the exact opposite of what I thought they were going to be. You'd think I would've stopped guessing at some point!" She threw her head back and roared with laughter.

Those delightful, random conversations happened multiple times almost every day. It didn't matter where I was. I loved it. I guess what I'm saying is I loved being the center of attention.

Dick and I came up with some great boys' names, and I thought that was a sign from the universe that we were going to have a son. Whatever we were having, we wanted a cool, nature name, like Willow, or Sky, Brook or River. Something that would speak to who we were. No "Johns" or "Pams" for us. We were finally free to be ourselves, to create our own path in life. Conventions be damned! We were leaving the old ways behind without apology or explanation.

Actually, Forrest was at the top of our list if we had a boy. Problem was the only Forrest we knew was a local logger named Forrest Sweat. (True story!) He had a few missing teeth and a serious drinking problem, so we thought better of the name.

I wasn't completely surprised when that first contraction hit me because the baby had been rumbling around in my uterus like a wiggle-worm the whole night. I hadn't slept much because of it. The little thing must've known something big was about to happen. I was twenty-five at the time and thought I was well prepared to give birth. We'd gone through all the Lamaze classes and had done our breathing homework regularly.

While I was pregnant, Dick and I lived with Rena. She was very dear and pretty hip for being in her seventies. The other reason Dick and I were crashing at Rena's was because our rock house wasn't quite finished. The eaves hadn't been sealed off yet, so there were big gaping holes where cold air, bugs, and the occasionally resourceful varmint got in.

Late that September morning, when that first contraction hit me, Dick woke up too. He was a light sleeper on the best of nights due to insomnia. We timed my contractions. They came about ten to fifteen minutes apart, or thereabouts. So, we lay in bed, talked, and practiced our Lamaze breathing when needed until the sun came up. The contractions continued, getting stronger and closer together.

Later that day, we said our sincere "thank yous" and "goodbyes" to dear, wacky Rena.

"Oh, my goodness," she said. "It was nice having y'all here. Now go on, take care of business. Good luck, you two!" Rena couldn't figure out why anybody would want to have a baby. "Too hard on the body," she told me once. I got the feeling she was happy to have her 'cat house' to herself again.

We drove from her place in town out to Ananda. We wanted to announce the news to our old friends, who were thrilled and almost as excited as we were. Then we drove to Penny's house, not too far from Ananda's farm. Penny was the community's very own, self-proclaimed midwife. She and her seven children lived with Michael, her second husband and father of three of them.

Under the pretense of being a strict, traditional Hindu husband and father, Michael was in actuality a misogynistic tyrant who was not above abusing his wife and children. They lived in a three-bedroom, ramshackle, slapped-together old house with lots of East Indian tapestries and standard Hindu and hippy-type paraphernalia. Penny was a kind, soft-spoken woman from Wales, who, she said, learned everything she needed to know about midwifery from her grandfather, who was a doctor.

Almost all our friends at Ananda wanted to come to the birth when we announced that I'd gone into labor. Dick and I had been planning a home birth from the beginning (unbeknownst to my obstetrician in town). He was our just-in-case, "backup," plan B guy. Our friends asked if they might join us at our almost-finished rock house for the big event, to celebrate, meditate and chant the new little being into the world.

So, always the accommodator, of course, I said, "Sure, the more, the merrier!"

My contractions had gotten stronger by the time we settled in at the rock house. The sun was getting low in the sky, and the house began to grow dark. I lay on the mattress on the living room floor and managed my breathing through each contraction while Dick and Penny got everything ready. Since we had no electricity, they lit kerosene lamps and candles and even incense while about twenty or so people traipsed into the house and settled around me. Penny checked my progress periodically, and Dick was my Lamaze coach. As each contraction hit me, he'd direct my focus to the breathing.

Now, labor is a wicked, painful son of a bitch, and anyone who tells you otherwise is either lying—so they can look somehow better than you—or they have the pain threshold of a toilet seat. So, there I was naked and spread eagle with way too many friends, and several total strangers, watching my every move. "It'll be fine," I told myself— forever the optimist.

Now, you might think that a vacant, funky, unfinished, ill-equipped rock house, full of building dust, debris, and God knew what all in the creepy-crawly department, on a bare mattress on the floor, surrounded by far too many freaks, hippies, and germs, not to mention being at least an hour's hellacious drive away from doctors and hospitals, wasn't the safest environment to give birth in—and you'd be right—but we were flower children. Everything natural was just as "Mother Nature" intended. After all, women had been giving birth for centuries under every imaginable and unimaginable circumstance.

I performed nearly flawlessly for my audience. I did the proper breathing through each contraction for hours and hours and fucking hours. Hard labor. Yeah; no fun. But what choice did I have? I'd made my bed, as it were.

Eventually, I didn't give a damn who was in the house, couldn't remember who was watching me bare my soul as well as my most private body parts. I was exhausted and fucking tired of being in so much fucking pain.

About seventeen hours after my labor started early that morning, Penny checked me again and announced, "OK, Reedy, you're almost ready to push. You're about eight centimeters, just a couple more to go—you're doing great." Finally, I was in the home stretch. But I was in no mood to say anything, didn't even know if I could speak words. So, I nodded and tried to force some semblance of a smile. When you're eight centimeters dilated, you're supposed to get an irresistible urge to push the baby out (for those unfamiliar with the process).

It seemed like hours passed. I continued to breathe. Then more time passed. I continued. Then too much time passed, and I never got the urge, and Penny never told me to push, so I didn't. By then, I was outside my body, unaware of anything except the tremendous pain I was in and trying to control it with my breathing. My contractions were coming every three or four minutes, they told me. But time had no meaning.

Penny rechecked the progress of my dilation. Her normally calm, sweet face was no longer calm or sweet.

She looked worried. "Your cervix seems to be closing."

What? My mind cramped up. *Wait… isn't my cervix supposed to be opening?* Her words didn't make sense. Suddenly, my contractions intensified. My insides felt like they were being ripped out of my body. I wanted to scream like a madwoman, pull out my hair by the roots, and curse God and everything. Instead, I jerked and twisted, trying to escape the excruciating pain.

In the dim glow of candlelight, dark shadowy figures lined the rock walls. Faceless forms watching, closing in on me. I imagined their expressions and nasty, holier-than-thou thoughts:

"She's doing it wrong."

"If she'd meditated more, she'd be done by now."

"She just isn't spiritual enough, never has been."

"She could lose a few pounds. Look at those thighs."

I tried to focus on the faces, tried to recognize somebody, but couldn't. I wanted them all gone.

I lay there, my body wet with sweat, and continued to writhe. I'd allowed myself to be watched, to be seen at my most vulnerable and I regretted it—I was failing, and they knew it. I knew why they'd really come. They'd come for the show! They'd come under false pretenses. *Perverts!* I wanted to yell. I hated them all—the contractions came faster and faster. I couldn't take it anymore; I prayed for the agony to end.

"Wait, her cervix is what?" Dick asked Penny. "Is closing? Her cervix is closing? What's that mean? What do we do now?"

"I'm sorry." Penny turned to me. "We're going to have to take you to the hospital, Reedy." She had a look of concern, almost panic, on her face, and spoke with such urgency, instead of her usual soft, calm voice. I got scared. I remembered all the horrible stories I'd heard from people trying to warn me about home births: the infants dying, the mothers dying, both dying.

"What?" I said through my panting. Penny stood up as if her work was done. She leaned in close to my ear.

"We need to get you to the hospital as quickly as possible." The words registered. *You mean I have to stand up? Put on clothes… Fuck. I have to walk?* I stopped breathing mid-contraction.

"No, I can't…." I whimpered.

Penny grabbed my hand and squeezed it. "Reedy, we need to leave now," she said.

"Can't you do something?" Dick pleaded.

"I'm afraid there's nothing I can do. We really must get her into town as quickly as we can."

"Fuck!" Dick took a deep breath, looked at me, and attempted to smile. Then he leaned in close. "Honey, we have to go now. What do you need?"

"Whaa? Uh, whaa?" were my exact words, I believe. Dick sprinted up to our room, grabbed the bag I hadn't unpacked yet, ran back down, and we did it. I did it. I don't remember doing it.

But in the dead of night, in the midst of debilitating contractions, I got my poor confused body up—with major help from Dick—put on clothes—I think it was a nightgown or robe or something—and we made our way to the truck. I was out of my mind or wished I could've been.

As soon as I got in, another contraction hit me, and I attempted to do the breathing—that lasted for about a second. Then a nonstop barrage of erratic, unbearable contractions hit me all at once, and that was it. I gave up. I growled, squirmed, and contorted my poor body like a mortally wounded animal for the entire ride into town. Dick was beside himself with fear and drove faster than he ever had. It sounded like our poor old truck was going to fall into a million rusty pieces.

Dick didn't care. Neither did I.

When we got to the hospital, Dick helped me in—by then, he was hysterical. A couple of nurses put me in a wheelchair and took me to a delivery room. They must've thought I was ready to deliver due to my mental state, or that something was very wrong. They helped me into a bed as my contractions continued.

Finally, my doctor came in to examine me. I'd been seeing him since I was two months pregnant. He was a tall, rather imposing man in his fifties. His brown hair was cut military-short, and it was going gray around the edges of his big pink face. He was one of those authoritative doctors who talked down to you and didn't listen because he had all the answers. He was way too straight-looking for my taste, but he did have pretty green eyes and a nice set of teeth—when he allowed himself to be a mere human and smile for a second.

It took every bit of strength and self-control that I didn't know I had to stop panting and squirming in pain, so that he could examine me. After which he said, "You're only three centimeters."

First of all, What. The. Fuck?! When I left the house, I was very close to ten centimeters, according to Penny. Did he just say three centimeters? My foggy, nearly suicidal brain tried to make sense of the information. *Three centimeters? Wait. Am I starting over?*

At the very first appointment with my doctor, seven months earlier, I told him emphatically that I wanted to have a natural childbirth. Dick and I made sure he knew that under no circumstances were drugs of any kind to be involved.

But now, everything had changed, and my doctor didn't know any of it. He didn't know why I was behaving like such a child. He had no idea what I'd just been through, no idea I'd already gone through one entire labor, and then a reverse labor. He didn't know about that hellacious ride I'd had to endure, or that, not an hour earlier, I was almost ready to deliver. I wanted to tell him everything, but I couldn't. I couldn't tell him about anything because I'd lied to him from the beginning. I had promised him that I wasn't one of those hippie freaks who wanted a natural home birth.

They attempted to move me to the delivery table. "Please, I can't—" I whined.

"She needs drugs," Dick clarified. I wanted to yell in the doctor's face that I'd take anything to stop the pain because I was starting labor number three! I would've settled for a sledgehammer to the head.

The doctor had told me early on that he knew all about those "foolish women" delivering their babies willy-nilly out in the woods or wherever. In fact, during my first appointment, he asked me point-blank: "Are you planning to have me deliver your baby here in the hospital?" He didn't wait for an answer. "Or are you planning to deliver it yourself at home?" He had nothing but disdain for "those ignorant young people" up on the ridge willing to risk the lives of mother and child by giving birth in those filthy, primitive, backwoods dwellings. I nodded that, of course, I wanted him to deliver at the hospital. This was one foolish hippie who did not want to lose her backup plan B.

I was certain my doctor wouldn't have understood the notion of giving our newborn a peaceful candlelit entrance into the world, in our own home, even though it's natural and wholesome, and the way women have been doing it for centuries. I believed that if I'd told him that I wanted a natural home birth, and that I was just using him as a backup, he'd have dropped me like a hot potato and refuse to deliver my baby under any circumstances. Then the word would've spread, and I probably wouldn't have been able to secure another obstetrician within 100 miles.

My doctor thought I was only in the beginning stages of labor, and already, I couldn't take it. I wasn't woman enough to pull it off. All those high and mighty things I'd said about natural drug-free childbirth. I could almost hear his thoughts when he discovered I was only three centimeters dilated. His expression said it all. "Look at that big crybaby, tsk, tsk, tsk, how pathetic."

He said to the nurse standing nearby, "Give her a para-cervical." Then he shook his head, removed his rubber gloves with a loud snap, and walked out of the delivery room.

Once he left, a nurse told me the shot would be given directly into my cervix and would numb the area for an hour so I could rest. I couldn't wait! Once she gave me the shot, I fell asleep instantly.

When I woke up from my drug-induced nap, which seemed only seconds long, I felt like a red-hot poker was ripping through my gut. I tried hard to do the breathing, but I was exhausted, and the contractions were coming on top of each other. I was in too much pain; I couldn't do it.

So, I went back to writhing and flailing about.

Dick alerted the nurse, who had come to check on my progress. She immediately called for the doctor, and as soon as he stepped into the room, I heard her whisper to him, "Something's wrong." She was right about that.

Long story short, the doctor examined me, and my cervix was doing it again—it was closing.

Turned out the doctor had to stretch my cervix around the baby's head with his hand. Then he told me to push, and I gave it my all, even though I never got the urge.

One hour later, Meadow arrived. My beautiful baby girl was all I could think about. It was love at first sight! Everything that happened before that moment was just a horrible nightmare that I hardly even remembered. Meadow was the name a friend suggested a couple of weeks before she was born. And as soon as she appeared, we knew that was her name.

Back in the early 1970s, after a delivery, they just swaddled the baby and handed it over to the mother. I remember like it was yesterday. Meadow looked into my eyes the moment the nurse put her in my arms. She continued to stare at me, didn't even cry or make a sound, just looked me straight in the eyes like she knew me and had been waiting to see what I looked like. She recognized me. Funny thing, I recognized her too. I knew she would look like she looked. She had lots of long black hair, beautiful milky-blue eyes, and perfect tiny features. I knew her! And I knew my life would never be the same.

CHAPTER TWENTY-NINE

1972

New Life

It was October 2nd, another beautiful fall day. My tiny, two-day old Meadow slept peacefully in my arms. I couldn't believe the depth of my love for her. I was terrified.

Driving back to our rock house from the hospital seemed unreal. The colors, the sounds, the smells were unworldly. The world outside was brand-new; I barely recognized it. It felt like my first day on earth.

We drove down the mountain and crossed over the Yuba River. I rolled down the window, and the roar of the rushing water thundering over boulders beneath us was exhilarating. Its sweet spray filled my lungs. A handful of nude hippies splashed in the icy green water.

We drove up the other side of the canyon, along the twisty mountain road where the silver poplars shook and sparkled in the afternoon sun.

We got to the top of the hill and turned onto the straightaway. The few remaining red and gold leaves flew off the oaks and maples like flocks of birds.

I was a shuffle of thoughts and feelings. A sense of complete bliss overcame me, then a deep ache, a longing to be the perfect mother to my perfect, precious daughter, followed by a deep fear and sadness—I knew I was far from perfect. The vibrant leaves cascaded down. Then a breeze caught them, and they spun and fluttered everywhere.

I thought back—to the birth ordeal, amazed that I survived it. After I was finally able to push my daughter out of my confused, anguished body, I was in a blurry stupor. The only thing I could think about, the only thing in the world that mattered was her—the little wiggle-worm in my arms. I was overwhelmed, joyful, and horrified at the same time. Amazed that somehow, with stamina I didn't know I had, I managed to live through unimaginable drama and excruciating pain and come out of it with an actual living human child—a priceless treasure. I felt 100 years older.

Two days earlier, we'd left the hospital only hours after Meadow was born, much to my doctor's dismay. He'd recommended I stay for at least another day or two, as was the norm, but we had other plans. We were grown-ups now, no longer children playing at marriage, pretending to be mature adults, acting like we knew what we were doing. Now, life was serious.

The world was different—we were a family.

Immediately after giving birth, I was out of my mind, not surprisingly. Through my entire twenty-five-hour labor, I'd slept only an hour, divided up into little catnaps. Dick was almost as exhausted as I was, so we stayed in a cheap motel in town for a couple of days. It was a lot less expensive than staying in the hospital.

Those two days went by quickly. I was in a dreamy daze most of the time. I ate, slept, and happily nursed Meadow while watching TV—the last I would see for a very long time.

We could've stayed with friends who lived in town. We had a couple of kind invitations and were tempted, seeing as how it would be free, but decided we needed to be alone and on our own schedule without being obligated to hold to anyone else's, or to have to form actual words and direct them at other humans.

Then we stocked up on groceries and supplies and hit the road back home. While Dick drove the truck, I spent most of the time watching the tiny person in my arms. I wanted to squeeze her too tight, wake her, and gaze into her beautiful eyes forever. And her smell! Her sweet baby smell was intoxicating!

The drive to our rock house was peaceful. Dick looked over at us from time to time. He and I were both lost in thought, both consumed with unfathomable love.

When we got close to home, Meadow finally woke up. I looked down at her tiny face—her perfect nose and cloudy newborn eyes, long black hair, and soft pink lips—and became overwhelmed again. Tears filled my eyes. I'd been so blessed and found my purpose in life—but one thing continued to nag at me: would I ever be up to the task?

Seconds after Meadow woke up, I felt a truly alien sensation, like a spigot inside my body had turned on and was filling my breasts. It continued to fill until they ached.

I had nursed Meadow the first couple of days before my milk came in, secure in the knowledge that colostrum was filling her sweet body with all the nutrients and antibodies it needed to grow strong and healthy. But now, suddenly, I had these two rock-hard containers protruding out of my chest. I suppose I shouldn't have been quite so surprised. I'd heard stories about when a mother's milk comes in for the first time, but when it actually happened to me, it wasn't like anything I had imagined.

Some years before, when I was home from Chicago during a break from classes at Goodman, Mom and I were chatting over a late break-fast. Dad was at work, so it was just the two of us. I was talking Mom's ear off.

"We're learning about method acting, and it's so interesting, Mom! You know, like how to authentically embody a character, become who they are deep down."

"Oh." She nodded and leaned her head to one side. Mom was a good listener. She appreciated everything artistic and always made an effort to understand.

"Yeah, and at the Club," I said, referring to The Three Arts Club where I was living at the time, "I got together with some of the other girls who go to Goodman, and we did this intense fear exercise."

"A what? What's that?"

"Mom, it's wild! You have to curl up in a little ball on the floor," I said. "You know, like sort of a fetus ball."

Mom chuckled. She had a wonderful laugh, my mom. When she found something funny, she'd throw her head back, let out a loud cackle, and her whole body would shake.

I continued. "Then you close your eyes and go through this rebirth process. And man, I mean, it takes a while to really get into it, like you have to get in touch with this deep, gut-level human fear. It's so scary."

"My goodness," she said. "Huh. That reminds me. Did I ever tell you? A couple of days after Packy was born, I woke up out of a sound sleep, flat on my back. You know, those hospital beds were pretty uncomfortable back then. But I remember the reason I woke up was because I got very thirsty in my dream, so thirsty I woke up." Mom took a sip of her coffee. "I tried to sit up because I saw a cup of water on the nightstand. So, I reached for it." Then she looked at me wide-eyed. "But I couldn't move." My mouth fell open. "I was literally pinned down, couldn't turn over or sit up or anything. I was terrified."

"Oh, my God, what was wrong?"

"It felt like something huge and heavy was sitting on the middle of my chest! So, I called for the nurse, but nobody came. Not a soul came in to help me, and I panicked."

"What the hell? Were you dreaming? Was it a dream?"

"No, it was real, honey. And I reached up to feel what was on me, what was holding me down, and I was shocked. It was my bosoms. They were hard as rocks. They didn't even feel like they were mine. And the pain—they hurt like the dickens." Mom had gigantic boobs, so I could only imagine. "Well, I grabbed hold of the bars, you know, on either side of the bed, and tried to pull myself up, but I couldn't.

I tried to wiggle myself around so I could lift up even a little, but nothing worked. So, I just started screaming 'HELP' as loud as I could and kept on yelling." She told me that a couple of nurses eventually ran in expecting the worst, only to find poor Mom struggling under her humongous jugs. Mom said both nurses laughed with relief and told her that her breast milk had just come in. That was 1930. Things were very different back then. Not much was talked about.

Suddenly, on the ride back home, with my brand-new Meadow in my arms, she woke up and started rooting around—she was hungry. More than happy to accommodate her, I pulled out one of my leaking, aching boobs and offered it to her. She latched on with fierce intensity—and oh my God, my nipple felt like it was on fire. Milk shot into her tiny mouth. She immediately started choking and pushed me away. Then my milk sprayed everywhere with bullet force like it was a weapon! It blasted Meadow right in the face, and she screamed and gasped for air.

"Dick! She's choking! Stop the truck!" Meadow continued coughing and started throwing up and screaming louder. I panicked. "Dick!" I turned Meadow over and pounded on her back.

"OK, OK!" Dick said and pulled over. I got out, milk from my boob squirting everywhere. Dick got out, ran around the truck, and took Meadow from me. I grabbed a diaper, wadded it up, and covered my breast. Then the other breast started spraying milk. So, I lifted my shirt and spread the diaper over both boobs. I took Meadow back and bounced her over my shoulder, trying to calm her down, but she would have none of it. She started shaking and screaming louder.

"Honey, what should I do?" Tears stung my eyes.

"Here, let me have her." He reached for Meadow.

"No!" I yanked her away. She got even more hysterical, sounded like she couldn't catch her breath. I totally freaked out, but pulled myself together and held her close, and we sobbed.

Fortunately, there was only one house in the area, and it was across the street. An older woman came out of the house wiping her hands on a towel. She walked out to the road.

"Everything alright?" she yelled. I contained my hysteria and nodded. "Yoo-hoo!" she called again. "You need help?" She waved her towel to get our attention.

"Yeah, no," I yelled back, sniffling, bouncing Meadow and trying to keep the soggy diaper over my squirting boobs. "It's fine. We're fine. Sorry… just, just a little n-n-nursing incident!"

The woman smiled and waved, but continued to observe.

"Well," she called. "If you need any hel—"

"We're fine," Dick screamed. "Go back inside!"

Her smile disappeared. I shot Dick a look.

"Sorry," I yelled to the nice lady. "But… but thank you anyway!" She waved again and went back inside. Dick took Meadow and rocked her in his arms, but she would not be soothed. I took her back, got in the truck, and offered her my breast again. She stopped crying and latched on, thank God. I silently cringed from the pain, but closed my eyes tight and made a concerted effort to relax. Meadow was drenched in breast milk. I got another diaper and wiped her sweet face while she nursed. I covered her with another blanket and realized again about how completely ill-prepared I was to be a mother. My heart ached. I regretted not listening to the doctors. I should've stayed in the hospital for at least another day or two, or maybe a week, or a year, or until they kicked us out, whichever came first.

Meadow nursed for quite a while. When her belly was full, she fell asleep, undoubtedly exhausted from the nightmare I'd just put her through. But she was alright; I could breathe again.

After Meadow's birth, Dick seemed to have a whole new attitude—most of the time. He was more loving, talkative, thoughtful, and mellow—perhaps having a child was the answer to our troubled marriage, I thought. Could this little one be the answer to everything?

Although, to be perfectly honest, there was something else nagging at me. Even though the old desire to revive and pursue my acting career *had* all but vanished—mostly thanks to Dick's enthusiastic discouragement—there was still a tiny, pea-sized yearning deep down in my secret place. I couldn't let it go, despite my new and totally all-consuming role. Somewhere in me, that determination to keep it alive, albeit barely, in my "hope chest" for another lifetime, after child-rearing (and marriage), in some pie-in-the-sky future, still remained.

As we drove the last four miles back the treacherous gravel and dirt roads to our house, my mind cramped up with hormone-induced thoughts—some euphoric, some not so much. I tried hard to keep a positive perspective. Tried not to think about the things I feared, the what-ifs. What if Dick reverted to being his constantly grumpy-silent-pissed-off self? And since he still worked in town as a drug counselor, Meadow and I were going to be stranded every day with no car, with our closest neighbors, whom we did not know, a good mile away. And since we had no phone, or electricity or plumbing—what if the austerity of the situation, the extreme isolation was too much? What if the dark, winter months ahead drove me insane? The news had predicted more rain than any year in over a decade. Or, oh my God—what if Dick was a bad father? After all, he tended to be hypercritical and was prone to depression.

What if I had doomed my daughter to a tormented father, a lost soul? Did that make me a horrible mother before I even began?

I dug deep, forced myself to think happy thoughts, to look at the bigger picture: we were about to introduce our baby girl to her new home surrounded by trees and a lovely green meadow (her namesake), with a creek running through it, and the cleanest, freshest air in the world, all on our own twenty acres. Could anything be more perfect? I looked down at Meadow and held tight to those good thoughts.

Meadow was a good sleeper from the beginning. She usually slept through the night, only waking when she was hungry, and I'd nurse her back to sleep. She took three long naps every day, so I had plenty of time to take care of all my chores. I worked hard, did my best to grow into what I thought I wanted to be: a responsible pioneer wife and mother. I adored my time with my daughter, loved bathing her, holding her slippery tiny body in the sink, washing her soft-as-velvet, flawless Italian skin. She enjoyed her baths, too. She'd kick her little feet, splashing water everywhere, then break into a big smile when I poured the warm water over her.

Those mostly dark days passed slowly during the first few months in our rock house. While Meadow napped and the house was quiet, I had plenty to do. I'd split logs to feed the fire in our fireplace—our only source of heat. I washed diapers and hung them to dry inside the house on a wooden drying rack. I cleaned the house, try to keep it as neat and tidy as I could, so Dick would be less angry. I'd watch bubbles rise from the yeast I'd sprinkled over warm honey-sweetened water to make bread. As the yeast would soften, the kitchen would fill with the odd pungent aroma of it coming to life. When I added the whole wheat flour and begin kneading, I'd remember Denise and Mary, my old friends and fellow cooks at Ananda's retreat. Then when Dick got home from work, well after dark, we'd have dinner.

During those cloudy winter days, the house was dark as dusk all day long because we lived in the equivalent of a rock cave. In the heat of the summer, though, the house was wonderfully cool, still fairly dark, but nice and cool. Because we had no electricity, we used kerosene lamps, but they didn't brighten much of anything.

I always looked forward to our weekly or every other Saturday drive into town to do laundry and food shopping. Sometimes we'd even visit friends.

One cold, gloomy November afternoon, I was rocking Meadow by the fireplace while she nursed. The blazing fire kept us toasty while the light in the house began to fade. Finally, she pulled away from my breast. She looked like a little angel in the golden light of the fire with her chocolate-brown eyes, her sweet satisfied smile, and her honey-colored hair. The long black hair she was born with grew in lighter week by week. She stared into my eyes, and a tiny drop of milk dribbled down her chin. I wiped it off, overflowing with love. I leaned in, poked her chubby cheeks, and said "Boo," and she laughed for the first time! Her laughter shattered the loud silence that overwhelmed our house. "Boo," I said again, and she laughed again! So simple. So perfect. I couldn't believe it. I kept playing with her, and she continued to laugh. My heart was all but out of me. When Dick got home that night, I told him about it. "It was amazing," I said. "And she just kept laughing!" He reached out for her.

"What'd you say?" I handed her over to him. "What was so funny?" he asked Meadow in his best baby voice.

"Nothing. That's the thing. I just pinched her cheeks and said 'boo,' and she thought it was the funniest thing!"

Dick made a face and looked down at her. "Who's a funny girl?" He poked her tummy. And she laughed again! It was moments like those that kept me going. It reminded me that it was worth it, all of it. Any hardship I had to endure didn't matter because we were a family.

One dark rainy, predawn morning a couple of months later, in the dead of winter, I watched Dick leave for work out the upstairs window. The sky brightened slightly. The sun had been buried beneath dark threatening clouds, but was now struggling to come up somewhere in the distance. I watched the truck skid around in mud puddles as Dick backed up our badly rutted driveway. Constant icy rain poured down outside. It was going to be another day of isolation for Meadow and me. This was the first sign of the sun I'd seen in weeks. Meadow was still asleep.

Earlier, in the freezing pitch darkness, I bundled up, put my quilted flannel shirt over my nightgown and robe, and felt my way down the spiral staircase. The staircase was built by Ron, a local artisan and friend. He made it fit in the only available space left to access the second floor.

A thick metal pole at the center of the staircase held the wood steps in place, and thin metal bars running vertically were attached to each one and at the top. It went nicely with our house's rustic, homemade feel, but it was not the safest.

In the blackness, I held tight to the metal bars and walked where the steps were widest. When I got down to the kitchen, I lit two kerosene lamps which shed dim light over the kitchen area. I could almost see what I was doing.

Dick brought in chopped wood, piled some in the fireplace, and built a huge fire to start the house warming up. I made him breakfast. He wasn't a morning person; we spoke only necessary words. Then he left for work, and I went back upstairs and watched him through the window as he drove off.

I heard Meadow stir. This was my favorite part of the day. I pulled her warm body from the small wicker crib and held her close. I inhaled her sweet baby scent while she stretched and made precious waking-up squeaks. I kissed her plump cheeks, brought her to our bed, and changed her diaper quickly because the house was still an icebox. We snuggled down under lots and lots of blankets. Then she nursed until we both fell asleep while the house slowly warmed.

CHAPTER THIRTY

1973

Tiny Swimmers

The fact that Dick liked everything neat and clean all the time no matter what wasn't really that big a problem until a child entered the scene. Then I realized how much pressure the incompatibility placed on our already-strained marriage.

In my defense, raising a kid in a typical household with modern amenities and conveniences kept a mommy very busy. But maintaining a spotless home while caring for a little one without plumbing and electricity, was, well, near impossible—according to me.

We had no bathroom or plumbing whatsoever, but Dick built an outhouse and a small sauna building where we did a family sweat and bath once a week or so.

The winters in Northern California were very cold and very wet. So, when I had had it with pumping and hauling water day after rainy day, Dick bought a huge barrel to catch rainwater and built a platform for it just outside the kitchen window. Then he rigged it so the rain would run down our steep roof through gutters into the barrel, then into the kitchen sink.

On yet another dreary, winter day, I went to get a glass of water—I was still nursing, so I was always crazy-thirsty. Just before I took a drink, I noticed something, or *somethings*, moving around in the glass.

I threw it out, of course, and refilled it. And there they were again! I took a closer look to find that the water was thick with what looked like millions of tiny swirling swimmers, gyrating every which way. Well, you can bet I went thirsty until Dick got home.

As soon as Dick walked through the door, I handed him the glass. "Look!" I said. I was still in my old yoga pants, faded ripped gray sweatshirt, and ragged slippers that used to be a pretty green, but were now poop brown. I smelled like baby puke and sweat and hadn't had a second to even run a brush through my hair. I'd just plopped the long, dirty mess on top of my head in a tangled, half-falling down knot with a barrette. (Trying to fit in any amount of self-grooming was out of the question under the circumstances).

After I showed Dick the yuck-infested water, full of God knows what all, I picked up Meadow, who was screaming like a banshee. "This is what we've been drinking," I said to Dick, trying to remain calm so Meadow wouldn't freak out even more. I had already started imagining wild symptoms from drinking the crap. I had a strange feeling in my stomach. Something weird and unsettling was going on in there, and my tongue felt fat. Then I realized I had been giving that bug-infested-water to my baby daughter too. I was horrified!

To make matters worse, it was suppertime, and suppertime, as every mother knows because it's a universal fact, is always that special time of day when infants go bonkers. They start fussing and carrying on because they're either over-tired, hungry, teething, all of the above. Or none of the above. But they always pitch a long, miserable, inconsolable fit. That's just the way it is, and Meadow was doing a good job of demonstrating my point. She was in her little, blue, flowered onesie with ruffles around her middle—a gift from Mom and Dad. She was about to grow out of it. There were tiny holes around the toes. I'd just changed her diaper, hoping it would soothe her somewhat. It did not. But at least she was clean and dry.

She twisted and squirmed in my arms, making it darn near impossible to hold on to her—a greased, wiggly baby pig comes to mind.

It was getting dark in the house. "Jesus!" Dick yelled and lit the kerosene lamp on the kitchen table and pulled out his flashlight. "How the hell am I supposed to see anything?" He shone the light into the glass of nasty bug-water.

"See? What the hell? We're all gonna get sick!" Meadow got fussier until I sat down at the table and nursed her. That shut her up for about five seconds.

"Mosquito larvae," Dick said, looking into the glass. "I think it's just mosquito larvae." He continued to watch the gyrating water.

"Oh my God! How long do you think we've been drinking them?!" I put Meadow down on the wood floor in the living room and went back into the kitchen. Well, that pissed her off big time. She started crying as loud as her little lungs would allow.

"Doesn't matter. It's fine. I'm pretty sure our stomach acid kills bugs and things." I picked Meadow up again. She put her arms around my neck and sobbed.

"You're *pretty* sure?" I said and got in his face. "*Pretty* sure?! We need to get that water tested as soon as possible!" I turned to Meadow. "Sweetheart, what do you want?!" I carried her to the cabinet above the stove and got out a bottle of scotch whisky. I knew that she was cutting a new tooth, a molar—they're the worst. I shook some scotch on my finger and rubbed it on her poor, sore gums to numb them. She stopped crying and shivered.

"No, we don't need to have anything tested." Dick continued peering into the glass. "I'm sure it's mosquito larvae." He lifted the glass in a celebratory gesture, then drank it down.

"Delicious." I watched in horror. "Nothing to worry about," he said. "A little protein in our water. Probably do us good."

CHAPTER THIRTY-ONE

1973

Cabin Fever

It was a cold, rainy, late February day, five months after I'd given birth to Meadow. Dick had left for work in the truck, our only vehicle, before it was light out. I still missed living at Rena's house. Missed it because she had electricity and indoor plumbing and a telephone. I missed Rena, having the odd little chats with her throughout the day. I also missed my easygoing strolls I'd take from her house, over the creek and through the neighborhoods into downtown Nevada City. No more running into old friends or enjoying spontaneous lunches with new ones. I missed being near other humans.

Our isolation was now complete. We still had friends at Ananda, but it was five miles away and took over a half hour to get there due to the never-maintained, washboard gravel road you had to travel on. No one had telephones on the ridge, including us, and occasional "drop ins" from visitors were few and far between. Dick was gone most days because once his drug counselor job with the city ended, he found work with local residents on building projects. Often on weekends, he'd drive into town for music gigs. So, Meadow and I spent most of our time alone together. It was a special time with my precious daughter, but those long, dark, dismal winter months took their toll on both of us.

Meadow was having a terrible time because, at only five months old, she was cutting her first tooth. I could see it pushing its way through her poor swollen gums.

To make matters worse, she had a nasty diaper rash covering her entire little bottom, and it wouldn't go away no matter what I did. An acquaintance had told me that I should be using disposable diapers, and it would promptly clear up. I just couldn't bring myself to because they were such a disaster for the environment. They stood for everything we hated about the modern world: "As long as it's convenient and easy, screw the planet!" But I did try every goo and potion on the market, as well as any home remedies for diaper rash I could get my hands on. Finally, as a last resort, I decided to keep Meadow diaper-less. I hoped some fresh air would help her sore, red bottom heal.

She'd been miserable all week, almost to the point of being inconsolable. She wouldn't let me put her down for a minute during the day without screaming her lungs out and woke up so often at night that I was a sleep-deprived wreck. I hadn't had a moment to even run a brush through my long-tangled hair or get out of my old robe, and throw on some clothes.

I held tight around Meadow's waist while I jostled her on my hip and stirred a small pot of pureed broccoli and potatoes on the wood-burning stove with my free hand. She continued to whine and squirm. I thought a little food in her tummy might soothe her, help her fall asleep. But even with the homeopathic teething remedy and a couple of baby aspirin, she refused to go down for naps. And if she did, they'd last five to fifteen minutes tops. In fact, she'd hardly slept and hadn't eaten much solid food for a couple of days. She was exhausted, in pain, and pissed off.

I continued to bounce her while I dumped the mixture into a small bowl. It was only two in the afternoon, and the house was already dark. I could barely see what I was doing. Finally, I gave up and lit two kerosene lamps.

"My poor baby bird," I crooned. "You just don't feel good." Baby bird was what we called her because when she was hungry, she looked just like a baby bird waiting for its mamma to feed it.

She fussed and rubbed her eyes. "I know, I know, honey. You're so tired. So's Mommy, precious girl. But look what I've got—potatoes and broccoli!" I sat down at the table and put her on my lap. I took a spoonful of vegetables and touched it to my lips to test it for heat. Then I blew on it and offered her a bite. "Here you go, baby girl, open up." She opened her mouth, shook her head, and slapped the spoon right out of my hand. It went sailing across the room, potatoes and broccoli flying everywhere. She turned her head away, leaned back, and wailed. And then she peed on me. I grabbed a diaper (they were everywhere) and sopped up as much urine as I could. She continued to cry. I took a couple of long deep breaths. "Just another puddle on the floor," I said to myself. "Nothing to worry about." I hadn't had a second to clean up any of them. I did some calming yoga breathing for a moment, took Meadow in my arms, and we sat in the living room rocking chair by the fire while she nursed. Thank God. I leaned my weary head back and closed my eyes.

The next thing I knew, I woke up. I had no idea how long I'd slept, but Meadow was out cold still attached to my breast. And the fire was almost out. I wanted nothing more than to sit there and let her sleep in my arms for as long as she could. But the house was beginning to cool, so I had to feed the fire. I also had to go to the bathroom, badly. I'd had to go for over an hour, but the outhouse was twenty yards from the house, and I couldn't very well take my little one out into the freezing rain and manage to do my thing with her in my arms. I had to take care of business while she slept.

I extracted my nipple from her mouth—and watched her little lips suckle sleepily at the air—after which I slowly stood, carefully tiptoed up the spiral staircase, and laid her gently in the crib. I didn't dare fuss with her too much for fear of waking the beast. I slipped rubber pants underneath her precious body, arranged a couple of clean diapers loosely around her, and covered her with blankets. Then I crept to my room, changed out of my urine-soaked robe—it smelled like a gas station bathroom, as did the rest of the house—and threw on my long flannel nighty. Then I hurried quietly back downstairs, put a few logs on the fire, and slipped on my noisy, still-wet rubber raincoat, my hat, and my boots. I stopped, listened, and heard a low squeak. I froze. *Was she awake?* This was my one and only chance, and I had to take it because I really, really, really had to go. Mamaw, my maternal grandmother, told me once that if you hold in your bowel movements for too long, there could be serious health consequences. But she said a lot of crazy shit, and I never knew what was true or what was just the paranoid ramblings of a neurotic old worrywart.

I pushed the front door open, and the frigid wind pierced my face like a thousand razor-sharp needles. I turned away and rushed out into the pouring rain. My feet flew out from under me, and I fell flat on my back. I lay there and fought back tears. I wanted to scream. I was furious with myself—how on earth could I forget about the slippery, ice-soaked ground?

After some ridiculous attempts to stand, slipping and sliding like some circus clown, I got up and made my way, step by cautious step, to the outhouse. I went in, scraped off as much mud as I could, hiked up my mud-covered raincoat and nighty, and sat my bottom down on the frozen toilet seat.

It took my breath away. "Motherfucker!" I whispered. I had to pull myself together. I took care of business fast, but as soon as I left the outhouse, I heard Meadow crying. My heart broke. I wanted to rush in and scoop her up in my arms, but I had to navigate the icy path back to the house carefully. By the time I got inside, she was hysterical. I threw off my gear, kicked off my boots, grabbed a clean diaper, wiped the sludge off my hands, and ran upstairs. I picked her up, and after a few minutes, she calmed down and nursed for about a minute. Then we went back downstairs, and I continued walking my unhappy girl around the house. That was the last of her naps for the day.

Later, when Dick got home, we had a dinner of cheese, crackers, and a simple salad. That's all I managed to throw together. Then I whined and complained about our day, told him how frustrated I was, and gave him an update on Meadow's teething progress and diaper rash. She was actually sitting in her highchair eating mashed bananas with her hands, and making a huge mess. But at least she wasn't crying.

"Dick, I gotta… I don't know, spend some time in town, you know, see some friends, talk to people, do things."

"Why?" He wolfed down huge mouthfuls of salad. "What's wrong now?"

My restless dissatisfaction had become a sore subject.

"I just need a break, is all. Meadow's miserable because of her teeth coming in and—"

"Uh-huh." He glanced at a pile of wet, smelly diapers. "Is that why it stinks in here, and the house is filthy?"

"Yes!" I yelled. Meadow jumped at my little explosion. Her bottom lip started to quiver. "Oh, I'm sorry, baby bird," I said and kissed her little head. She sniffled, then went back to eating her banana. I turned to Dick. "I can't do anything; she won't let me put her down for a second. What the hell am I supposed—"

"Have her teeth broken through yet?"

"No, they're taking their sweet time. And she hurts, poor baby." Dick stuck his finger in Meadow's mouth and felt around.

"Dick, stop!" Meadow fussed, pushed his hand away, and went back to eating her mashed banana—that was her favorite.

"Wow, they're almost in, baby bird."

"Yeah, but she fussed all the way through her morning nap again, completely missed it, finally went down around two o'clock, for about ten minutes. I had to run to the outhouse before she woke up because I'd had to poop for over an hour. Then I slipped and fell in the mud. Man, I fell hard, too, hurt my neck and my butt."

"Hummm." Dick nodded and munched on some crackers.

"And by the time I was finished, she was awake and screaming bloody murder."

Dick looked at Meadow. "No big deal, she's fine. You're OK, right?" She fussed a bit and continued eating.

"Oh my God! Did you not hear the part about how I fell? And, by the way, waking up with me gone was traumatic for her!"

"Oh, she's OK."

"Dick!" I was about to explode into a million pieces of blood and guts. "You don't know what it's like being cooped up here all day, ice-cold rain pouring down outside, while you're off doing whatever, and we're here in this dark, cold house try—"

"Doing whatever! Doing whatever?" He stood up. "How about working! How about making money so we can eat!" Meadow started to cry again. I picked her up. *Damn it. I'm such an idiot!* He was right. Dick was nothing if not a hard worker. He was great at finding jobs and learning and honing new skills. And he was doing his part just the way he planned it.

And I was doing what I always did, following the loudest, most aggressive voice. Once again, I didn't think about what I wanted. I hated myself at that moment, hated the whiny pathetic victim I'd become.

"Shhhh, it's OK, sweetie." Then I turned to Dick. "I'm sorry. I know. Oh God, I'm sorry. You're right. You're working, of course. I'm sorry. I just…" I took a deep breath. "It'd just be really nice to have indoor plumbing for a day or so, that's all. And it stays so dark in here. Maybe we can stay at a motel for a night? Or maybe for a few days since the weather's so—"

"What?" he snapped. "Jesus Christ! We can't afford that! What's wrong with you?" Good question. What was wrong with me? Was

I stupid? Weak? But wait, all I was asking for, what I desperately needed, was a reprieve, a day or two of ease—or what most people would call an average day with average amenities, like electricity and plumbing, and maybe even a damn telephone. Was that too much to ask? I decided it was not!

I was at the end of my rope. "I fucking don't care!" Meadow started screaming at my outburst. I shoved her into Dick's arms. He grabbed her. Then I raised my fists, shook them in his face, and at the sky, and stomped into the living room, raging. "I can't fucking go on! I can't! I'm going fucking crazy! Fuck you! I need a Goddamn fucking break!"

"OK! Jesus Christ, alright already! Settle the fuck down." I glared at Dick, slapped the tears off my face, and took Meadow back, who was screaming and miserable again.

The following day was Saturday, time for our every-other-week trip to town for supplies.

All rain-geared up, Dick and I traipsed through mud puddles packing everything into the truck's cab because, again, it was pouring. But I was more than happy to do whatever. I pictured the day in town, didn't care if it was snowing or raining piss, just wanted to be among people. Ahh, humanity!

With our piles of laundry, our overnight and diaper bags jammed into the cab of the truck, there was barely enough room for the three of us. Thankfully, Meadow slept most of the way into town. Car rides usually knocked her out, even when she was suffering.

Midway into town, the temperature dropped, and the rain turned into snow and ice. Navigating those curvy mountain roads was tricky. The trip took us longer than usual.

By the time we got to town, Meadow was awake, on my lap and fussing when the argument started.

"Let's stay at the Sunrise. They have bathtubs." I never liked showers; they seemed wasteful. All that nice hot water just running down the drain. Baths were my thing. I could relax, soak my tired, sore muscles, and dream.

"No, it's too expensive. We'll go to Night Arms." Dick was an even bigger penny-pincher than I was.

"Honey, I really need to take a nice long bath. Come on."

"You can take a shower—"

"No, I can't! It's not the same. I need a bath."

"Oh, for Christ's sake! What the hell's the difference?"

"A lot, there's a lot of difference to me! How much more does it cost, anyway?" While we argued, Dick drove slowly onto an ice-covered bridge. I saw a car coming straight toward us, and, before I knew what was happening, it crashed into our truck. My head broke through the windshield on impact, but my arms remained tight around Meadow—I hadn't even tried to brace myself from crashing through the glass. Meadow started screaming, and I realized her face might've bumped the dashboard. The man who was driving the car walked over to us.

In a state of shock, I watched him try not to slip and fall on the ice when he opened my door. Bits of glass cascaded out of my head, and blood gushed everywhere.

"Oh my God!" the man said. "Are you alright?" Dick took Meadow from me.

"Jesus Christ, you're bleeding! Shit!" He tried to wipe off some of the blood. "Oh, fuck! I've got to get you to a hospital!" Dick pulled a clean diaper out of the bag and barked orders at the man. "Hold this over my wife's bleeding head. And put some pressure on it."

"Of course, of course! Lady, I'm so sorry." His hands were shaking as he put pressure on my head. "The ice on the bridge… I lost control."

I noticed he was a nice-looking older man. Then the pain started, and I watched Dick run off with Meadow toward the houses on the other side of the bridge.

"Yeah, I know. Is she OK? Is my baby OK?"

"I don't know. I think… she's probably just scared."

I went into a painful daze, couldn't hear all his words, only Meadow's screams in the distance. "You know," I mused. "I wouldn't mind dying as long as I know she's alright." The poor man looked at me in horror.

"Oh, no, you're not going to die!"

I laid my head back and closed my eyes. I didn't care about the pain or the truck or what was going to happen next. All I cared about was Meadow. She was everything to me. She was precious and pure. She was brilliant. She had to be alright.

Dick took care of business quickly, as always. He had an ambulance there in no time, and we went to the emergency room. I got twelve stitches in my head after the painful removal of many glass shards.

The doctor inspected the stitches on my forehead. "You're going to be fine. Doesn't look like a concussion. You might have some scarring by the hairline. But your daughter…" I held my breath and silently prayed—*Please, God, please make Meadow be alright.* "Because she's so young, we just have to wait and see. We should know more within the week. No need to keep either of you in the hospital, but you need to stay someplace nearby, so we can keep a close eye on her."

Dick and I were sick with fear. The first night in the motel (with a bathtub), we all slept together. We cuddled with Meadow until she finally fell asleep. Dick and I cried and held each other tight.

"Honey, I'm so sorry. I don't know what I would've done if anything terrible happened to you or Meadow. I love you so much."

That was the hardest week of our lives, but it brought us close and put things into perspective.

We lay there together, didn't sleep much, just meditated, chanted, and prayed that Meadow would heal and be perfect again.

The next day, Meadow had two black eyes—dark blue bruises had developed overnight. We continued to stay in close contact with the doctor, and slowly, she got better. Her two bottom teeth pushed through, and she started sleeping again. By the end of the week, the doctor gave her a clean bill of health, and we were so thankful and beyond ecstatic as we drove back home.

After that, things were much better for a while. Meadow grew more beautiful every day. She got more teeth that weren't as painful growing in, and she started walking and talking.

Several months later, Dick got a gig teaching yoga at a community college every other week in Sacramento. So, we'd all climb into the truck and drive there together. Meadow would chatter on about our trip most of the way.

"Be go Sac-er-ment-o?" she asked over and over again. We laughed, and she'd continue to babble until she was babbled out and fell asleep. She was becoming her own person with a strong, unique personality and a remarkable sense of humor. She was the sunshine in our lives and kept our marriage together. At least for a while.

Spring came, then summer, and life got easier, better. We had a well dug and hand-pumped our water for a year or so. Eventually, we got a gas-generated water pump. Our lives were slowly getting a little less primitive, thanks to a lot of whining on my part. We got to know our neighbors and were invited to parties. We had playdates with our new friends and their kids, and I became a more relaxed mother. Meadow and I spent lots of time outside in the summer sunshine while Dick worked.

We had decided before Meadow was born that we liked the idea of having two kids, so the first would have a companion to play with. By Meadow's first birthday, things were still good, so we got busy planning for another child. Within a couple of months, it happened.

One night, shortly after I got pregnant again, Meadow seemed crankier than usual. So, I took her temperature, and it turned out she had a 103-degree fever. Now, for an infant, that's not terribly high, so we thought it was probably just her tiny body's reaction to more teeth coming in, and didn't think anything of it. It was close to sunset; the house was getting dark, and Meadow fell asleep while I was nursing her. I took her upstairs and laid her in the crib. As soon as I did, she let out a strange sound, and her body started convulsing. I freaked out.

"Dick!" I yelled. I picked her up and wrapped another blanket around her. "Oh my God! Dick, something's wrong!" I hurried down the stairs. "She's shaking! Shit! Come on, we have to get her to the hospital!"

"What?" Dick was sitting at the table finishing his dinner. "What's wrong?"

"It's—I don't know! I don't know… she's… she was shaking and jerking when I put her down!" Dick jumped up and looked at Meadow. I gently handed her off to him, and she started crying.

I grabbed our coats and the diaper bag. Dick blew out the kerosene lamps, and we left everything the way it was. He tore out of our long driveway. The truck slid around spraying mud and rocks everywhere. He drove like a mad man over the slick, badly rutted road.

When we got to the washboard gravel part of the road, Dick drove faster than he ever had on it, like it was nothing. I held Meadow tight so she wouldn't get scared amidst the violent bouncing and deafening racket. Our poor old truck rattled like it was going to explode into a million pieces.

I thought about the fetus inside my body, afraid I was in danger of miscarrying. But my only concern was Meadow and getting to the hospital as fast as we could. We were terrified we were going to lose our daughter. When we got to the two lane highway all the rattling stopped. Meadow eventually dozed off. I continued to check her breathing, scared to death it would stop.

Forty minutes later, we arrived at the emergency room in Nevada City. I rushed in with Meadow in my arms while Dick parked. The nurse immediately took Meadow's temperature.

Her fever had dropped to just above normal, thank God! We told the doctor about her high fever and the convulsions. He removed the blanket and her clothes and diaper and gave her a thorough examination. Meadow screamed and shivered, and her tiny naked body went stiff. She wasn't happy about any of it. The doctor said she was alright and wrapped her back up. He said we'd done the right thing by exposing her to the cold air. That was what caused her fever to break.

I didn't miscarry, thank goodness, but the whole horrifying incident was a wake-up call, and I took it to heart.

The winter of my second pregnancy wasn't nearly as cold or rainy, but it was very snowy. Meadow and I often played outside in the winter wonderland with our friends and neighbors.

Spring came, then summer, and Meadow, at almost two years old, was talking up a storm. She and I discussed the baby growing in my big belly a lot, and she was so excited about "getting" a little brother or sister.

CHAPTER THIRTY-TWO

1974

Jeremy

I WENT INTO LABOR IN LATE SEPTEMBER, A FEW DAYS BEFORE MEADOW'S second birthday. We got packed up and ready to make the trek to the hospital in Grass Valley. I was taking no chances with this pregnancy. I wanted to be in a hospital in plenty of time, being all too familiar with my body's quirks.

Before driving into town, we dropped Meadow off at Charlotte's house. Charlotte and Michael were good friends who lived on a huge, beautiful compound a mile further back the dirt road.

Michael was a wildly talented artist, and Charlotte was a true Earth Mother. We met them a few months after Meadow's birth. They had four children ranging in age from one year old to nine, and Meadow was happy to join the party for a day or two, depending on how long it took me to pop this second kid out.

When we got to the hospital, the doctor examined me and informed us that I was having false labor, but that it was very common to mistake it for the real thing. Even so, Dick wasn't happy. He scowled at me. I was mad at me, too, and disappointed. I really did think I was in labor. It felt like labor. Maybe, without being consciously aware of it, I was paranoid that my last labor experience was going to repeat itself, so I was overly sensitive to the signs. Meadow's birth was only two years earlier, and the nightmare was still fresh in my mind.

I felt terrible. I'd wasted our whole day. I apologized to Dick. We drove to Charlotte's house, picked up Meadow, and explained the situation to everyone.

Dick had little tolerance for mistakes. He liked everything to be on schedule and handled in a timely manner. He refused to accept that some things, like birth (and life), were unpredictable.

At home, things went on as usual. I waddled around the house, followed by Meadow, my little assistant, who helped me with some chores, like making bread. She loved to knead the soft, spongy dough, loved the way it smelled and tasted. "Momma," she said. "It feels like I'm rubbing somebody's soft tummy!" We laughed because it was true. And when I made fresh yogurt, she liked stirring the warm milk into the culture and would get excited seeing that it had turned into yogurt the next morning.

"Look, Momma!" she'd say and giggle. "It got all jiggly and stiff!" We had to test it out with nuts and honey to make sure it was good. It was our special breakfast after Daddy left for work.

On Meadow's big day, we had a birthday playdate with our neighbors Eva Grace and Michael. They were friends who also lived back the dirt road. Eva Grace brought their five-year-old daughter, Kia, and their one-and-a-half-year-old son, Ropi, over to our house to play. I made lunch for us and baked Meadow's favorite: a white cake with thick, rich chocolate icing. Eva Grace and I chatted while the kids played. It was a warm fall day and a lovely birthday party. We did have to break up a couple of skirmishes, but it was mostly fun and games.

When it got close to suppertime, the children got hungry and cranky, but did not want the day to end. Whining and crying started, and all of a sudden, without saying a word, Eva Grace jumped into action. I watched in awe as she hustled a crying Kia into the car, then proceeded to chase, catch, and wrangle a flailing, hysterical Ropi into the car. She slammed the car door, trapping the screams inside.

Then, breathless, disheveled, and as though she had nothing left, she threw the following pearls of wisdom at me. "Having two kids is about five more than one," she said. "Sorry to run like this, but I've got to get some fucking dinner in these little monsters fast." She sped off, leaving a trail of dust in her wake. I picked up a crying Meadow and while I comforted and fed her, I thought about Eva Grace's words. "Five more than one…" It was bitingly hilarious, yet terrifying and I would soon be experiencing it for myself.

On October 6, a week later, I went into full-blown labor in the late afternoon—there was no doubt about it this time. Dick was reluctant to go through the whole time-consuming ordeal, fearing I was mistaken again. I convinced him that I was sure, so we dropped Meadow off at Charlotte's house, and drove into town.

Once at the hospital, a friendly, middle-aged nurse named Sheila escorted me to my room. She was short, thin, had dark, brown eyes, and a dyed brown pixie haircut with a line of stark white roots showing. There were lots of tight, little curls encroaching on her narrow face. And she had a gruff voice like she'd been a smoker for far too long. She questioned me about how close my contractions were while she wheeled me to my room.

"Is this your first?" she asked.

I told her it was going to be my second child and told her all about Meadow. She said she had three boys who were now grown men. She was chatty. I knew pretty near everything there was to know about her and her family by the time we got to my room. I liked her. I could picture us having Thanksgiving together. Maybe she jabbered on the way she did because she was trying to make me feel safe, like she understood, knew the ropes, and was going to take good care of me. It worked. I felt like I was in good hands. Dick didn't say much, as usual, but then he always was a man of few words.

When we arrived at my small, bland, gray cubical, I was underwhelmed. It smelled to high heaven of disinfectant, but at least it was all mine. I did as I was instructed, got undressed, slipped into my hospital gown, and settled into the stiff, crisp-sheeted bed. Nurse Sheila examined me and confirmed that my labor had indeed begun. Then I slipped into another nasty contraction.

When it subsided, I realized how much more relaxed I was. As much as I disliked hospitals, I knew that if my body started pulling the same shit, at least this time I wouldn't be caught off guard and have to go through two agonizing labors like last time.

After several hours, my contractions were coming closer together and getting more intense by the minute. I was wild-eyed, straggly-haired, sweat-saturated, and fucking exhausted. Dick was about to go out and alert someone, when Nurse Sheila came back into my room to check on my progress. Through heavy panting, I told her that I really thought it was time.

She examined me, then shook her head. "No ma'am," she said with a chuckle. "You've got quite a while to go, darlin'. Why, you're only three centimeters dilated."

"What?" Dick said. "No, that can't be right. Check again."

How could that be? I wondered. I couldn't believe it. I was three centimeters when I got to the hospital eight hours before! Now my contractions were coming nonstop! Nurse Sheila was no longer my friend.

"Nope, don't need to check again. I'm sure." Then she stood there, arms akimbo. "Listen, kids. I've been doing this now for thirty-two years and—"

"Get the doctor," Dick ordered in no uncertain terms. The nurse looked at Dick in shock.

"OK, but—"

"Doctor, now!" he said.

She smirked, shook her head, and left the room. Another mother of a contraction hit me hard, and I returned to the Lamaze breathing. Dick took my hand and sat next to me on the bed. I looked behind him out of the only window. It was pure blackness. I panted and prayed for the pain to stop, unsure if I could survive another second of labor.

While I panted, twinkling lights outside came into focus. Flashes. Were they traffic lights? Warning lights for airplanes? Halloween decorations? Stars? Planets? The contraction finally subsided, and I turned on my side to face Dick.

"Shit." I whispered. I barely had any energy left. The pain was far worse than I had remembered.

Between contractions, Dick and I commiserated about what a half-wit, know-it-all Nurse Sheila was, and how much we hated hospitals, and Western medicine in general, and how, if my body wasn't so damn weird, we could've had both of our babies at home the way God intended.

Next thing I knew, Dick abruptly stood up and reached over my body. "Stop! What is that? What are you doing?"

I turned to find Nurse Sheila had crept back into the room and was about to shoot a large hypodermic needle full of something—I later found out it was Demerol—into my exposed, unsuspecting hip.

"What the hell do you think you're doing?" Dick raged. He was my protector, and I was happy to have him.

"This is just going to relax you, dear." Nurse Sheila went in for a second attempt.

"Get away from me!" I yelled, or as close to a yell as I could muster. I wiggled as far away from her as I could without falling off the bed.

"I want my doctor. Now!" Another contraction hit me, and I went back into my breathing. Nurse Sheila crossed her arms and stormed out of the room.

Not ten minutes later, she appeared with my doctor, and he proceeded to examine me. After a few minutes, he smirked and glanced up at Nurse Sheila, who was looking quite sure of herself.

"Sheila, that's the baby's head you're feeling." Then he turned to me and said, "Let's get this baby out, shall we?" He got up and turned to the nurse. "Get her to the delivery room."

Yes! Finally! I thought. I felt validated and relieved. I knew my own body, and I knew Nurse Sheila was dead wrong. She looked utterly baffled at the doctor's pronouncement. Her expression completely changed, and she instantly wheeled me out, down the hallway, and into the delivery room, all while actively avoiding eye contact with me.

In Nurse Sheila's defense, I wouldn't be at all surprised if my odd cervix threw her off. But I hoped she learned that she needed to listen to people, and that she didn't have all the answers all the time.

By the time they got me into the delivery room, I was a sweaty, stinky mess, fully dilated and in seriously hard labor. Then my cervix pulled the same bullshit it had during Meadow's birth—it started to close! WTF? The doctor seemed confused at first, but quickly figured it out.

He inserted his hand and slid my perineum around the baby's head. Then he looked at me with wide eyes and nodded. "Ok, time to push."

It didn't take long to squeeze the little person out. And there he was in all his glory. Jeremy, our brand-new baby boy! We already had a boy's name picked out, and as soon as we saw his little "package" (which wasn't so little—took after his daddy), we were over the moon with joy. We were now a complete family. We had ourselves a sweet little daughter and an adorable son. Perfect!

I felt that overpowering love for my precious new bundle, and we were ecstatic. My body was exhausted, in pain, and falling apart, but I didn't care. Nothing mattered except our wonderful new son and our darling little girl waiting to meet her new baby brother.

Nurse Sheila cleaned Jeremy up, swaddled him, and handed him over to me. Immediately, he started fussing, and I offered him my breast. He latched on with such force, it damn near took my breath away. Eventually, we fell asleep together in a mist of sweat and tears.

Soon after I awoke, just before dawn, Dick helped me get my things together, and we left the hospital. I was sore and frazzled, not to mention exhausted, but sweet Jeremy slept. On our drive home, Dick and I watched in speechless awe as the sun rose over the hills. I was anxious to share our new arrival with Meadow. I missed her terribly.

The moment we pulled up in front of Charlotte and Michael's house, Meadow came running out. "Momma!"

"Hello, my love!" Jeremy was sleeping in my arms. "Look what I brought you!"

She giggled, and I slowly got out of the car and sat on the porch steps so she could meet her new sibling. "This is Jeremy, your baby brother." I hugged her tight and kissed her plump little cheeks.

She looked at him with wonder. "Hi, Jeremy." She stroked his tiny hand and gently kissed him. My heart exploded with love.

Charlotte and her whole crew surrounded us, and everything was absolutely perfect. Dick and I were exhausted, though, so we didn't stay long.

Before we left, Charlotte took me aside so the kids were out of earshot and gave me some of her homegrown advice. "You know, Reedy, a word to the wise; you're going to have to devote a lot more attention to Meadow than you could ever imagine any child would need or want." She was referring to the natural human inclination to dote on the newborn infant and somewhat neglect the older child. I'd seen it on display with other families. I'd seen the older sibling chastised for trying to steal a tiny bit of attention for themselves. Shameful. I followed Charlotte's advice most of the time, devoting an overabundance of special attention to Meadow—although I have to admit it was hard sometimes—but she always lapped it up.

Jeremy was the sweetest baby imaginable. He was happy and content and absolutely adored his big sister, which suited her just fine.

Life was kind of perfect for a couple of years. We were actually a happy family.

Then slowly Dick's and my relationship began to backslide. We fought a lot. Everything started to fall apart. We tried to hold it together. For a while.

CHAPTER THIRTY-THREE

1977

The Last Straw

It was a fairly normal day—except that it was the second day of my period, and the world, and everything in it, looked bleaker and more hopeless than ever. I was hanging on by a very thin thread. In a moment of clarity, I realized I could use my raging hormones to my advantage—maybe for the first time ever.

Dick and I weren't speaking, so it was business as usual. Well, we *were* speaking, but only enough to get through the day, logistically. It was Saturday, and Dick was home all day instead of working at one of our neighbor's places building or repairing something or other. The pit of my stomach was full of paralyzing fear, but I had decided that day was the day I was going to leave.

I was determined, scared beyond reason, but determined.

It had been one year, almost to the day, since I had gone to a two-weekend self-help seminar in San Francisco—against Dick's wishes. I took a Greyhound bus and stayed with Jocelyn, my oldest and dearest friend. It was a hard sell because the program was expensive, and with the added cost of the bus ride, I had to do some pretty fancy footwork to get him to agree to letting me do it. He took care of the kids all week so I could attend the seminar. Now I was an emotional wreck. I cried daily. It was bad. I was on the verge of something big—running away, a nervous breakdown, a killing spree, something—and Dick knew it.

I explained to him that the workshop was supposed to be amazing. That it might be just what the doctor ordered. Maybe it would get rid of my depression and even help our marriage. I lied.

I would've said whatever I had to. I was that desperate. I figured if it didn't help our marriage, which I doubted seriously it would have, I might at least come away from the seminar happier and with some emotional tools, so I could stay that way. I even suggested that Dick do it with me. We could have one of our friends take care of the kids while we go through the life-altering experience together. That's what people were saying about the program.

But Dick said, "No way!"

I wasn't surprised. I knew why too. First, it had been recommended by my sister Sally. And to say that Dick and my sister didn't get along, didn't see eye to eye about anything, would've been like saying Adolf Hitler and Mother Teresa probably wouldn't have agreed on much. Sally flat-out hated Dick, and the feeling was mutual.

Reason number two was that Dick believed he and our marriage were perfectly fine. That it was me. I was the bad apple, the problem that needed fixing. Reason number three, he already knew everything there was to know about everything, so why should he pay good money for something when he already had all the answers? And number four, it wasn't free. So, no, he would not be joining me at the seminar. And, truth be told, I was extremely relieved.

My experience at the seminar was profound. I became enlightened, saw the world for the first time through new eyes. I spent most of the four-hour Greyhound bus ride home in tears. I was in complete awe of the magnificence of our world. I'd been reborn!

Dick and the kids picked me up at the bus station, and it was brilliant to see them again. I had new hope for our life together. During the year that followed, I tried really hard to use the tools I'd learned in the program to start over, to be a new and better wife and mother. I gave it my all.

I stopped blaming Dick for my unhappiness. I even got a job in town as a waitress in a sweet little natural food restaurant a few days a week. Dick wasn't crazy about the idea, but I was growing, and he was trying to be open to it. Also, I listened to his criticisms and complaints instead of arguing and defending myself or making excuses. Thanks to the program, I stopped resisting and tried to put myself in his shoes. I looked at the issues from his perspective. I used the techniques as best and as often as I could.

Funny thing, though, a week before that 'fairly normal day' I spoke of earlier, when I had decided I was done, I had a revelation and finally spoke my truth. It was during one of our many battles about what a crappy housekeeper I was, and how the place was always a big fat mess when he got home.

"What the hell do you do all day? Goddamn it! Why is it always such a mess in here?!"

I took a deep breath. Didn't want to react defensively like I usually did. So, I looked around, and realized he was right. It was a big cluttered mess.

I thought for a moment. "You know what? You're right. Yeah, I get it. I understand. Frankly, I don't know how you put up with me." I heard the kids playing in the living room, and I shrugged. "I just want the kids to be healthy and happy. I don't really care much about having everything be neat and tidy."

First, he looked surprised, like he didn't know how to respond. Then, he shook his head, pulled his fist back, and... stopped himself. I don't know how to express the sounds he made. It wasn't words. It was more like a deep, guttural growl. And it changed everything.

The following week, the Saturday in question, Dick was out chopping wood, and the kids were happily playing outside. Before I got started doing the thing I'd been avoiding for years. I took a long, slow look around. That's when it hit me. This was going to be the moment of truth. If I walked out that door, it might be the last time I'd see our beautiful rock house. I'd miss it. My eyes filled with tears. I realized I'd miss many things about my life in the woods. My friends, for instance. Would I still have any after I left Dick, or would they all side with him?

After all, I was the deserter. Not only was I leaving my husband, I was leaving the lifestyle, and moving to the forbidden "Big City" where I'd have conveniences like plumbing, electricity, and a telephone, for God's sake. I'd be able to watch the "idiot box" as it was referred to. All the things the community as a whole railed against.

I got shaky and overwhelmed. Tears welled up, and I thought about our neighbors. I remembered them welcoming us to the community, many offering to help us with anything we needed while we built our rock house. I remembered designing and building our own home, how it had been a wild adventure. I remembered working our butts off, finding rocks in ravines, hauling them by hand, and loading them into our 1949 Ford pickup truck.

I stopped myself. I didn't have time to reminisce. If I got sentimental, I'd be in danger of getting sucked back into our disaster of a marriage.

I did love our rock house. Along the whole side wall, spanning the living room and kitchen, were three sets of old, glass-paned French doors. They gave the house a lovely open feel and let in a good amount of light. On the French doors in the kitchen area, the one we used to enter the house, we attached a deer antler for the door handle. We'd run across it in the woods and were thrilled that we'd discovered a way to incorporate it into the house. It was a personal touch, a natural representation of who we were at the time.

I straightened up and wiped my tears. I had to muster up some courage so I could continue with my plan, despite my fears and doubts.

I looked out the French doors at Meadow and Jeremy playing in the sandbox Dick had built for them. Oh my God—the gravity of the situation hit me again, and tears filled my eyes. I had to rescue us from the disaster of our marriage. Dick and I could no longer agree on anything. My mind began racing a million miles a second. Would it be better for the kids if I stayed in the marriage? Some things worked OK. Why was I about to destroy it all? Dick was a loving dad.

But we fought so much of the time. The atmosphere had become toxic. I decided. Again. I couldn't stay. I couldn't put our little ones through the daily hell. My mind fogged over. A dark, tangled rat's nest of conflicted feelings swelled up, choking me, and ripping apart my insides. I didn't know if I'd be able to speak. If I did this thing, if I left Dick, it would change everything.

Forever.

I knew Dick all too well. He would not give up easily, and why should he? He didn't force me into anything. He didn't hold a gun to my head.

I had to be stronger than I'd ever been in my life, stronger than I'd ever imagined I could be. I talked to myself silently so I wouldn't collapse under the fear and guilt and dozens of other emotions. I closed my eyes, pulled up memories of our fights. Bile filled my mouth, and I knew I had to keep going.

I looked down at our marble kitchen floor and thought back to when Dick first had the idea. He collected leftover scraps of marble from building supply stores. Each piece was a different shape, color, and size, and he used them to create a beautiful, mosaic floor. I gazed at our natural wood counter. It was three inches thick and ten feet long. It ran along the entire kitchen wall. We coated it with something that made it shiny and easy to clean.

The kitchen sink was in front of a giant paned window facing the woods. Daily, I'd look out while doing dishes, and see deer grazing, or raccoons, or possums scampering around. Occasionally, coyotes would slink by. Our old Wedgewood stove was next to the sink. We'd found it at an antique store in Nevada City. It was a real beauty. It had both wood and propane ovens and burners. I turned to see the spiral staircase going up to the second floor. It was a work of art made of wood and iron.

After the incident the week before—when Dick almost clobbered me—I decided to clean the place thoroughly—my little secret goodbye gift. But really, I did it so Dick would have little to bitch about before I destroyed him with my exit.

I was sad to be leaving my life out there in the woods, for many reasons, but I knew deep down I had no choice. I hated conflict, which was why I had avoided the inevitable confrontation for so long. All I ever wanted to do was please people, make them happy, whatever it took. And this was not going to make Dick happy.

"Be a broken record," my sister Sally told me. "Listen to him, agree with him, don't say too much, and keep coming back with these words, 'I just have to get away for a few days.' Don't get caught up in anything he says." Her words kept running through my mind. "Don't engage! Whatever you do, don't let yourself get seduced into an argument."

I finished cleaning the kitchen. My eyes burned. They wanted to close, to cry, to escape. I'd hardly slept for days.

Dick brought in some firewood and was stacking it by the fireplace in the living room. The smell of freshly cut oak filled the house. I loved that smell. It brought back happy memories of Christmases at Mom and Dad's. *Good*, I thought. *We're both in the house.* It was time to start.

Ready, set, go! I hoped I might be able to spare the kids the worst of it. I gathered all the courage I could muster.

"Dick." I tried to keep my voice from trembling and used an old acting technique. I forced air through my vocal cords and spoke loud and clear. "I need to get away for a few days."

"What?" he asked from the living room. Logs banged on the floor as he stacked them, and I flinched every time.

"I just need to get away for a little while," I said. "I'll stay with—"
Another log dropped.

"What are you talking about?"

It started. I'd started it. I got chills, and the knots in my stomach twisted tight. Maybe I should wait. It was already too hard, and I was just beginning. Maybe I should wait until—

"Barbara," I forced out. "I can stay with Barbara for a couple days."

Dick stormed into the kitchen. "Why? What's going on?"

How on earth could he be surprised? We hadn't spoken in days. The tension around the house was palpable.

"What's this about? What the hell's Barbara got to do with anything?"

Barbara was a Godsend, but Dick wasn't a fan. I met her the year before while doing the self-help program. I felt an instant kinship with her. Barbara lived on the outskirts of Nevada City with her husband of many years. People had come from all over the country to do the workshop, and I couldn't believe Barbara lived near Nevada City. She and her husband, Ed, had a healthy marriage and grown kids. Barbara and I became good friends.

"No, nothing, I just—" I started to lose it. *Breathe!*

"What are you saying?" His temper started to flare. The kids were playing not far from the house, and I got worried they'd hear us. "What? You wanna go somewhere?"

"Just for a couple of days." He stared at me for what seemed like forever.

"FUCK! What the fuck! How can you…" He paced around the kitchen. It's what he did when he was pissed off, or anxious, or frustrated. Which was often. Then he stormed outside, slamming the door behind him. I ran outside to the kids.

"Goddamn it!" he yelled, stomped around, arms flailing. Jeremy started to cry. Then Meadow joined him. I picked them up and brought them inside.

"It's OK, my loves." They were no strangers to our fights or Dick's outbursts. But this was different, and they knew it.

"Goddamn motherfucker!" Dick hollered at the top of his lungs. "You're fucking gonna ruin everything! Stupid cunt!" The kids grabbed onto me, and their cries turned into screams. Dick continued to yell obscenities outside. I carried the kids up the spiral staircase into their room, and we all sat down on the floor. They hung on to me, crying.

"What's wong with Daddy, Momma?" Jeremy asked through his sobs.

"Oh, sweetheart." I held them close and kissed their sweet little heads. "Daddy's just upset right now, you know. But it's going to be OK."

"Son of a bitch!" Dick yelled. "Goddamn motherfucker!" Our bedrooms had no doors, no way to stifle Dick's tantrum.

"You Goddamn bitch!" I held the kids tight and covered their ears. Our closest neighbors were Eva Grace and Michael. I prayed they weren't home to overhear our nightmare. Finally, the yelling stopped, and we heard the downstairs door open and close.

"Guys," I whispered. "I need to go talk to Daddy."

"Noooo, Momma," they cried and grabbed on to me. So, I carried them down with me.

Dick was sitting at the kitchen table.

"Daddy?" Meadow whimpered while still holding tight around my neck.

Dick looked up. His face was wet with tears. He wiped it with his shirtsleeve and came over to us.

"How can you think about doing this?" His voice was feeble and horse. "Please give us another chance… please." He looked so sincere, so vulnerable. He promised everything would change. I'd seen that look and heard those promises so many times before, and because I was a big fat coward, I had given in every time. Until now.

The kids held on to me. Dick just stared at us. I hadn't seen such desperation in his eyes since he faced serious jail time. He smelled like he usually did, a combination of dirt, BO, and grease. He was out of breath.

"Look, maybe we can move into town like you wanted to." How many times had I pleaded with him, told him over and over that I was going nuts being so isolated? But he always came up with reasons why it was impossible. We didn't have the money, or he'd lie and tell me he'd try to find a place when he was in town, and that would be the end of it. So, now he was ready to bargain. "Come on, how about it? We can go look for a place this week."

"…Yeah… OK… that sounds good. After I get back, I just need a couple of days."

Dick kneeled down in front of us. "No, you don't have to go." He took my hand in both of his. "Please, don't do this…" He started to cry again. "Please? I'm sorry. We can make this right, come on. Please…"

I was so close to giving in, but then I looked down at my children—their bodies shook from so much crying. Their little faces were contorted in terror and pain, and their precious, chocolate-brown eyes were red and swollen—I decided, right then, I could no longer do this to them. It was killing me. Somebody had to stop the nightmare.

Then time slowed. I saw Dick's tears falling, and his lips moving, but I couldn't make sense of his words. I saw something I'd overlooked all those other times. This was his game. This was how he got what he wanted. All those lies he'd told his parents and gotten away with. Art and Toni had provided the perfect training ground for Dick to develop his art of seduction, of manipulation, of getting his way. I came back into real time and knew I was going to do what needed to be done. Now Dick just looked pathetic. I remembered my sister's words. "Don't engage in any arguments. Keep repeating that you just need to get away for a few days."

"OK, good, I just need a few days to clear my head."

I knew the kids were hungry. It was later than they usually ate. I got up and sat them down at the table. They hung onto me and whined. I kneeled beside them. "It's OK, sweethearts, I'm just going to get you guys some supper. Everything's OK now." They sniffled and looked up at Dick, who watched us with sad, red, puppy-dog eyes.

I warmed up some spinach and potatoes with cheese I'd made earlier and dished it up in two little bowls. I put their dinners on the table and sat between them. They calmed down enough to eat. Dick sat down on the last step of the staircase. He put his hands together and leaned on them.

It looked like he was thinking—probably scheming—trying to come up with another plan, wondering why his strategy had failed this time around. The kids watched their dad and me while they ate.

"We could sell the house… That's what we'll do. Maybe buy a house in Nevada City."

"Uh-huh… yeah, maybe. We can talk about it when I get back." For a second, I got scared. Was I engaging too much? I had to give him something. Create the illusion that if he played his cards right, maybe I would stay. A few years before, during one of our bloody battles, he told me that if I ever left him, I'd never see the kids again. That threat bought him a few years.

"Maybe we'll sell the house and move back to Louisville." That was totally out of left field. Live near my folks? He couldn't stand my family, and the feeling was mutual. I was surprised and a little taken aback. He must've seen my hesitation, a glimmer of 'maybe' on my face. He stood up. "What do you think?" He wiped his face. "Probably sell the place pretty quick, you know? Be out of here in a couple of months."

Dick was going for broke. This one-sided conversation continued while the kids finished their dinner. I just listened, nodded my head, and said we'd look into it when I got back. I told him I wanted to take the kids with me, that Barbara had a large home, plenty of room. But he said no, he'd keep them. I didn't object because I didn't want to arouse suspicion. I had to make sure to be sweet, nonconfrontational, and even try to seem easygoing because I needed him to drive me to Barbara's house in town.

We only had the truck, one vehicle, and if things went south, I'd have to hike half a mile to Grace's house and ask for a ride. That would've opened up an enormous can of worms. My secret would be out! I didn't know if I was strong enough to withstand Dick's reactions and the impending scrutiny from friends.

I told Dick I was going to throw a few things together and went up to our room. I sat on the bed and said another prayer, then grabbed the small bag I had already packed.

Meadow and Jeremy were confused and upset on the ride into town. My heart broke at the thought of leaving them, but I had work to do in town, and I knew Dick would take good care of them.

"Where we going, Momma?" Meadow asked. I wiped the kids' faces and helped them blow their noses.

"Yeah, whew we going, Momma?" Jeremy asked. "I got a tummy ache. It weally huwts too."

I knew why his tummy hurt. Mine hurt too.

"Oh, honey, let Mommy rub it. Here, put your head in my lap." I turned to Meadow. "Honey, do you mind if your brother lays across your lap?" Meadow shook her head, and Jeremy wiggled around until he got comfortable. I rubbed his tiny tummy. "Just relax, my love," I said in a soothing voice. "Now, breathe nice and deep. Let me feel your tummy go up when you breathe in, and down when you breathe out. Like this." I inhaled and expanded my stomach until it almost pushed Jeremy's head off my lap. The kids both laughed, and Jeremy followed my example.

When Dick dropped me off at Barbara's house, the kids got sad again. Barbara opened the door and waved to us from her porch.

"Hey, guys, we'll see Momma in a couple of days when we pick her up."

"Yeah, don't be sad, my loves. I'm just going to visit my friend Barbara. See?" I turned around, and we all waved to her. "I'll see you guys real soon, OK? Here, give me big kisses! I love you so much!"

"Yeah, good," Dick said. "See you soon, Momma." And they settled on the seat next to their dad. Then I went around to the driver's side window and gave Dick a piece of paper with Barbara's phone number on it.

"Thanks, for the lift, Dick... I'll talk to you soon."

He looked so sad, eyes red and puffy. "OK. We'll miss you." And he slowly drove off.

"Bye, Momma! I love you!" Meadow and Jeremy yelled.

As the truck disappeared down the block, I started to crumble. I wanted to run after them, take it all back, turn it around, go home, and forget the whole thing.

"Reedy?" Barbara came out, put her arm around me, and we both waved. Then, the second they were out of sight, I lost it.

She ushered me inside. "Come on. Let's get you inside. It's going to be alright, dear." I was falling apart, splintering into a pile of broken pieces. But because of Barbara's kindness, I was finally able to calm down. I told her the whole ugly story, bit by bloody bit. We talked far into the night. In fact, over the next few days, we never stopped talking. Barbara counseled me, helped me figure things out and strategize, so I'd be prepared when I saw Dick again. We tried to think of all the possible scenarios and to come up with the best way to end it, if that's what I needed to do, with the least amount of pain, especially for the kids.

CHAPTER THIRTY-FOUR

1978

Saint Barbara

SOME PEOPLE COME INTO YOUR LIFE, IT WOULD SEEM, DIRECTLY FROM heaven. Barbara was one of them.

After the soul-crushing goodbyes between Dick, the kids, and me, I was a complete basket case. I was convinced I'd done the most fiendishly selfish, horrendous thing a wife and mother could ever do to her loved ones. The sobbing faces of my poor children haunted me day and night; sleep was next to impossible.

"I can only imagine how horrible this must be for you," Barbara said while she stroked my hair. Barbara was from Boston and still had enough of a New England accent to suggest that she never left. We were sitting on her couch with a big box of tissues between us.

The afternoon sun poured through her large bay window, and the house plants on the shelf just below it glistened in the sunlight. Barbara loved African violets. She had dozens of them, in all different colors. The sunshine filtering through her jungle, created abstract designs in shadowy grays on the wall behind us. Leafy images slowly shifted upward as the sun moved lower in the sky. The soothing colors in her living room were varying shades of whites and pale yellows with a soft green trim.

I was still wavering. I put my head on Barbara's shoulder.

"Dear, do you mind if I ask you something?"

"Of course, anything."

"Good. Now, I know you're busy beating yourself up, and far be it from me to interrupt your self-torture." I laughed; she hit the nail on the head. "But you told me how hard you've been working on your marriage, close to a year now, isn't it?"

"Yeah," I said between sniffles. "But, see, that's the problem, Barbara. I thought things were getting better. I thought it was working."

"I know, I know," she said. "So, tell me what changed?"

"Oh, God, I don't know. It just stopped working. Everything. Nothing I do makes any difference. I try so hard, but Dick seems to get more grumpy and unhappy every day, and I just… I just feel like a failure all the time."

"Uh-huh, I see, dear." Barbara called everyone 'dear.' "You do realize, don't you, that Dick's the only one that can make himself happy?"

"I know that. Yeah. It's like walking on eggshells all the time. But I can't help taking it personally. And how can I not lose my will to live around somebody who's always miserable and pissed off? It's like living in a storm cloud. I cry all the time." I continued to whine and spill my guts, and Barbara just listened.

We talked until the wee small hours of the morning.

Eventually, Ed, Barbara's husband, stumbled into the living room to check on us. He was in his bathrobe, and his gray hair, what little he had left, stuck straight up. He stifled a yawn, blinked several times and tried to smooth down the thinning mop on his head. Barbara introduced us.

I sat up and wiped my tears away. "Hi, I'm so sorry to steal you wife from you."

"No, no," he said and waved his hands like it was no big deal. "I'm happy to share her for a few days. It's giving me some well-needed time to myself."

I laughed. Barbara smiled and shook her head. "Go on back to bed, dear. I'll be in directly."

Ed waved. "'K. Night, ladies."

"Barbara, you should go to bed. I'm sorry."

"Oh, stop. This is important. Ed's fine. He'll appreciate me a little more since he's not my main focus for a few days. Now go on."

"Well, see, I know the kids need their dad, and Dick needs them. That's why this is so hard."

"I think you're forgetting one thing, dear. Yes, the kids need both of you, but they'll still have you both. Look at it this way; let's say you go back and continue living with Dick. The kids will spend their entire childhood around the constant fighting and tension. Do you really think that would be healthy for them? Would it create happy, healthy human beings? Ones that would choose healthy, happy spouses? Trust me, what you choose to do now will affect their entire lives." Her words hit me like a wrecking ball.

The next day, I walked over to see my friend David. David was a young photographer and jazz enthusiast I'd met a year earlier when I came to hear Dick play at Tony's Jazz Club in Nevada City. He would often appear wherever Dick and his band were playing. David and I became friends, and eventually, I confided in him how unhappy I was in my marriage.

A few months before I had decided to leave Dick, David and I were sitting together at Tony's enjoying some drinks and Dick's trio. The place was packed with excited, boozed-up jazz lovers, and it was smoky, too. I could hardly see David across the table. The band had just finished playing a number, and the whole crowd erupted in applause, hoots, and whistles.

Once the cheers subsided, David leaned in and whispered, "How are you guys doing?"

I teared up. Dick and I had just had another nasty fight earlier.

I tried to keep my voice from shaking. "We're OK." The smoke got to me, and I started to cough. David suggested we step outside to get some fresh air. The area behind the bar was dark and deserted. I looked around, then up at David, and tried to smile, but couldn't stop the tears. He hugged me. Then he looked at me with such compassion that I was overcome and leaned in to kiss him. (I should mention here that someone once told me that the best way to get through a breakup is to have an affair. Don't remember who it was, but whoever it was, I blame them for my moment of indiscretion).

"No," David said and pulled away. He looked around, moved in close, and lowered his voice. "Uh-uh, I'm sorry, I won't be your excuse. Look, if you're going to end your marriage, end it on your own. I won't be part of it."

"I'm sorry, I'm sorry. You're right. That was so stupid of me. I'm sorry."

"Don't worry about it." Then we went back inside the club. David and I remained friends, and he kept my secret.

The morning after Barbara and I talked, I walked over to his apartment. I had finally gotten a good night's sleep and felt somewhat renewed.

When I got to David's, I knocked on the door, and after a few minutes, he opened it.

"Well, hello," he said. "What's going on?" He looked around for a car or Dick or whatever.

"I ran away from home."

"Oh, wow, you finally did it."

"Yep."

"Damn, come in," We went inside and sat on the couch. "How ya doing?"

"Been better, thanks. But I'm good."

"Was it hard?"

"Hardest thing I've ever done. And it's not over yet." I took a good breath and made a gesture of strength with my fists. "I just wanted to ask you if you know of any apartments for rent?" He thought for a minute, and I couldn't believe what happened next.

"Well, I'm leaving town in a couple of days, got a big shoot in Utah. Be gone about a month. You want to rent this place while I'm gone?"

"Oh, my God, yes! Would that be OK? I'll take good care of it." It was a sign. A definite sign, I was sure of it. David agreed to let me sublease his place and gave me the rundown on everything I needed to know.

David's apartment was small, but nice and clean. I'd saved up enough money from waiting tables so I could afford it. It was exactly what I needed—exactly! A quiet place, already furnished with everything I needed, so I could figure out my next move. It was only a one-bedroom, but was plenty big enough for the kids and me. It was perfect.

After I left David's apartment, I walked two blocks to The American Victorian Museum. There was an elegant restaurant in the basement, and I'd always thought it would be a great place to work. So, I asked one of the servers if I could speak to the manager. He pointed to a hallway and said it was the last door on the left and that the manager's name was Pete. I thanked him and immediately marched myself through the hall and knocked on his door.

"Come in," a voice from inside said. I opened the door and peered in. I was relieved at what I saw. Pete was at his desk surrounded by a clutter of paperwork and didn't even look up. He was writing down something with the intensity of a college student studying for finals. Next to him was a half-eaten sandwich on a tiny paper plate and a bottle of beer. The office smelled like a boozy picnic. It was small with nothing on the walls, a cushy chair in front of a desk, and a file cabinet in the corner. Eventually, he looked up. He was nice-looking, probably close to forty, and had a straggly mop of wavy, brown unkempt hair. When he stood up, a few papers flew off his desk.

He looked surprised to see me. "Hi, um, hello, can I help you?" He went about picking up the papers while still more flew off his desk. I stifled a giggle. He was wearing a sweatshirt and khakis.

"Hi Pete? I'm sorry to bother you." I offered him my hand. He rushed over and shook it.

"Oh, no, it's no bother," he said. "I was just—please sit." I sat in the cozy, old chair that looked like it had come from a Goodwill store, or his grandma's basement.

"Well… I'm looking for work. I just moved into town." He got up, walked around his desk, and bumped into the corner of it.

"Ow, damn it. I keep doing that, got a big purple bruise on my hip." He smiled and rubbed the spot. Then he sat down in front of me. "Chair is new, too big for this stupid office. My mom gave it to me, said I needed something comfortable in here."

"Oh, yeah? It is comfy." I bounced on it a couple of times.

Pete smiled. "Where'd you move from?"

"The ridge."

He looked shocked. "You're kidding. I have friends up there. How come you left? I thought everybody loved living up there."

"Yeah… no… yeah, we do. It's… well… I left my husband and—" I couldn't believe I blurted that out. Pete let out a nervous laugh. Then his smile disappeared, and we stared at each other for a long moment. "Shit," I said. "I'm sorry. I shouldn't have… I haven't been sleeping well. I'm so sorry."

He stood up, went back around his desk, bumped his other hip, and sat in his chair.

"Shit! No, it's OK. I understand." He rubbed his other hip. "Believe me. I know it's tough. Been there. Um, what kind of work are you looking for?"

"I have experience waiting on tables," I told him. "I worked at Toffinelli's in Grass Valley."

"Oh, yeah? I love that place," he said. He told me that his waitstaff was full, but then gave me a look of compassion and grabbed a large ledger-type book. He started rooting through it, seriously searching for something. "What do you think?" he said and looked up at me. "Can you start day after tomorrow?"

"Really?" I said. "Oh, Pete, thank you!" I got up and hugged him. That was an awkward moment. But he was funny and sweet, and I told him I'd be available whenever he could fit me in. I thanked him several times over until he playfully shooed me out of his office.

As I walked back through Nevada City on my way to Barbara's house, a feeling of euphoria swept over me. Birds were singing, bees were buzzing, and all was right with the world. A sweet, overpowering aroma of blossoms hung heavy in the air, and I was overcome with appreciation and gratitude. I felt sure for the first time that I was doing the right thing. That whatever happened, the kids and I, and even Dick, we were all going to be OK.

The next morning while Barbara and I were sitting at her kitchen table having tea and talking, the phone rang. My stomach knotted up, and I looked at Barbara with dread.

She answered the phone. "Hello?" Her eyes got wide, and she mouthed the words, "It's Dick." Then she said, "Yes, she's right here," and she handed over the phone.

Now, after all the role-playing, practicing dozens of scenarios with Barbara, I thought I was prepared for anything Dick could throw at me. I also thought that Dick had to have at least an inkling of what was coming next, considering the state of our marriage. But I guess I was a better actress than I'd realized.

"Hello?" I said.

"Hi, babe," Dick said. "We're here, so I'll swing by and pick you up, and we can go have lunch somewhere before we head home."

OMG! He was acting like nothing had gone down! Like everything was fine and dandy! In fact, he sounded happier than he'd been in months. *Shit, shit, shit!* Barbara was watching me. I made a face at her, like I couldn't believe what I was hearing. She got up, arms out, eyes wide.

"What?" she mouthed.

I forced myself to focus. "Um, no, Dick," I said. "I'm not coming home."

"What do you mean you're not coming home?"

"I'm staying in town. I got—I'm going to sublease an—"

"What? What the fuck are you talking about? Goddamn it! Just hold on! I'm coming up there!" He hung up, and Barbara and I stared at each other. I started to panic.

"Way to go!" she cheered and clapped her hands. Then she noticed the expression on my face, and her applause stopped. "Uh-oh."

"He's—they're coming up here. Now!"

"He's got the kids with him?"

"Yeah! Oh God, it's starting all over again!" I started to pace around her living room.

"Oh, dear, but it's OK. You can do this."

"No, I can't… I can't!" I ran to the guest bedroom and started throwing my clothes in my bag.

"I've got to get out of here!" I wanted to run away, disappear, but I couldn't do that to my little ones.

Barbara followed me into the bedroom and took me by the shoulders. "Reedy, dear! Breathe." She took several big breaths with me, in and out, in and out. "Come on now. We worked on this, remember?"

"Yeah, but—but—" I stammered. "He acted like, like…"

"It's OK. Look at me, dear. Look at me." I looked at her sweet, calm face. It was a little pink, undoubtedly from dealing with my soap opera. As usual, she had no makeup on. Her eyes were soft and brown, and her short, straight, gray hair framed her face nicely. She always smelled clean, like soap mixed with the tiniest hint of gardenia.

She mostly wore pastel button-down shirts and long pants and she always looked like what she was: a kind retired social worker ready to do whatever it took to help out.

Dick and the kids came to Barbara's house, and I went to meet them in her front yard. Meadow and Jeremy ran to me, and I hugged them fiercely for a long time. Then we all went for the worst walk ever.

I tried to remain calm and focused on the task at hand. I tried desperately not to think about the earth-shattering tsunami I was about to cause. Every inch of me pulsated with fear and self-loathing. I tried to remember Barbara's wise words, "Do it for the kids."

"I just need some time, Dick. A friend of Barbara's is leaving for a month for work, and they've agreed to let me live in their apartment while they're away."

Dick got hysterical and went in for the kill. He fell on his knees and started sobbing. "No, no, you can't!" he pleaded. Right in front of the kids, in the middle of Barbara's lovely neighborhood. My babies' reactions broke my heart. They held on to me and cried the whole time. How could he do this? How could he use the kids to force me to stay in our nightmare of a marriage? This was low, even for him.

My brain started spinning. Maybe I was a horrible person. I was the one who started this whole disaster! Me. All because I'd been a child from the beginning. A cowardly, pigheaded, ignorant baby who was too chickenshit to do what I knew I should do, what everybody else told me was the right thing to do—get out! All because I was afraid of being alone, afraid to grow up, afraid that nobody else would ever love me. I knew what was ahead. Dick would hate me, and put me through a living hell.

"Dick, you know how unhappy I've been."

"I know, but—"

"No." Tears streamed down my face. "Barbara's friend will be back in a month. Maybe by then... I need more time."

"Please, we can do this together!" I held the kids tight.

"No, I'm sorry, but I can't, not yet." He looked me in the eye, and maybe that "Not yet" gave him hope because something shifted, and I saw a kernel of understanding, or maybe it was surrender or acceptance. Then, there was silence for about a minute. Finally, Dick wiped his face and stood up.

"OK guys," he said. He nodded his head and took a deep breath. "OK, give your mom a hug. We'll go have some lunch."

"Momma?" Jeremy looked up at me with red, tear-filled eyes and sniffled. "Whew awe you gonna go?" I kneeled down and wiped tears from his precious little face. I hugged them both.

"My sweethearts, don't cry anymore," I said. "Everything's OK now. But I've already had my lunch, so you go have something good with Daddy. Maybe you can go to Toffinelli's. Remember? They have that delicious chicken salad you love so much."

"Oh, yeah," Meadow said through her tears. "Remember, Jer?"

"Yeah, but Momma's got things to do here in town." I could hardly bear to look at their sweet faces, knowing I wouldn't see them every day. "Hey, you know what? I bet after lunch Daddy'll take you guys to get some ice cream!"

They looked at Dick, then back at me.

"Can we get some ice cream, Daddy?" Meadow.

"Yeah, sure we can," he said. I wiped their wet faces and hugged them again.

"I'm gonna get stwabewwy!" Jeremy said.

"Yeah! Yum, strawberry's my favorite!" I said.

"Me too," Jeremy said.

"I'm getting vanilla, my favorite!" Meadow said.

"Yum, I love vanilla too! And I'll see you two in just a few days, OK?" I held them for a long time while secretly my heart broke into a million pieces. Then we all walked back to Barbara's house and they got in the truck and drove off. The kids continued to wave until they were out of sight.

I ached from head to toe. Thought my head would explode. I sat down in the grass and wilted.

I wanted to keep the kids with me so bad, but Dick wouldn't have allowed it. He told me he'd bring them in on the weekend. I had to trust him. I knew how much he loved our babies; I hadn't a doubt in the world that he'd take good care of them.

Soon after, Dick and I worked out a temporary schedule to share the kids. And eventually, we got on with our lives. We'd talk briefly when he dropped them off, and it was always cordial, even friendly, both of us on our best behavior. Then Dick told me he wanted to do the same self-help seminar I had done.

"I think it'll be good for me." I was shocked at first. Until he added, "It'll be good for *us*." Then I knew it was a ploy to get me to come back, to get what he wanted. That's how he operated. I encouraged him to do the seminar, but made no promises.

Dick stayed with Jocelyn in San Francisco, the same friend I'd stayed with when I did the seminar. Jocelyn was great. We'd known her and her ex-husband, George, almost as long as we'd known each other. They'd gotten a divorce a couple of years before Dick and I separated.

After Dick did the program, he told me he was glad he did it and that he got some good things out of it. But clearly, he didn't think it was the life-transforming experience I did. I talked to Jocelyn about when Dick stayed with her while he did the program.

"He had a very different experience than you did," she said with a chuckle. "I remember you couldn't say enough good things about it. Him, not so much."

"Oh, you've got to tell me everything." Even though Jocelyn was more my friend than Dick's, I could tell she didn't want to betray his confidence. So, she said he didn't talk much about it. But I continued to try to drag information out of her.

"Well, I remember one thing he said." She took a minute and smiled. "After the first day, he complained about the trainer. He hated her, said she was a real bitch and just downright mean."

"He had a woman trainer?" She nodded. "Oh, my God!"

"Yeah."

"Oh, no! She must've been a real ball-buster!"

"I guess, And afterwards, he bitched some more for about an hour. So, I told him, 'That's so funny because Reedy said she loved every minute of it.' Then he just shook his head and said, 'Jesus, that dingbat would have fun doing anything.'" Jocelyn and I looked at each other for a second, then burst out laughing.

PART THREE

CHAPTER THIRTY-FIVE

1978

Recovering

"She had to leave. I know that now." Dick's bloodshot eyes shifted from Dr. Jean to me and back again. It was our third session with our marriage counselor, and our fifty minutes were almost up. We'd been coming twice a week, and according to her, we were "making progress."

"Good. That's very good, Dick. Coming to a realization like that is a big step."

I figured Dr. Jean to be in her fifties. She was a bit on the plump side with graying brown hair cut in a loosely curled bob, and she always seemed to be calm and collected.

Her office was in Grass Valley, not far from a small house I'd rented with Anne, a soon-to-be-divorced, fellow escapee from the ridge. Dr. Jean's office was a cheerful space all done up in greens and aqua. Sheer curtains hung over the windows with lots of sunlight filtering through.

Dick looked down at his hands like he was ashamed, or maybe that was just my optimistic interpretation of his body language. "I do understand. The house is isolated, too far away from everything. And what with raising the kids with no plumbing, or electricity, or even a telephone, it makes her depressed." Hearing him say that he understood was a shock. I thought perhaps this new expression of insight was genuine.

He had cleaned himself up, actually looked attractive, handsome even, and was much more presentable than usual. He was wearing newish-looking jeans, a nice plaid shirt, and had tidied up his beard. And he smelled like soap instead of grease. "I think we should sell the place." He looked at me with puppy-dog eyes—those big baby browns I fell for back on the streets of Chicago.

I tried not to show surprise, or any emotion.

"Maybe move into town. Or back to Louisville near your folks."

And there it was—his big concession. Considering the fact that he couldn't stand my family, the mere suggestion of us moving near them was a dead giveaway. I tuned him out, refused to listen to any more of his bullshit. Instead, I glanced around Dr. Jean's office.

She had hundreds of important-looking psychology and philosophy books on the tall shelves next to her desk. My eyes slid over the titles. *Modern Man in Search of a Soul* by Carl Jung, *Beyond Good and Evil* by Friedrich Nietzsche, *The Seven Storey Mountain* by Thomas Merton.

Thomas Merton was a Catholic monk who embraced Zen Buddhism. He was one of Dick's gurus. There were also a few colorful abstract paintings hanging on the walls and, behind her, a framed Child & Family Counselor certificate.

In the early, carefree, stoner days of our relationship, Dick and I regularly went to a small Zen Buddhist temple close to our apartment in Chicago, where we practiced Zen meditation. That was my first foray into Eastern philosophy. We went with Jocelyn, a school teacher and my best friend and her husband, George (Dick's drummer buddy). We all loved our sensei, Reverend Matsuoka. Often, he would invite us to join him for a sukiyaki bash at his temple, which doubled as his home. The four of us would bring food and drink to the party, where we would indulge in great, drunken, mind-bending dinners. Upon our arrival, Sensei would always smile, seeing the bottles of sake, then heat it up, and keep it flowing freely throughout the evening.

I tuned back into the session just as Dr. Jean turned and looked at me. A smile took over her sweet, round face. A smile of recognition, I hoped. I had an inkling that her expression meant that she had seen something different about me, a glimmer of a backbone, maybe a smidge of growth. I took it as confirmation, and sat up straighter. Dr. Jean gave me a slight nod, looked back at Dick, put her hands together, and declared, "Really good work today."

I left the session somewhat less burdened, felt more confident that everything would work out, and that I was maybe on the right track.

Dick and I continued to work with Dr. Jean for a few more months. She was great. She managed to keep alive an inner strength within me, while at the same time effectively counseling us as a couple. Nothing could repair the damage we'd done during our marriage, but at least we were able to communicate better. I knew Dick's goal was to resume our marriage. I also knew that I'd sooner cut my own throat than get back together.

Dick and I finally agreed on a plan. We would sell the rock house, move back to Louisville, and give our marriage another chance. (At least that's what I led him to believe.) If he had known that my real plan was to get a divorce, he might've made good on his promise to disappear with the kids, and I'd never see them again. I couldn't let that happen.

Lying was not in my nature, so I had to rely on my acting skills. The stakes were too high to fail.

Mom and Dad couldn't have been happier about us moving back to Louisville, but were dead set against the reconciliation part. Mom tried her best to convince me to leave the marriage. Little did she know she and I were on the same page. I hated keeping my plan secret from her, but we were planning to stay with Mom and Dad until we found a place of our own, and I couldn't trust Mom to keep her big trap shut if she and Dick got into one of their head-banging brawls. I could easily imagine Mom yelling something like, "See? That's why Reedy's divorcing you!" Or some such other spoiler alert. She could expose my entire plan in a wild fit of rage.

As soon as we got settled at Mom and Dad's house, Dick and I got busy. He went to all the jazz clubs in the downtown area to look for music gigs, and the first thing I did was call my old pal director Doug to see if I could get a job with Shakespeare in the Park again.

I called him from Mom's place. "Hello?" said a deep, male voice.

"Doug?" I knew it was him. I hadn't seen or talked to him in a good eight years, but I would've recognized that gruff voice anywhere. Doug was a serious smoker. I can't remember ever seeing him without a cigarette in his hand. "You'll never guess who this is," I said with a laugh.

There was a pause. "Reedy?"

"Yes! Oh my God, how'd you know?"

"I remember that laugh," he chuckled. "Well, as I live and breathe. Where the hell have you been hiding? Last I heard, you and Dick were out in the woods in California with some cult or other."

I filled Doug in on the abridged version of my life with Dick. I told him about the California Shakespeare Festival, our years at Ananda, about buying our own twenty acres, and building the rock house. I told him all about Meadow and Jeremy and about how Dick and I just got back together after a long separation.

"Oh, interesting. You know, back when you and Dick were part of the company, I thought you kids were an odd mix of personalities. He was so intense and serious, and you were always lighthearted."

"Yeah, I know. Opposites, right? Anyway, we just moved back to Louisville and… well, might you have any work for an old friend?"

He chuckled again. "Well, I've started casting for the summer productions, mmm… would you be interested in auditioning for the role of Kate in *Taming of the Shrew*?"

"Oh, my God, Doug! Yes! I am Kate! I tell you, this year, I have grown into a powerful woman. That role is exactly what I've been preparing for!"

Doug laughed.

The next day, I went to Doug's place, the same tiny, filthy, cat-stinky, gag-worthy, wonderful apartment I'd gone to so many years before, and auditioned for him. It was a warm and friendly reunion, and Doug loved the strength I brought to the role. He hired me on the spot to play Kate.

I was back. I was making it happen, felt like some kind of super-hero. I felt unstoppable.

A couple of weeks later, on a cool, sunny Tuesday in late May, while Dick, the kids, and I were still living at my folks' house, I was getting ready to meet Doug and my fellow actors at the Shakespeare stage. It was the first day of rehearsals, and the kids were finishing up breakfast.

I came into the dining room to hug them goodbye.

"Whew ya goin', Momma?" Jeremy asked. "Can we come?"

"Yeah, can we come?" Meadow chimed in. I'd gotten to spend most of the week with the kids, so I felt pretty OK about leaving for the next several days of rehearsals. I was a little concerned about Mom and Dick getting along, even though they'd promised to be on their best behavior for everyone's sake. I still had my doubts.

"No, sweetie pies, sorry, Mommy's got to go to work. But I'll be back in just a few hours." They whined a bit; then Dick came in the dining room.

"Hey, who's ready to play ball?"

"Me!" Jeremy squealed and ran out the back door. "Bye, Momma."

"When're you coming back, Momma?" Meadow asked.

"I'll be back by dinnertime, honey." I kissed her sweet face.

"Hey, Meads, let Momma get going," Dick said and offered her his hand. "Come on, ball time!"

Meadow and Dick hugged me. Then she grabbed her dad's hand, and they ran off.

"Have a good time, Momma," Dick yelled. I waved. I was touched by how supportive Dick was being. He was really trying.

I went into the kitchen, where Mom was at the sink doing dishes. I hugged her from behind and whispered in her ear, "Thanks, Mom. Are you gonna to be OK? I mean with Dick?"

"Of course, honey. Now, go on. Have fun."

I drove to Central Park and found a parking place directly in front of our old apartment on Saint James Court. It was still my favorite street. I strolled down the grassy median in the middle of the long block, and remembered walking to the Shakespeare stage for rehearsals and performances eight years earlier.

There it was in all its glory: the stage, in the middle of the park, surrounded by large, old oak trees. It hadn't changed much—except that it seemed larger, fancier, more vivid. I was a little early—and very anxious, full of butterflies. I could hardly believe the way things had fallen into place. I was back doing what I loved, what I had wanted to do all along. I'd made it happen.

A sweet breeze rustled through the trees, and everything smelled like springtime. I saw people lounging on the audience seats in front of the stage, and I knew they were the actors. Snippets of conversations drifted my way: "…got so nervous I was sick to my…"

"…it was the first play I ever did…"

"…this crazy-assed director, you cannot imagine…"

Doug sat in a large, throne-like chair in the middle of the stage, looking over some paperwork.

I was giddy with anticipation. When I reached the stage, I sat in the front row and looked back at the other actors. Some were in groups chatting, some were reading, and a few were curled up on the benches napping. Since I was early, I pretended to be studying my script while I checked out the crowd for possible Petruchios. Several men looked the part. Then I noticed an actor a few aisles back talking to an actress. He looked perfect for the role. He was handsome, with a fresh, masculine baby-face, shoulder-length, wavy, blond hair, wearing cut-offs, and a T-shirt with the word "BLOOMINGTON" printed on it.

Suddenly, a burst of laughter broke out. Everyone turned, and Doug looked up to see what was going on. The laughter came from the actress sitting next to the actor I hoped was going to play Petruchio. When all eyes were on him, he stood and took a grand bow. Everyone laughed.

"Hello, Ron… well, if you're quite finished entertaining your lady friend, can I get on with it?" Ron gave an "it's all yours" gesture and sat down. Doug stood and asked us to introduce ourselves and tell everyone which role we were going to play. There were to be two other Shakespeare plays in production for the summer repertoire: *Julius Caesar*, who Doug was going to play—this I couldn't wait to see—and *The Two Gentlemen of Verona*.

When it was Ron's turn, he stood up, introduced himself, and said he was playing the role of Petruchio. YES! I was thrilled. I later found out that his name was spelled Rohn, but pronounced Ron.

Why the extra letter? My hilarious friend Joann—who later became my improvisational partner—called him Rohon. But he was not only perfect for the role of Petruchio; he was also a fine actor. He was only a couple of inches taller than I was, but he had a strong voice, broad shoulders, and a dynamic personality. There was something irresistible about him.

Rohn and I hit it off right away. He was passionate about acting, and his work ethic was infectious. He was inspiring. When we'd work on our scenes, I'd forget everything else and immerse myself in my character. Rohn exuded confidence and brought a real command, and unique sort of arrogance and swagger to the role.

A few days into rehearsal, everyone in the cast sat on stage out of breath, and mopping the sweat off our faces—Louisville's extreme summer heat and humidity had kicked in, and we were all dripping with perspiration. The actors had gathered in groups discussing their scenes and where to have dinner.

"Great rehearsal," Rohn said. "Thanks, Doug."

"Yes, sir." Then, in a voice loud enough to be heard over the ensuing chatter, Doug said, "Good work today, everyone. Great job. Now you kids go have some dinner and study your lines. I mean it. Get 'em down. I expect you all be off-book by the end of the week. See you in the morning." Then he left.

Rohn leaned in close to me. "Hey, you want to grab some dinner and go back to my place? I want to keep working. You up for it?"

"Oh, I'd love to, Rohn, but I told the kids I'd be home in time to have supper with them."

"No problem. I really like where the scene's going."

"Me too! Maybe we could work after rehearsal tomorrow."

"Yeah, great, that'll work."

The next day after rehearsal, Rohn and I grabbed a couple of sandwiches from a nearby Italian deli and walked along the other side of Central Park to his place. I'd heard that Rohn was in college, but that's all I knew about him. During our walk, he told me he was in the third year of his master's at Bloomington. He said the program was rigorous and that he was carrying a full load while doing several leading roles on their main stage at the same time. And that he loved it.

So, while Rohn was deep in training, expanding his mind, working his butt off for his craft, I was out in the woods canning fruit, giving birth, changing poopy diapers, and fighting off severe depression.

I was scared that I was seriously out of my league. What if I'd forgotten everything I knew about how to break down a script or how to act in general? What if Rohn acted rings around me, and I was exposed as the fraud and amateur I was?

We walked past all the quaint little houses across from the park— chatting about our different acting experiences. Then he led me up a sidewalk to an old apartment building, and down some stairs. His dark studio apartment had no air conditioning and was hotter than hell. It was also pretty messy, and all the furniture was old and well-used. There was a double bed in one corner, a couch, a small TV, an overstuffed chair, and a tiny kitchenette with a table and one chair. We unwrapped our provolone and salami sandwiches—the smells of olive oil, fresh herbs, and Italian bread overwhelmed me. My mouth started watering, and I realized I was starving.

Rohn went to his mini-fridge. "Want a beer? Or a coke?"

"No, got any wine?"

"Ah, yes, leftover chardonnay."

"Perfect." He filled a mug with wine and handed it to me. "Thanks! Here's to Kate and Petruchio!" I tapped my cup against his bottle of beer, and we drank. I'd always been a lightweight when it came to booze, unless I had plenty of food in my belly to soak it up. Otherwise, it would go straight to my head, and I'd get moronically giggly. But I decided I needed a drink to shut my monkey brain off and calm the fuck down. Also, I thought it might lower my inhibitions and allow me to access all the things I used to know about acting. Maybe even spark some creative genius I'd always hoped might be hidden deep within my psyche.

We took bites of our sandwiches while running lines and working on our scenes. We weren't off-book yet, so we often had to stop and check the lines. It was choppy. We talked in-depth about our characters, what drove them, and their motivations.

"Well," I said. "I think it's obvious that Petruchio goes where the money is. That's *his* motivation."

"Agreed, he is an opportunist, but he's also in search of adventure."

"Uh-huh, yeah, he's open to it wherever it takes him. And… I think he's kind of looking for something deeper too, you know?"

"I do. So, who is Kate? Why do you think she's so mean and feisty?"

I thought for a second. "She is mean. Hmmm, yeah." My mouth was half-full of sandwich. "It's like she has no tolerance for human frailty." I took another big guzzle of wine.

Rohn raised his finger to emphasize a point. "Kate does not 'suffer fools!'"

"Ah, yes. But why is she so angry?" The sun was getting low in the sky. Stark white rays shone through Rohn's basement window, creating light patterns on the floor and wall.

"I submit that Kate is really smart," he said. "Smarter than the rest of her family, or any of her would-be suitors."

"Interesting. Maybe that's why she's older and still unmarried. Maybe she simply can't abide the dumbasses that want to court her."

Rohn chuckled. "And then along comes Petruchio. They spar intellectually and physically and—"

"Kate has met her match!" I said. "And... I'll bet she's still a virgin. I bet she refused to entertain any of the morons around town, much less bed them."

Rohn looked at me wide-eyed and nodded. "Let's run the scene now, without scripts." He grabbed mine and tossed both on the floor. "Don't worry about getting the lines right."

"Really? But..." is all I got out. I didn't have a chance to be nervous. Rohn just took my hand, and we did it. We ran Kate and Petruchio's meeting scene. Yeah, some of the lines were far from perfect, and we fumbled a lot, but the timing, the intention and intensity, and the depth was brilliant. Everything clicked. "Oh, my God!"

We sat on his bed in silence and marveled at the perfection we had just created. We ran through the same scene again and again, each time feeling more freedom to improvise and delve deeper, allowing the connection, and our characters to grow, finding more nuance with each run-through. Finally, exhausted and out of breath, we collapsed on Rohn's bed. I'd never experienced such an authentic connection with a character or a scene partner. I got goosebumps and felt more alive than I'd felt in years. Rohn moved in close to me and gazed deep into my eyes. Moments passed. We couldn't stop smiling. Then, slowly, we leaned in and kissed.

I can't explain it. I was no longer Reedy—wife and mother of two. I was Kate—the brilliant, virginal bitch who had been waiting too long for her equally brilliant knight in shining armor to come and rescue her. And Petruchio, oh, Petruchio was the only one man enough to take her on, to tame her, to satisfy her. We had transformed into our characters. Our kiss grew deeper and deeper. Then we surrendered to the moment.

A morning bird sang as I left Rohn's apartment in the wee small hours of the morning. I walked through Central Park, swimming in the memory of the entire evening. It played over and over in my mind. What a night! I thought. I'd reawakened the actress in me and felt desirable again, worthy of love. Deep inside, it seemed as though something had begun to heal. I needed that night. It nourished me, fed my soul. I deserved it, I told myself.

When I got to the car, I remembered I should've been back at Mom and Dad's hours ago. I had to focus, concoct a story in case Dick woke up. But of course, we were rehearsing—which was true. Sort of. Mostly.

The house was dark when I arrived, but I managed to slip inside quietly and quickly, wash up, and climb into bed without waking Dick. Then I fell into a sweet dream with a big smile on my face.

CHAPTER THIRTY-SIX

1979

Actors Stage

Finally, I was doing what I loved: working in a good theater company—with the bonus of playing one of the most dynamic and coveted female roles in history. My creative juices were exploding, after having been suppressed and slowly dying from neglect due to years of hardship, isolation, and childbearing. Now, I was learning and growing in my craft. I felt more alive than I had in almost a decade.

Spending time with Rohn was exhilarating. He stimulated and inspired the best in me creatively. And as a woman, he treated me like I was beautiful and desirable after years of feeling invisible. Our affair continued through the run of the play. We both knew the relationship was temporary. As soon as the play closed, he would be gone.

Soon, I found a ferocious custody divorce lawyer and set up a meeting.

Later, when rehearsals for *Taming of the Shrew* were over, and it was playing in rotation every third night, I tried to contact Mark, the artistic director of Actors Stage, a very prestigious local theatre. When Mark took over the theater several years earlier, he moved it into a large building in a more prominent area and developed two other theater spaces within the new facility. Now Actors Stage was renowned and celebrated.

I was first hired to do a play at Actors Stage back in 1968, ten years earlier, shortly after I played Juliet in *Romeo and Juliet* at Shakespeare in the Park. Back then, Actors Stage was a small, obscure theater. So now, almost a decade later, I was determined to meet Mark and schedule an audition with him. I called his office about ten times, but hard as I tried, his secretary, Anita, would block my way.

Her rote response was, "Mark is not in currently. May I tell him who called and what this is regarding?" She was the gargoyle at the gate.

"I'd like to speak with Mark, please. When will he be in?" Anita would always respond that she didn't know. So, I'd thank her and tell her that I'd try again later. Next day, I'd finally had enough of her dismissive attitude. I dialed the number.

"Actors Stage, Anita speaking, how may I help you?"

"Hello, Anita, this is Reedy calling again. I'd like to set up an audition with Mark."

"I see, and from where are you calling?"

"Louisville."

"And how long are you planning to be in town?"

"Oh, no, I live here."

She stifled a snark. "I see. Well, I'm sorry… Rita is it?"

"Reedy, R-e-e-d-y," I said clearly.

"I'm sorry, Rita, but Mark only hires his actors out of New York City."

"Huh," I said. "Well, then, I'd like to make an appointment to come to his office and meet with him personally."

"No, that won't be necessary. Perhaps you didn't understand me. Mark only hires actors out of New York City. Bye bye now." And she hung up. I couldn't believe it. I was furious, and made up my mind right then and there that, one way or another, I was going to get a goddamn audition with Mark come hell or high water.

The next day, I was totally free, no rehearsals, no performance, nothing. So that morning, I made a big pancake breakfast for Mom, Dick, the kids, and myself, and we enjoyed a lovely meal together.

"Hey, guys, I need you to help me choose an outfit because I'm going to the big theater downtown to see if I can get some more acting work."

Meadow jumped up. "OK!" she said. "You should wear that pretty blue dress, Momma."

"Yow gonna get the job, Mommy!" Jeremy said.

"Yeah, 'cause you're the best actress!"

Dick, the kids, and Mom and Dad had come to see me in *Taming of the Shrew* on opening night. The consensus was unanimous. They declared me to be the best actress in the world!

The kids and I chatted while I got all dolled up. I took Meadow's suggestion and wore the blue dress. Then we hugged, and I drove to Actors Stage. When I got there, despite the hundreds of butterflies in my stomach, I marched myself right up to the administrative office.

Anita looked just like she'd sounded: in her mid-fifties, very thin, too thin really, with sharp bony features, and a tight, graying ponytail. She was wearing a dark maroon and deep forest green willowy blouse with a collar halfway up her neck. I decided that Anita was an artsy-fartsy, upscale version of The Wicked Witch of the West. Her tiny old head behind her big old desk was a sight for sore eyes. Her hands looked like those of an eighty-year-old.

"Hello," I said. "You must be Anita. I'm here to meet with Mark. Is he in?"

"I'm afraid he is not. Do you have an appointment? What's the name?" She looked in her big appointment book.

"No, I do not have an appointment," I said without apology. She looked at me, puzzled, and cocked her head to one side.

"The name is Reedy. I spoke to you yesterday." I ignored my heart pounding in my ears. The old me would've seen the roadblock—Anita—and immediately retreated.

"Ah yes, the local actress. Well, as I told you—"

"Oh, I remember what you told me. What time will Mark be in?"

"Well, I don't know. He may not be coming into the office at all today."

"I'll wait." I sat in one of the three handcrafted wooden chairs along the wall next to her matching desk. She looked somewhat stunned and watched me with a stern, disapproving expression. I paid no attention. I took out my script of *Taming of the Shrew* and proceeded to pretend to study while I waited.

A couple of uncomfortable hours dragged by with Anita occasionally shooting me the stink-eye, when the office door opened, and a nice-looking, casually dressed man in his early fifties walked in. He grabbed some mail off Anita's desk and proceeded to sort through it while he walked past me and continued down the hallway.

I jumped up. "Excuse me, Mark?" He had just opened a door when he turned.

"Yes?"

"Oh, good. Hi, Mark, I've been trying to reach you." I walked over to him and stuck out my hand. He shook it and ushered me into his office. Just before I went in, I glanced back at Anita, whose mouth was hanging open, and gave her a 'thanks for nothin', bitch' smile.

Mark's office was spacious and beautiful. The walls were a pale, burnt umber, and the afternoon sun blasting through three tall windows bathed the room in a sunset pink. It was like walking into a flower. The windows overlooked the Ohio River and healthy-looking Ficus trees stood in two corners of the room. Dozens of huge, artfully framed posters of some of the plays they'd produced over the years hung on the walls: *Tartuffe*, *A Christmas Carol*, and *The Miracle Worker*, just to name a few.

Mark sat down behind his handsome, modern desk and looked at me. "Have a seat." He gestured toward a luxurious, brown, leather couch. I sank into it. It was the softest, most comfortable thing I'd ever sat on. Then he looked me up and down. "Hi." He watched me with a pleasant, albeit hungry, look in his eye. I reminded myself to breathe. "Who are you?"

I laughed. "Um, I'm Reedy, an actress, and I just moved back to Louisville after living in Northern California for several years."

"Huh. Where in Northern California?"

"Oh, you may not have heard of it, Nevada City?"

"Ah…yes. No, I have heard of it." He folded his arms and sat up like his interest had been piqued. "Lots of hippies live up there."

I raised my hand. "Guilty as charged. We lived at Ananda, a yoga commune out in the boonies for a couple of years." Mark's eyes were laser-focused on me, like I was the most fascinating thing in the world.

He nodded. "Hmm. Tell me more."

"Well, before moving to Ananda, we worked with the California Shakespeare Festival in Los Gatos, California. Then, we bought some land and built a rock house. And, oh yeah, we didn't have any electricity, plumbing, or telephone while we had a couple of kids and… now we're back."

"Wow, that's wild. What was that like?"

"Well, let's see. How can I put this? It *was* wild and fun, sometimes, and harder than I thought it would be. That's why we're back." He nodded. "Mark, I've got to say, what you've done with the theater is remarkable. You know, I worked at Actors Stage ten years ago when it was in the old building by the railroad tracks."

"Ah, that was before my time. I think I was at the Guthrie then."

"Oh, well… I would love to audition for you." I pulled my picture and résumé out of my bag, climbed off the couch, and placed them on his desk. He looked at my eight-by-ten, then at me, then back at my picture.

"You know, you're so much prettier than your picture." I felt blood rush to my face. I'd heard that Mark was married with three little kids, and according to the gossip around town, he was not above using his charisma and artistic status to procure the affections of many aspiring young actresses.

"Well, thank you."

"Seriously." Then he jotted something down on a piece of paper and handed it to me.

"Give Stephen a call, tell him I sent you. He's an excellent photographer. Really knows what he's doing."

"Oh, wonderful. Thank you."

Our meeting went beautifully. We talked for quite a while—I admit that I used the knowledge of his philandering ways to lure him in. I told him that my marriage was in trouble, and, being new in town, I alluded to the fact that I was emotionally vulnerable and could use a strong masculine shoulder to cry on.

I was getting pretty good at using my feminine wiles and my wits to get what *I* wanted, for a change, instead of perpetually feeling compelled to blurt out something no matter what light it shed on me. I was finally looking out for myself. (Trained by the best.) Within a half hour, I had an audition appointment and had laid some groundwork for a special relationship with Mark.

I called my sister Sally the instant I got back to Mom's after my meeting with Mark. "I did it," I said. "I'm auditioning for Actors Stage next week!"

"Fantastic," she said.

"But, oh my God, I'm so scared!"

"No, come on now. You're gonna do great. You've got your audition pieces ready, right?"

"Yeah, but—"

"Yeah, but nothing. Just work on your pieces, and remember, *pretend*. That's the key. When you go in for the audition, just breathe, stand up tall, and *pretend* you have confidence."

So, I did. I had the whole week to work on my monologues and pretend. I studied and practiced every day, sometimes in front of Mom and the kids, who were always my best and most appreciative audience.

The day of my audition, I was a wreck. I had hardly slept the night before, and eating was out of the question. One piece of dry whole wheat toast was all I could force down. Fortunately, Mom understood my nervous state and got busy with Meadow and Jeremy. She created a still life scene on the dining room table: a vase filled with colorful flowers and a bowl of fresh fruit on top of an apple-green scarf. She set up paints, colored pencils, and crayons. Meadow and Jeremy were thrilled. They stayed happily preoccupied with their art project while I prepared for my audition.

I left early to avoid any possibility of being late and keeping Mark waiting. I got there and took my time walking into the theater. With every step, the butterflies that started in my stomach doubled, then tripled, then filled my entire body. I repeated my mantra: "I'm confident. I'm confident. I am confident."

When I got to the theater door, I took many deep breaths.

"Hello, Reedy," came a voice from behind me. I jumped and spun around.

"Shit!" I giggled. "Oh, hi, Mark, sorry, you scared me!"

"Did I? I'm sorry. You weren't expecting me?" I laughed, and he looked at his watch. "You're nice and early. That bodes well." He opened the theater door, and we went in.

It was beautiful. The seats were designed perfectly so the audience could see the entire thrust stage from wherever they were seated, no matter how large the person's head was sitting in front of you.

While we strolled down the aisle, Mark and I chatted about insignificant things, like traffic and the weather. Then he settled in a middle, third-row seat, and I went up on stage.

"What'ya got for me?" I inhaled deeply before I spoke.

"This is one of Kate's monologues from *Taming of the Shrew*." By then, I knew her character inside and out and loved her. I thought about Rohn playing Petruchio. I paced around the stage, got emotionally connected to Kate's arrogance, and then burst forth with the first couple of lines.

The more my wrong, the more his spite appears.
What? Did he marry me to famish me?

I continued ranting and raving, using the entire stage with ferocity. I got inside Kate's mind, held nothing back. I became Kate! When I finished the monologue, Mark smiled, gave me an 'attagirl' look, nodded his head, and took some notes. I felt invincible. But I was sweating profusely and my face felt hot.

"Well done."

I could feel the adrenaline coursing through my veins. I was on fire.

"This next piece was from *Beyond Therapy* by Christopher Durang." I took a moment to change character, then went into it. *Beyond Therapy* was a contemporary, quirky play, and the monologue was odd and goofy. Mark laughed several times, always a good sign. Once I finished the piece, relief from the anxiety I'd been carrying around for days, hit me like a sweet, powerful wave in the chest—I could breathe again.

"Excellent," he said. I couldn't stop smiling. "That was some fine work, Reedy." He asked me to join him for a late lunch. A picture popped into my head: Mark and I seated in a dark corner of a fancy restaurant, him gazing into my eyes and stroking my hand on top of a white tablecloth.

"Oh, I'm sorry, Mark, I would love to. But Mom's staying with the kids, and she has to dash off to her prayer meeting when I get home, so I'm afraid I'll have to take a rain check."

"Of course, we'll do it another time." I knew I had to make a quick getaway because I'd gotten the distinct impression that his invitation was a loosely veiled attempt to lure me into his seduction plan—if

I'd been unaware of his reputation, I might not have seen it coming. Before I left, though, I thanked him again and gushed over how much I'd love to work with him. Then I got the hell out of Dodge.

The ride back to Mom's house was euphoric. I'd done my very best work, and I could tell Mark was genuinely impressed. When I got home, I told Mom, Meadow, and Jeremy all the details, and we celebrated me for a job well done. Then Mom made one of her famous pot roasts with celery, carrots, onions, potatoes, and a ton of parsley. I made up for the couple of meals I'd missed, having been too nervous to eat, and ate like a monster.

The following afternoon, the phone rang, and Mom picked up. "Hello?" she said. The kids and I were just heading outside to play.

"Reedy," Mom whispered. "I think it's him!"

My stomach tensed up, and I took the phone. "Hello?"

"Reedy Gibbs?" said a manly voice.

"This is she."

"This is Mark calling from—"

"Oh, hi, Mark," it was Mark!

"Hello." He was as calm and collected as I wanted to be, but wasn't. "Reedy, I'm calling to check your availability. I would like to hire you for the upcoming season." I about fell off my chair!

He hired me for the first three plays of the new season, as well as one of only three cast members of his high school touring company for the remainder of the season. That meant I'd been invited to work with a very prestigious theater for the entire season, and be getting paid for it! Me, a *local* actress! I was almost speechless. But I gathered my wits about me and tried not to get tongue-tied or make a fool of myself—I did not succeed.

"Oh, Mark, that's amazing!" I said a little too loud. I pictured him pulling the phone away from his ear. I lowered my voice. "Thank you, I mean, yes, I'd love to!" After we hung up, I laughed hysterically—I was floating on air.

"What happened, Momma?" Jeremy asked.

"Mommy got a job, sweetie pie! I'm a working actor! Yippee!" I scooped him up and his sister, and we did a happy dance with Mom all around the house.

CHAPTER THIRTY-SEVEN

1979

Creating Stuff

It was beautiful out, the perfect fall day. Since I had time off from rehearsals, I suggested to the kids that I make some sandwiches and go to the park and have lunch.

"We'll have a nickpic!" Jeremy squealed. After Meadow and I stopped laughing, she jokingly corrected her brother. Then we made our lunches; chicken and cucumber sandwiches with plenty of mayo on whole wheat bread, of course, and drove to the huge park near Mom and Dad's house. The kids instantly bounded out of the car, and the party began. We romped and ate at the same time while their dad went to check out another house for rent.

It had gotten pretty tense at Mom and Dad's, not surprisingly, with all of us living there. They loved having the kids and me around, but Mom wasn't good at pretending she liked somebody when she absolutely did not.

Her patience was wearing thin when Dick was around—there were a few near explosions. It was absolutely time for us to find our own place.

The problem with finding the right area for us to live in was that Dick hated the suburbs—and my family, for that matter. And since I refused to live isolated out in the country again, we decided to split the difference. We agreed to look for a house just outside the city.

When the kids and I got back to Mom's, Dick was there, and he was excited. "I found it," he told me. "This place is the one. It's perfect. An old, two-story farmhouse. And it's only twenty minutes away."

"Hmmm, only twenty minutes, huh?" I tried to look happy.

"Maybe less. I think we should take it before someone else snatches it up."

"No, I want to see it first."

"You never have time. It just came on the market today, and you're rehearsing the rest of the week. The agent said he has two more showings today and three tomorrow."

"Dick—"

"Reedy, I've been looking for weeks, and I'm telling you this one's perfect." He stared at me with that annoyed look, like he was about to lose it. "So, tell me…when you can squeeze it in, huh?"

Fuck!

"You swear it's just twenty minutes away? How far from the theater?"

"Oh, for Christ's sake! I'm telling you, it's close enough, alright?" That 'thing' inside myself that hated confrontations, especially with bullies, started to waver. Against my better judgment, I gave him the go-ahead to sign the lease.

The next day, I had rehearsal all day, so Dick went to the real estate office and signed a six-month lease. The following week, I had a day off, so we packed up our stuff, said our farewells and "thank yous" to Mom and Dad, and drove to our new home. There was no traffic, and I kept a close eye on the clock.

As soon as we pulled into the long driveway, I glared at Dick. "Dick, it took us fifty minutes to get here," I said. "Without traffic." The house was an old, two-story, spooky-looking place set way back off the road. The kids got excited and rushed out of the car to romp in the huge front yard.

"Yeah, because we drove from your folks' house."

"What? Mom and Dad live in Louisville—"

"Just come in. You gotta see the inside. The kitchen's huge." He got out of the car and called to Meadow and Jeremy. "Hey, guys, let's go see your new room!"

I sat in the car, seething. I felt so stupid. I couldn't believe I'd fallen for his trickery again. Yeah, maybe it was twenty minutes from Louisville, if you drove 100 miles an hour. That did it. I was done. I let go of any lingering guilt or doubt I'd had about getting out of the marriage. His manipulation game wasn't ever going to work on me again.

We moved into the old farmhouse, and I used the long drive to the theater to calm myself and prepare for rehearsal.

My first day of employment at Actors Stage was the table-read. I took my time driving to the theater and arrived very early. I talked to myself on the drive. "I can do this. It's going to be great. *I'm* going to be great; I project confidence."

Whose Life Is It Anyway was a new play about a quadriplegic man written by Brian Clark. I played Nurse Jean Saddler and had several scenes with James, who was amazing as the bedridden patient. I had seen him on several TV shows. Even though I had lots of lines and blocking to memorize, the character I played wasn't demanding. It was a supporting role.

Any breaks I had from rehearsals, I managed to squeeze in appointments with Phil. Phil was the attorney I had painstakingly searched for and hired to handle my divorce. He was in his late forties, obese, balding, with a tidy comb-over, and the best custody lawyer Louisville had to offer, according to my research. Phil spoke slowly, and the timbre of his voice was deep and almost hypnotic. He made you feel safe and that he could be trusted. He was incredibly brilliant and tough as nails. He would get to the core of the issue and present everything in such a way that his solution would look like the obvious and best choice. I'd found him by asking everybody I knew for referrals for lawyers specializing in difficult custody cases. Phil was the best of the best, and Dick knew nothing about any of it.

The second play of the season was *The Runner Stumbles* by Milan Stitt, a very serious drama. I played Erna Prindle, the impoverished daughter of an old woman who dies suddenly. To become my character, I had to do some serious soul-searching, find that vulnerable place inside me so that I could connect and respond with real, emotional authenticity to my mother's unexpected demise. I dug deep into my psyche and found it: Packy's suicide. After all the years, it was still as fresh as if I had just gotten the news. That memory had everything I needed: shock, denial, and violent hysteria. It was perfect. The role was deeply satisfying. But after each performance, I was exhausted and emotionally spent.

It was during these rehearsals that I met Howard. Howard was a great guy and fine actor who loved improvisation. He was a dynamo—always turned on and ready to play. We got to know each other, and talked a lot during rehearsals about our lives and career goals.

He wanted to write and produce his own shows, and his enthusiasm was infectious. We clicked.

One Sunday night in November, after our last performance of the week—Monday was our day off—Sherri had invited us all over to her apartment. Sherri was the actress they'd hired out of New York to play one of the lead roles in *The Runner Stumbles*.

It was snowing outside, and her apartment was warm and cozy with a big fire burning in the fireplace. Most of the company was there and had broken up into small groups chatting away. The alcohol was flowing freely, and there were snacks galore.

Howard and I were chatting, when suddenly, he reached over me and snatched a joint from Jack, who was passing it around.

"Huh, you're welcome, Howard," Jack said, and we laughed. Jack was an older actor who had been part of the company for many years.

"Yeah, thanks, Jack," Howard said. Jack just rolled his eyes. Howard took a couple of long slow tokes, then offered it to me. I declined.

I'd promised myself I wouldn't smoke in social situations because I learned long before that I turned into an insecure, paranoid nutjob when I got stoned in certain situations. Not a flattering look at parties.

"Oh, come on." So, I took a small hit, just enough to satisfy his insistence. "I want to create my own improvisational show, maybe put it up at a nightclub or maybe rent a theater." He started pacing. Howard was a good six feet, five inches tall, and he expressed himself with wild intensity even when he wasn't stoned. But when he was, he became incredibly loud and alive. You couldn't help getting excited just being around him. "See, we'll start out…"

'*We'll* start out?' Was he saying that the two of us were going to create something together? Then I realized that that tiny hit of the joint I took was affecting me; I was stoned. Uh-oh!

"We'll start out with a fight, see," he said. "Catch the whole audience off guard—"

"Ooooo, that's good, Howard! Then what?" He turned to face me.

"Then we'll run up on stage, and that'll be the beginning of the show! We'll surprise 'em!"

"I love it! Let's do it!" And that was the beginning of AD-Glib—our comedy show.

Howard asked Mark if we could borrow the Actors Stage rehearsal space when they weren't using it, and Mark said, "OK." So, we squeezed in time whenever we could between rehearsals, performances, and family duties, to bounce ideas off each other and play. I felt like a kid again.

The feeling of creating something, in the moment, from nothing was like no other feeling in the world. And it turned out I was pretty good at improv. Who knew? We created many scenes.

For example: a stoned hippie couple trying to remember where they were headed in their car, and why they were dressed like animals; a patient with multiple personalities—one of them being a sheep—who tries to mount me, his psychiatrist; a very proper father and his young daughter sitting at dinner politely discussing premarital sex.

While Howard and I rehearsed with the rest of the company's cast during the day and performed the shows at night, we still managed to continue our work together whenever we could. We created more material and slowly arranged the sketches into a one-hour original show.

The third play of the season at Actors Stage was *A Christmas Carol* by Charles Dickens. I played Martha Cratchit, and it ran during most of December. In certain scenes, we sang Christmas carols, and at the end of each performance, the entire cast sang "We Wish You a Merry Christmas" in harmony to the audience. It was an absolute blast.

During those rehearsals, I got to know Bob.

Bob played a weaselly beggar who sneaks in and pilfers belongings from the newly dead. He was disgustingly brilliant. Bob was a thin, lanky, attractive man with incredible acting abilities. He was from Oklahoma City and had quite a bit of Cherokee Native American blood in him. He was a divorced father of two little girls and was eight years older than me. He was also newly remarried.

Bob was like nobody I had ever met before. He was quiet, reserved, very mysterious, and a good listener. There was something about him. I knew that anything I told him, no matter what it was, would remain between the two of us always. If I told him I had robbed a bank or killed someone, he wouldn't have turned me in. He would have figured I had my reasons. Bob and I talked about everything: his divorce; his girls; his current wife, who had been his college sweetheart, and currently lived and worked in Baltimore, MD. I told him about my troubled marriage and all about my little darlings, and I even confided in him about my secret plan to divorce Dick.

After every show, most of the cast would go down to the bar to party with audience members and unwind. Bob was never there. He would simply disappear after each show, and when I'd ask him why he never joined us, he'd say he liked to relax at home after a show.

One day, when rehearsal was over, Bob and I were embroiled in deep conversation about marriage and how hard it was, and we hadn't noticed that everyone else had left. The rehearsal hall was empty, except for us.

While we got our things together, I asked him, "Hey, why don't you ever have drinks with us after the shows? Is it really that you're just tired, or is there more to it?" He stared off in silence.

"I'm sorry," I said. "It's none of my business."

He looked at me like he was sizing me up, making sure he could trust me. Or wondering if I was ready to hear the truth. He looked around the room to make sure no one else was within earshot.

He took a deep breath, lowered his voice, and leaned in. "I'm an alcoholic," he said. "Haven't had a drink in over ten years. But I used to be a hopeless drunk."

I felt terrible. I thought I had crossed a line, stuck my nose where it didn't belong. He shook his head.

"I lost everything," he said. "My marriage, my kids, my house, and career, and almost my life."

"Oh my God. How'd you stop?"

"Well, my doctor told me that if I didn't stop drinking, I was going to die. It was just a matter of time. The next day, my wife served me with divorce papers and left with my daughters. That same day, I went to a liquor store, bought bottles of scotch, vodka, and whiskey—as many as I could carry. I checked into a cheap motel, paid for the week, and locked myself in. I started drinking and didn't stop. I intended to drink myself to death. Couple of days later, at least I thought it was a couple days, I woke up choking on my own vomit. The room was pitch-dark and—ever hear of delirium tremens?"

"I've heard of them, but don't really know what they are."

"Yeah, well, it's nasty hallucinations. Happened a lot before I quit drinking. When I was drunk, the walls looked like dark, slimy swamps, and they'd be crawling with snakes."

"Jeez."

"When I woke up, I heard a deep voice say, 'Do you want to live?' My eyes felt like they'd been glued shut. But I forced them open and looked around in the darkness. I was scared. I wanted to connect the voice with a body. But nobody was there. Then the voice repeated, 'Do you want to live?' and I heard myself say, 'Yes.'" He looked off like he was remembering. "I was surprised. I thought I wanted to die. 'Just rest,' the voice said. And I passed out again."

"Wow, do you think you imagined it? The voice, I mean."

"Oh, no. No, it was real, alright. Never heard anything like it before or since."

"Maybe it was... you think it was God?"

He shrugged and shook his head. "Don't know, but it happened three more times that night. I'd wake up, and that voice would ask me the same question, 'Do you want to live?' and I'd say, 'Yes.' But then... and I don't know how many hours or days later, I woke up sober enough to stand and walk out of the motel room. It must've been very late because it was dark and cold, and the only light was the blinking motel sign. I knew a guy who lived pretty close, a friend. I'd done a play with him. So, I walked to his place and knocked on the door. It took a while for him to answer, but when he finally did, he took one look at me, held his nose, and told me to come around to the back. Then he told me to remove every stitch of vomit-soaked clothing and leave it all on the porch. I did as he asked, and he escorted me to the shower."

It was almost dark outside, and dinnertime. Bob looked tired, I was hungry, and I needed to get home to the kids. I picked up my things and started for the door. "What happened after?" I asked. "You mean you never had another drink?"

"Yep. That was it."

"Just like that?"

He nodded. "Just like that. I left the last alcohol I would ever taste in that motel room. Never touched another drop."

A couple of weeks later, after *A Christmas Carol* had opened, instead of joining the gang for drinks, I went to Bob's apartment. Things had gone from bad to worse with Dick, and I needed to talk to a friend who would understand.

Bob's one-bedroom apartment was on the second floor of an old single-family home converted into multiple units. It was in the artsy part of Louisville, not far from St. James Court, where out-of-town actors stayed while working the theater circuit. The owner of the building had furnished the main room with an older couch, an end table, and a small bookshelf. And there was a kitchenette with a table and two chairs. During the day, when the sun was out, the place was nice and bright with flimsy flowered curtains hung over the windows on the side and back walls.

But at night, with only two small lamps to light the room, it was dim and dingy.

Bob was a loner, so his small, no-frills apartment suited him. I got the feeling that I'd been the only person he'd had over that whole season.

We sat on his couch, and I poured my heart out to him. "I know the kids can feel it, and I'm sure Dick can sense that something's going on. The atmosphere is toxic." Bob nodded and stroked my arm. "I mean, the meetings with my lawyer are going well. Phil says he's pretty sure I'll get custody, and I know that's what's best for the kids. But I feel so guilty lying to Dick all the time. I don't know if…" I started to tear up.

Bob moved closer and hugged me. "Oh, honey, it's going to be OK, I promise. Hang in there." He said. "I remember when Bobbie—she's my youngest—when she was four and my wife was leaving me with her and her sister. Just before they walked out, Bobbie came over, hugged me, and stroked my face. She said she was sorry she had to go away with her mommy, but she promised she would come see me when I got better."

"Shit."

"Yeah… kids'll break your heart seven days to Sunday. It killed me."

Bob and I talked far into the night. He told me about his drinking days and the hellish breakup with his first wife, and about his current wife.

"It was only a few months after my divorce," he said. "I was getting my life straightened out, and I thought she was just an old friend helping me heal. She was newly divorced, and we were having a good time, but… then she accused me of using her." He looked down at his hands and shook his head. "I felt terrible and I just gave in." He told me he didn't have much hope for the marriage lasting. Then we commiserated about all the terrible things we had put our kids through, and the deep, unforgivable guilt and sorrow we carried around as a result.

I wiped my eyes and yawned. Then I noticed the clock on Bob's end table. "Oh God, I've got to go!" I stood up.

Bob took my hand. "Oh, honey, you're so tired, and you've got such a long drive." I sat back down. "Why don't you rest for a while before you go?" He laid me back on his couch, and we looked into each other's eyes. He leaned in close; I pulled him closer. We kissed. It was sweet, soft and gentle—and the beginning of something wild!

When the season was over at Actors Stage, Howard and I took our creation to The Fig Tree, an upscale jazz club in downtown Louisville.

The place was classy. The day we went to meet the manager, the first thing we noticed was the long, highly polished, hand-carved bar against the back wall. Behind it were booze bottles of all colors, shapes, and sizes. Row upon row of ornate glassware was on display from floor to high ceiling. There were delicately designed sconces sprouting out of the walls around the entire large room, creating the perfect lighting. A stage in one corner, usually occupied by a jazz quartet, was bathed in bright stage lights. Tables and chairs filled the rest of the room.

The manager of The Fig Tree loved our ideas and gave us a shot. We were scheduled to do our test performance on a hot July night, and we were super excited, also pretty freaked out, but raring to go. We'd been running our scenes over and over all week, adding new bits of business as we rehearsed them. That's the incredible thing about improvisation: since *you* create everything, you can change anything at any time, lines, blocking, intention, any of it, and the sketches always—at least ninety percent of the time—get better and better. The bottom line is you must trust your partner and stay immersed in the moment, ready for whatever occurs. Because the sketch is your baby and you're in it together.

Before entering The Fig Tree, we strolled arm in arm past a large sign out front:

"Tonight is a Special Night at the 'Tree!' Improv with AD-Glib! Come Join the FUN!"

The place was teeming with people. The room smelled like a combination of grilled steaks, shrimp, and other delicacies, rounded off with undercurrents of every alcoholic beverage imaginable. I heard the welcoming sound of ice cubes clinking in glasses and people talking.

Inhibitions were lowering, which made me a tad less nervous. Howard and I sat at the bar and ordered seltzer water with ice and lime slices (so that it would look like we were getting liquored up). No one knew who we were save the manager, who was pretending he didn't.

Howard and I chatted for a while and downed our drinks. Suddenly, a fight broke out—between us.

"Stop it!" I stood up, hauled off and slapped him.

He looked around the room, feigning embarrassment, then grabbed my arm. "Come here—"

"Get your hands off me!" I yelled and yanked my arm away. By then, some patrons were beginning to get alarmed, and we proceeded to give them their money's worth. We continued screaming at each other. Then I walked away again, he grabbed me again. (We had choreographed some very realistic looking hand-to-hand stage combat.) The tension was growing by the minute. Several audience members stood up, ready to intervene. Then I ran up on stage, followed by Howard, and we turned to the audience, smiled, and I announced into the mic, "Good evening, ladies and gentlemen!"

Then Howard said, "We are AD-Glib!" and we took a bow. The audience was stunned; you could have heard a pin drop. The few people standing slowly sat back down, and everyone broke out in laughter and applause.

We performed the whole show to a very alert and responsive audience. It was brilliant! We won them over. Toward the end of the show, we took audience suggestions for places and relationships and did some pure improvising using their ideas. The owners of the club loved our show and hired us on the spot. We performed there three nights a week for eight months before Howard was hired to play the role of Dracula in an off-Broadway production in New York City.

Bob came to our show when he was in town and wasn't performing, and he and I continued our private affair for a couple of years. He was a real source of strength for me while I made my way through Dick's and my final separation and divorce. Shortly after, Bob and his wife divorced.

Then, we both got busier. Bob went to New York to do an award-winning play that got its start at Actors Stage before it went to off-Broadway. Due to spending so much time apart combined with hectic schedules, etcetera, our relationship eventually ended. I saw Bob in a few productions after that, and we remained friends.

CHAPTER THIRTY-EIGHT

1980

Custody

It was a soggy, sweltering Monday in early August. I'd gotten the afternoon off from my waitress job and was on my way to my lawyer's office to meet Dick. I was a nervous wreck.

Phil was preparing to present him with the custody arrangement we had worked on—I hoped to God Dick would sign it.

Phil's office was old school: dark antique matching desks and furniture, and a huge, deep maroon, leather couch with plump, matching, paisley-designed cushions. On the stark white walls hung a few old black-and-white ink renderings of scenes from past centuries. Hazel, Phil's receptionist, sat at the front with one crisp green plant on the corner of her large desk.

Hazel was sweet and cheerful. She usually wore some kind of old-fashioned, colorful shirtwaist dress or blouse, probably bought decades before and meticulously maintained, with flowers, stripes, little animals, or inanimate objects on them. The office was highly organized and spotless. Hazel was probably in her sixties and very agreeable. She had short, white, wiry curls pulled back off her thin face and wore no makeup, except for bright red lipstick. The rooms smelled like fear—or maybe it was just me.

Phil was damn good at his job, and I had spent months, unbeknownst to Dick, pouring my heart out to him. Phil insisted on having all the relevant information about our case: why Dick and I married in the first place; why it had taken me so long to realize that I wanted out of the relationship; and what I believed were our irreconcilable differences. Phil did not let me get away with any bullshit. No blaming Dick for everything. He insisted on the God's honest truth, the whole truth, and nothing but the truth. Lucky for me, Phil was wise and nurturing and had excellent psychological skills. I shed a few tears in his office while I gave him the abridged version of my life with Dick.

Phil didn't mince words either. After our very first meeting, when I agreed to his terms and hired him, we chatted for a while. Then he asked me how I heard about him, and I told him that he came highly recommended by several people. He got right to the point and asked me what I wanted.

"Well, I can't imagine living my life without Meadow and Jeremy being part of it every day." He nodded. "But there's no way Dick will allow me to get full custody. So, I guess I'll have to be satisfied with joint custody."

"I see." He stared at me for a long moment. "You know, quite often, that arrangement doesn't work out so well for the children. And if Dick is anything like you described him to be, I believe joint custody would be a mistake." Truer words were never spoken. So, we went to work.

I arrived at Phil's office ten minutes early and went in. "Good afternoon, Hazel." I closed the door. The place was intensely quiet.

"Good afternoon, Ms. Gibbs." She had a sweet, singsong-y manner of speaking. "How are you today?"

I shook my head, took a deep breath, and blew it out my mouth.

She nodded with a smile of sympathy, then pressed the intercom. "Ms. Gibbs is here. You may go on in, dear."

I was relieved. I did not want to be sitting in the outer office when Dick showed up.

Phil had never met Dick, but with the information I had given him, he had come to the conclusion that perhaps the only way to get Dick to agree to my being awarded full custody of Meadow and Jeremy was to make it as easy on him financially as humanly possible. So, in the agreement Phil and I had worked on for weeks, we proposed a mere $200 a month in child support. And we offered Dick visitation rights every weekend. I was hoping that, considering the kids were going to a Montessori school in Louisville, and Dick was now living fifty miles out in the country, the arrangement would work out well for everyone.

Dick and I had sold the rock house and split the profit before leaving California. So, I still had a small nest egg to keep the kids and myself afloat after I paid Phil for his services. He was not cheap.

After the season at Actors Stage ended, I got a decent job waiting tables at the Bristol, a large, popular restaurant where the patrons usually tipped generously.

Phil and I ran through parts of the agreement when Hazel's voice came over the intercom.

"Dick is here, Phil. Shall I send him in?"

Phil pressed the button. "In a moment please, Hazel." Then he lowered his voice. "Remember to let me do the talking." He smiled and put his hand on mine. "And, considering that you seem to be nervous, I suggest you keep your eyes on me or on the contract."

I nodded and took a couple of deep breaths, hoping to ease my nervous stomach.

Dick came through the door. "Hi, Dick, this is Phil."

Phil stood up and reached out his hand. "Nice to meet you, Dick." They shook hands.

"Yeah." You could've cut the tension with a butter knife.

"Please have a seat, Dick." Phil handed Dick and me copies of our proposed agreement. "Let's get to it."

Phil read through the contract in his slow, methodical, soothing voice while I followed along.

After Phil had read the entire contract out loud, he looked at Dick. "Questions?" he asked. Dick seemed to think for a moment while continuing to look over the paperwork. I held my breath and looked up at one of the obscure drawings on Phil's wall. Two children appeared to be running from a bull across a large field toward a forest. They looked terrified, screaming with their hands waving over their heads, as the animal charged closer. A small herd of cows watched and grazed nearby. I got a chill.

"What exactly does this section mean?" Dick pointed to the document. "This here, about my visitation rights."

Phil deciphered the legalese and explained the part where I had agreed to drop the kids off at his house every weekend and pick them up Sunday evening.

"What about holidays?"

"Yes." Phil flipped a few pages. "That would be paragraph number… eight, right here." He indicated the part in the contract that stated we would share custody every other holiday. Making our way through the entire agreement had lasted about an hour and a half. By then, I was a sweaty, frazzled mess.

Dick continued to stare at the contract. The silence was agonizing. Then he looked up, glared at Phil for a moment, and finally signed the agreement—I nearly had a stroke.

"Thank you, Dick." Phil's voice had the nonchalant smoothness of a criminal. "We'll be in touch."

Dick nodded and left the office without a word. I was overwhelmed. When he was gone, Phil and I smiled at each other.

"We did good. Reedy, you did great."

"Oh, God! Thank you, Phil, thank you so much." I pulled myself together, wrapped my arms around his huge body, and hugged him.

Things went smoothly while we waited for our divorce to become final. In the interim, I found out that the midwife Penny—who almost delivered Meadow in our rock house on that horrible night when I had to be rushed to the hospital because my crazy-ass cervix was closing, that Penny—had moved to Louisville with her seven children and was staying at Dick's house. He casually mentioned it at a local café, after we discussed Meadow and Jeremy's school schedules.

"Oh, they're living with you?" He nodded. "Huh… when did that happen?"

He slurped his coffee. "Well, we've been talking for months. As soon as our divorce is final, we're getting married." The statement rolled off his tongue like he was ordering a deli sandwich.

My brain froze, and hundreds of questions bubbled up. First, what kind of knucklehead takes on—no, marries a divorcée with seven children? Especially when said knucklehead is a struggling musician who refuses to look for more practical and lucrative work.

I wasn't at all surprised that Penny had left her abusive, son of a bitch of a second husband, just that she and her brood had landed in my backyard. Dick was still talking, and I was absent from the conversation. I focused.

"…Yeah, she had to get the hell out of there."

Ah, then I understood; Dick was her knight in shining armor. I wondered if they had started up after I left him and moved to Grass Valley. Not that it mattered, or was any of my business. Once I left the ridge, I lost contact with everyone because no one had phones out there.

Dick seemed to notice the stunned, jaw-dropped expression on my face and added, "Don't worry. We're not having sex until after we're married." His Catholic roots showing.

"Uh-huh." Like I gave a shit.

"Yeah. I've been celibate for ten months now," he bragged.

"Huh." Then I thought for a minute. "But we've only been separated for six months."

"Oh," he scoffed with a chuckle. "I don't count the months after you complained about not having orgasms."

He was dead serious.

I choked back a belly laugh and wondered, *Am I on Candid Camera?*

Once I wrapped my mind around the new turn of events, things moved along pretty well. Dick and I managed to keep our relationship friendly. The kids seemed to enjoy their weekends with Dick, Penny, and their many new stepsiblings out in the countryside. However, Meadow told me that she and Jeremy didn't get to spend much time with their dad and rarely even saw him because he was always too busy. Apparently, the house was all about Penny and her kids.

When our divorce was final, Dick and Penny got married. I was not invited to the wedding, but Meadow and Jeremy loved being part of the ceremony.

I worked the waitress job for months while juggling my schedule around Howard's and my improv performances at The Fig Tree. But once Howard left for his acting job in New York City, AD-Glib ended. That's when I realized it had been my lifeline and got together with Joann and Robin, my brilliant and hilarious actor friends. We created Women's Glib, another improv show that we performed in clubs in Louisville and Cincinnati. As much as we loved doing it, and as much as audiences seemed to enjoy our shows, we couldn't find a steady place to perform, so eventually we went our separate ways.

So, I hustled to find whatever acting jobs Louisville had to offer, but it was slim pickings. And between my waitress job, taking care of the kids, and schlepping them to and from Mom's house, so Mom could babysit while I worked, I had time for little else. I did manage to land the rare nonunion, local TV commercial, and the occasional modeling job, or magazine spread. But while we lived in Louisville, it was impossible to support us solely with acting work.

Then Robin and Joann were talking about moving to Chicago. They had looked into it and talked about the endless creative opportunities available there. Literally dozens of auditions every week for national commercials, industrial films, voiceover jobs, and plays, not to mention every imaginable way to study.

There were Shakespeare workshops, scene study intensives, acting technique classes, soap opera and commercial study groups, casting showcases, play readings, you name it. There were also hundreds of theaters to audition for, and Second City was there! Apparently, the talent and casting agencies were always on the lookout for new faces. It sounded like *my* dream come true.

I was just sure I could support myself and the kids in Chicago by doing what I loved. But how was I going to sell the idea to Dick? I knew he had to be crazy-busy trying to support and deal with his new wife and huge stepfamily. I believed that Penny's kids ranged somewhere between the ages of eight and twenty. That's a shitload of teenagers to deal with, and a lot of mouths to feed, too.

Chicago was calling me, and I had to give it a shot. So, I scheduled a meeting with Dick at our usual café.

He was a few minutes late when he walked up to the table.

"Hi." He sat across from me. "What's this about?" He rarely looked pleased to see me, but today, he had his hackles up.

"Hi, um, well, I wanted to show you these." I passed a couple of Jeremy's reading comprehension quizzes across the table. "Look, Jeremy got 98 percent on these in Miss Mariam's class. She said he's doing so much better. It's like something finally clicked, and he's reading better than the rest of the first-grade class now."

Dick looked them over and actually smiled. "Wow, that's great."

"Yeah, he's happy about it. Pretty proud of himself, ya know?"

"Good, tell him I'm proud of him too."

"I will! Yeah, so, how are Penny and her kids doing? They all settled in?"

"They are. They really like it here."

"Good, good," An awkward silence set in.

Then Dick abruptly said, "Look, Reedy, I'm really busy." He readied himself to dash off.

"Yeah, yeah, I know." My nerves were taking over. "Wait, just… listen, Dick, I've been thinking about making a move, and I wanted to run it by you."

"What are you talking about?" A suspicious look took over his face.

"Well, there's not enough work here for me. Not enough acting work." Dick rolled his eyes and shook his head. Then I remembered what I'd forgotten. He hated me acting, didn't have much respect for the entire profession. He even thought my love of acting was the cause of our split. "I know, I know, but some friends are relocating to Chicago, and I'm thinking about maybe moving there too."

"What?" he yelled and stood up.

Shit, shit, shit! I fucking blew it! The other two couples in the café turned and watched. "What the fuck are you talking about? You want to move to Chicago? Fine, move! But the kids aren't going anywhere. They're staying right here with us!" He turned and started to rush out. I ran after him.

"Wait! Dick, please—wait, can we at least talk about it?" He stopped and spun around.

I almost crashed into him.

He looked me in the eyes, only inches from my face. "This is bullshit," he said. "I knew you were up to something. Look, you wanted a divorce, you got a divorce. You wanted custody, you got custody. That's it. I'm done!" And he stormed out.

I could feel people's eyes on me. I fought back tears and followed him out, but he had already gotten in his truck and was pulling away.

A few weeks went by. I wanted to give Dick time to cool down and let the idea germinate before I broached the subject again. Then a moment presented itself. I was picking up Meadow and Jeremy from his place, and Dick seemed to be in a pretty good mood, and Penny and her kids were gone somewhere. Meadow and Jeremy were romping in the yard.

I waved to them and walked up to Dick. "Hi, I've been thinking more about Chicago—" He shot me The Look. "Wait, just… what if you and Penny have the kids for the whole summer? And… and once a month, I'll drive them back to your place for a couple of days during the school year?" His expression eased up a bit. He still wasn't happy, but seemed to like the idea of having the kids for the entire summer.

A couple of weeks later, Dick agreed to keep Meadow and Jeremy for the week while I went to Chicago to check things out and get a lay of the land.

When I drove the kids out to Dick's house, they had lots of questions. "How long are you gonna be gone, Momma?" Meadow asked.

"Yeah," Jeremy chimed in. "How long?"

"Just a week, guys, not that long."

"A whole week?" Meadow said.

Jeremy pounded the car seat. "Momma, that's too long!"

"Oh, honey, you guys will have lots to do with all the kids."

"No," Meadow said. "Why can't we come too?"

"Yeah," Jeremy said. "We wanna come with you!" I pulled the car over to the side of the road and turned to face them.

"What's going on, guys? I thought you liked staying at your dad's." Jeremy was almost in tears.

"It's OK," Meadow said. "But what if something happens to you?"

Jeremy started crying. "Yeah, what if you don't come back?"

"Oh, sweethearts." I got out of the car, climbed in the back seat, and hugged them close.

"Mommy just has to find a place for us to live in Chicago." We snuggled for a while. "But hey," I wiped away their tears, "I'll hurry.

And I'll call you every day, tell you all about it, OK? And you know, your dad said something about helping you kids build a birdhouse this week."

The kids still weren't happy, but I told them more about Chicago, and how much fun it was going to be when we all lived there. And their sadness gradually turned into excitement.

By the time we got to Dick's house, they gave me big goodbye hugs and ran off to play in Dick's giant yard. He was nowhere to be found, so I said hello to Penny and went on my way.

CHAPTER THIRTY-NINE

1981

Bruno

THE NEXT DAY WAS SURPRISINGLY COOL FOR THE MIDDLE OF AUGUST. Good day to travel. I got all my stuff packed in the car, and before I hit the road for Chicago, I called Dick's house to say another goodbye to the kids.

Penny picked up. "Hello?" She had a soft, unmistakable voice, almost sounded like a child.

"Hi, Penny, are the kids around?"

"Hello, Reedy, they're out in the yard playing."

"Oh, huh. Well, would you mind telling them I'm on the phone?"

"Certainly, please hold on." I could hear Penny's attempt at yelling. "Meadow and Jeremy, your mother is on the line for you." I found it hard to believe that anyone would be able to hear her timid voice unless they were right in front of her face. "Meadow and Jeremy?" she called again. After a bit of a wait, Meadow picked up the phone, out of breath.

"Hi, Momma!"

"Hi sweetie pie." It warmed my heart to hear her precious voice. I was always amazed how much I missed my kids when I wasn't with them. Especially considering how I sometimes longed for a break from the little buggers when I was. "Are you having fun?"

"Yeah," she laughed. "When Jeremy kicked the ball, he fell on his butt!"

"Lemme talk," Jeremy said in the background. Then I heard lots of laughing and scuffling with the phone. "Hi, Mommy! Whew ah you?"

"Hello, my love, did you fall on your butt?"

"Yeah, whew ah you?"

"I'm at our apartment, honey, getting ready to leave for Chicago."

"Oh. Well, be cawful." His adorable voice was music to my ears. Jeremy couldn't pronounce his Rs yet. I assured him I'd be very careful. Then we talked about what he had for breakfast, and the game they were playing and with whom. I told them both how much I loved them, and we all three sent lots of kisses through the phone.

The six-hour drive was pretty uneventful, except for the fact that I was anxious as hell seeing how I was on a mission to find a new life in the dazzling city of Chicago. During the drive, visions of sugarplums danced in my head: me landing lots of acting jobs, me finding a sweet (cheap) apartment for us, me getting everything set up for the kids. But the first thing I had to do when I got there was find a place to stay for the week.

When I landed in Chicago, I stopped at a deli to grab a sandwich and ran into Lois. Lois was an old friend of Dick's and mine whom I hadn't seen in years. Back when Dick and I lived there, more than ten years earlier, Lois was married to Fred, a piano player friend of Dick's. As it turned out, they had divorced several years earlier, and Lois was still living in their big house.

When Lois found out that I needed a place to stay, she offered to let me crash at her house while I got my shit together. She said she was taking several classes at the university and was hardly ever home anyway.

Lois was ten or fifteen years my senior, and all her children were grown and off on their own.

Her house reminded me of my grandmother's—a messy version. The furniture was old and worn. Over the windows in the living and dining rooms hung yellowed lace curtains creating a dingy atmosphere. I always liked Lois and admired her. She was a dear person, kind and generous, but she didn't seem to have any sense of style. Or I suspected she felt that, as long as her house was comfortable, that was enough. She had plenty of friends who loved her for who she was, and I don't think she cared what anyone else thought.

The next day, I called Dick's house, but the phone just rang and rang. Eventually, I gave up. Figured I'd try again later. Then I gathered up my actor tools, my pictures and résumés, etcetera, tucked them in my shoulder bag, and went to one of the talent agencies that a friend had told me about.

The office was a bustling beehive of activity with actors, actresses, and models running in and out of the door nonstop. "Hi," I said to the middle-aged woman at the reception desk with bright, red-dyed hair.

"Hello." She glanced up at me. "How may I help you?"

"Hi, um, yes, may I please speak to someone about representation?" Just then, an older, gray-haired, slightly plump woman came out of a door holding some papers. She looked at me, down at her papers, then back up at me.

"Nan, who's that?" asked the older woman. The red-headed receptionist looked at her, but before she could get a word out, the gray-haired woman said, "Who are you, sweetheart?"

I looked behind me. "Me?"

"Yes, darling, you."

I told her my name and that I was new in town. She hustled me into her huge, well-lived-in office. "I'm Emelia, dear," she said. "And I need you to go to an audition for a commercial tomorrow. Can you do that?"

I nodded my head. "Yes, please."

"Good." She smiled. "Nan will fill you in on the particulars. Be sure to give her your name and contact information, love." Then she shooed me out of her office.

The audition was for an Aldi commercial. Aldi was a small grocery store chain, and I was to team up with an actor named Bruno, whom I'd never met. Nan told me to find him when I got to the casting office. The scenario: I was to play a shopper in the store, and my audition partner, Bruno, was to play a small angel on one of my shoulders, and a small devil on the other.

The next morning before I went to the audition, I called Dick's house again. After about ten rings, he picked up. "Hello?"

"Hi, Dick, it's me. Are the kids up?"

"No."

"Oh, well, OK. Darn… please tell them I called, and I'll try again later."

"OK."

"Yeah, thanks, and tell them I love them?" Damn it, I shouldn't have said that. He'd probably read something threatening into it.

"Yeah, OK." I heard a click. Par for the course.

I got to the casting office on time and found two men sitting in the waiting room studying what I assumed were their lines. One was unusually tall, rather strange-looking, and gangly. The other was short, plump, and downright funny-looking with slicked-back hair and an Italian mafia sort of snarl on his face. Clearly, the casting agent was looking for unusual character types for the role.

I approached the short one and leaned down. "Excuse me," I said. "Are you Bruno?" He looked up at me. Before he could speak, I heard a deep, velvety, sexy voice from over my shoulder.

"I'm Bruno." I looked up into the deep, brown eyes of a tall, muscular, handsome, European-looking man.

His expression read, 'How could you possibly think that shrimp of a man was me?' Bruno was very well built with broad shoulders and huge hands. He had brown hair, beautiful, brown, liquid, wide-set eyes, and was wearing a gaudy Hawaiian shirt—an obvious attempt to look like a character.

"Oh." I let out a slight laugh of surprise at the vision of manhood that stood before me. We sat and worked on our lines together. The script was supposed to be funny, but failed miserably. It was ridiculous, in fact. We read it and laughed at how stupid it was.

After we got familiar with our lines, I asked Bruno, "Do you have a comb I could borrow?"

"Oh, man." He shook his head. "Yeah… I'm sorry. It's really dirty."

"That's OK. I don't mind." I watched him reluctantly reach into his back jeans pocket, pull out a black comb, and give it to me. He was embarrassed, but did it anyway. I was touched.

He could've just lied, told me he didn't have one or made up an excuse like he had cooties, and it was contagious or something. But he didn't. He was compelled to tell the truth and hand it over to me, a total stranger, despite how it would make him look considering the state of it. I found that endearing and telling, like an intimate peep into his personality.

The comb was a bit disgusting, covered with gray dust and tiny particles of God knew what all. I suppressed my honest reaction and smiled. "Thank you," I said, then went to the ladies room and used my hand instead.

Bruno and I both thought the audition went well and decided to grab lunch afterwards. I told him about Meadow and Jeremy, and about my divorce, and he filled me in on his family. His parents were Lithuanian immigrants who had escaped from their homeland during World War II and traveled for over a year in a horse and buggy. He said they survived unimaginable hardships, including the loss of two children. Bruno was smart, funny, a good listener, and really seemed to like me too—all qualities on my newly revised 'must have' list in a man. He was so easy to talk to. I felt like I'd known him for years.

After a very long lunch, I was a bit smitten. Then he said he was going to go to Shirley Hamilton's agency, one of the top talent agents in town. He asked if I'd like to join him and that he'd introduce me.

"Yes, please!" Bruno laughed—a good sign. We walked to her office.

During the '80s, Chicago agents didn't always sign talent to exclusive contracts. So, we actors got to 'play the field,' as it were. That meant that whichever agency called us first for an audition got to represent us for that particular job, should we land it.

When we went into The Shirley Hamilton Talent Agency, I noticed it was a bit less chaotic than Emelia's office and seemed more organized. The dozen or more people sitting around the outer office appeared to be studying scripts. The agency itself was quite impressive. It was bright and colorful, and the afternoon sun filtered through several tall, leafy plants near the huge windows. Large framed posters hung on the walls, displaying top models in various provocative poses. The whole place was high-end. Bruno approached the front desk.

"Hi, Elaine, is Shirley in? Bruno," indicating himself. Elaine smiled and nodded.

Elaine was a stunning woman I guessed to be in her fifties—probably a successful model now past her prime. Her streaked blond hair was tied up into a tight twist, and her makeup and wardrobe were impeccable.

Elaine looked at me, smiled, and pressed the intercom. "Shirley, someone is here to meet you." Then she turned to us. "You both have a seat. She'll be right out."

Moments later, a door opened, and a tall, shapely, platinum blond came swishing out in a long yellow dress. She appeared to be in her sixties. Her hair was fluffy around her shoulders, and her entrance reminded me of *The Loretta Young Show*. I was giddy.

"Hello!" She looked me up and down. "And who might you be?"

"Hi Shirley," Bruno said.

She kept her eyes glued on me. "Hello, Bruno, who's your friend?"

"Yeah, this is Reedy. She's just moving here. Met her at an audition and—"

"How nice." Shirley cut him off. "Let me look at you, dear." Which she did. "Do you have any experience? Perhaps a picture and résumé?"

"I have, yes. I also have a videotape of some of the commercials I've done." I pulled them out of my shoulder bag and handed them to her. She looked impressed. My introduction to Shirley Hamilton was brief, but she said she would *definitely* be in touch.

As we were leaving Shirley's office, Bruno looked at me for a long moment and shook his head. "Jeez, that was quite a welcome you got. They didn't react that way to me." He made an angry face, then smiled. I laughed.

Bruno walked me to my car, and I got in and thanked him. Then I reluctantly said goodbye. But he just stood there looking down at me. "Um, tomorrow, I'm dropping off my pictures and résumés at some industrial film producers if you'd like to join me—"

"Love to! I mean, thanks, sounds like a great idea."

The next morning, I called Dick's house again. The phone rang for quite a while, and I finally gave up. Then I drove to Bruno's apartment to pick him up. He had a list of addresses of production houses, and we went to every single one. We gave our pictures and résumés to several receptionists, then ran into some luck and got to meet a couple of the big producers. I learned a lot that day. Bruno was very together and a real gentleman. When I got back to Lois's house, I tried to call Dick again. Penny picked up, and told me that Dick had taken the kids out to McDonald's for dinner.

"Oh, darn. OK. When would be a good time for me to call again?"

"I never know when they'll be available, sorry."

I called the next morning, but to no avail. I was getting uneasy.

I picked up Bruno, and we dropped off more pictures and résumés to the other talent and casting agencies. I was learning how to be pro-active with the lovely bonus of getting to hang out with my new crush.

Finally, after the long day, we rewarded ourselves by going to Andy's, a local jazz bar in the heart of downtown Chicago. The place was packed. We made our way to the bar and yelled our orders to the bartender, "Dewar's on the rocks with a twist," our newly discovered, shared favorite alcoholic beverage. Then we shoved our way, drinks in hand, into the middle of the mob where we stood close, unwound, and listened to some sweet, mellow jazz.

We hadn't eaten in a few hours, and the scotch was having its way with me. I looked up at Bruno, he looked down at me, and our eyes locked. Then he wrapped his strong arms around me, pulled me in tight, leaned down, and kissed me. His lips were the softest and sweetest I'd ever tasted. I wanted to stay there forever.

Later, we left the club. "Do you have to get home right away? You want to come over to my place? I don't think my roommate will be back for a couple hours."

"OK, sure." I parked the car, and he led me up the two flights of stairs to his tiny two-bedroom apartment. It smelled like a bachelor's pad. A few dirty dishes lay in the sink, covered with old, crusty food, with a pile of wet towels on the kitchen floor.

Bruno opened a cabinet like he was searching for something. Then he looked in the refrigerator. "Damn," he said. "Looks like all we have is some white wine. Would you like a glass?"

"Yes. Please." We took our drinks into his tiny room and sat on his unmade single bed.

The walls were bare except for a small painting hanging over his dresser of a lone, little house out in the country on a snowy day, with footprints in the snow leading up to the house. He said he saw it years ago at a gallery, and it spoke to him, so he bought it.

Bruno and I were in the middle of talking about our good luck at getting to run into the two big industrial film producers and decided that we impressed the hell out of them. Then all of a sudden, a deafening noise came out of nowhere. It sounded like a huge train was about to barrel into his bedroom. I looked at him in a panic. He laughed and hugged me until the racket subsided.

"Sorry, I forgot to tell you—"

"Holy mother of God! What the hell?"

"Sorry, that was the EL. The elevated subway."

"Jesus, how close are the tracks?" He indicated out his only window. I looked out, and there they were, not six feet from the apartment building. "How the hell do you sleep through that?"

He shrugged. "I'm used to it."

We talked for hours. I told him that Dick was royally pissed because I wanted to take the kids and move away. But I was determined to make it work.

Then Bruno told me that after he graduated college, he got a hospital job as a respiratory therapist for a couple of years working exclusively with terminally ill children.

"Great kids." He shook his head. "One summer, I arranged for a bunch of them to go to this camp with a few of us technicians. Got real close to a few of them, too."

"Really?"

"Yeah, it was great. There was swimming and boating, and all kinds of games, and this huge playground. For the kids that had Spina Bifida, us medical personnel would pound on their little chests while the other kids played musical instruments. We made their treatment part of the fun."

"What happened?"

Bruno looked down. "I quit. Had to. It was killing me to watch these kids get sicker and sicker and finally die. I couldn't do it anymore."

"Wow. But how'd you go from that to being an actor?"

"Oh, well, I went to boarding school. That's where I got interested in theater." Bruno told me he got in a lot of trouble during junior high, so his parents sent him to a Catholic boarding school in Maine.

The school was known for being especially strict on discipline, and it was where many Lithuanian families sent their bad boys. "The place had a ghost, a sea captain. Died in the 1700s."

"Really. You think it was true?"

"Oh, it was true alright. We'd hear him clunking around up in the attic. And one time, we experienced an actual visitation."

"Holy shit!" It was getting pretty late, and I didn't want to leave. "Um… would it be alright if I spend the night?"

"…Um, well." He blushed a little; then he looked away. "That'd be nice, but, the thing is, I think David will be home soon, and as you can see, my bed's pretty small."

I shrugged. "I don't take up much room."

He chuckled, and we got ready for bed. He had a new toothbrush that I borrowed and got washed up. Then I straightened up his covers, undressed, and climbed into his bed nude. I scooted down under the covers, and he came in the room. He took off his pants and started to put on his pajama bottoms.

"Really?" He stopped half naked and looked at me, one leg in his pajama pants and one leg out. "You really want to put on pajamas now?" With a slight smile on his face, he stepped out of the pants and crawled into bed next to me.

By the time Bruno came along, let's just say I'd sown my share of 'wild oats' and had gotten very comfortable being sexually aggressive with men. I found their different reactions fascinating. Some men liked it and had a great time with the whole role-reversal thing. Others became shy and slightly bewildered—like Bruno, my current victim. I had taken over their role as aggressor, and they didn't quite know how to respond. And still others seemed to be offended by my forwardness, or got pissed off, and the whole thing would collapse like a house of cards.

But that first night, once our naked bodies were lying together in his small bed, Bruno knew exactly what to do, and rose to the occasion, so to speak. And that, as they say, was the beginning of a beautiful friendship.

CHAPTER FORTY

1981

Sleepless

I didn't sleep much that hot Chicago night. I should've gone back to Lois's house, but couldn't bear to leave Bruno alone in his tiny bed. So, I took dreamy catnaps between the many elevated subways that blasted past his open window.

Something woke me up in the middle of a lovely dream. "G'mornin'," Bruno said in his deep, silken voice. (My lady parts vibrated.) The dim light of predawn created a tender magic. I could barely see his sweet face and shaggy, mussed hair. I inhaled his manly scent, and we kissed—his breath was sweet as a baby's. I pressed my naked body against his, and we made love again, then fell asleep in each other's arms.

A few hours later, the sudden sounds of someone banging around in the kitchen alerted us to the fact that we were no longer alone in the apartment. We glanced at each other like we had just been caught with our hands in the cookie jar. We silently giggled, rolled out of bed, and got dressed.

Bruno pointed toward the door and whispered, "My roommate, David. I'll go out first." I nodded. He closed the bedroom door behind him, and I heard the muffled sound of voices. I sat on the bed and thought about our previous hours together. I couldn't stop smiling.

I ran my fingers through my tangled hair, opened the door, and went into the kitchen.

"Hi, David." He turned around from the stove where he was scrambling eggs and looked at me. Then he looked at Bruno, and back at me.

"Hi," David said.

"Reedy," I said, indicating myself. And I stuck out my hand.

"Yeah, David, Reedy. Reedy, David." That broke the tension, and David offered to make me breakfast. I almost accepted until I remembered that I hadn't spoken to the kids in a few days and started to miss them. So, I thanked David and explained that I had to go. Bruno walked me to my car. He pressed himself against me, and we kissed. My whole body filled with butterflies. Then we made plans to meet for dinner.

When I got back to Lois's house, she was getting ready to leave for a class. "So, where did *you* sleep last night?" I smiled. "Been whoring around, have you?"

I laughed and nodded.

We had a quick 'girly' conversation about boys, and I told her about my wonderful night with Bruno. Then she told me about her current crush on a man in one of her classes, and off she went.

After she left, I picked up the phone and called Dick's house.

"Hello?"

"Hi, is this Anna?" I asked. Anna was the oldest of Penny's seven kids.

"Yes?"

"Oh, good." I was relieved that someone, anyone, finally picked up the phone. "Hi, Anna, would you tell Meadow and Jeremy to come to the phone, please?"

"They're not here."

"Oh, where are they?"

"Gone."

"Gone? Huh, well, may I please speak to your mother then? Or Dick?" I heard voices in the background.

"No." Her voice had taken on a hard, disagreeable quality. "No one's here but me."

"But I hear people talking… sounds like somebody's there—" Then I heard a click, then a dial tone. She had hung up on me. I couldn't believe she hung up on me! I called back immediately, but no one picked up. I was furious. I rushed around Lois's house in a fit of rage—I felt helpless.

Then I stopped, took some deep breaths, and reasoned with myself that I'd only been hung up on by a teenager. A snotty, messed-up teenager. I started to cool down and decided I'd just keep calling. And if necessary, I'd drive back to Louisville and confront the situation head-on.

Later, Bruno and I met at a new restaurant in Old Town. It was a sushi place, a completely different culinary experience for both of us. Our waiter helped us decide what to order and suggested we start out with some hot sake. Raw fish and hot alcohol—who knew it would become our favorite place to eat?

I told Bruno about the maddening phone call. "I couldn't believe that little bitch hung up on me! I'll tell ya what, though, I'm going to let Dick know how rude his stepdaughter was, that's for sure."

"Well, you know, those kids have been through a lot—abusive dad, moving across the country, and getting yet another father. You might want to give them a break."

I stared at him. "Hey, whose side are you on?" He laughed, and so did I because we were both pretty soused on that delicious hot hooch. After dinner, we went back to his place for a lovely, drunken roll in the hay.

The next morning, I tried calling Dick's house several times, but no luck. Bruno found a few apartments in the newspaper that were within my price range, and we went to see them. A couple were real dumps, and the others were in scary sections of town. We continued to search each day, and I continued to try to reach the kids. I had been in Chicago for almost a week and hadn't talked to Meadow and Jeremy once since I got there. I was starting to feel desperate.

Finally, I called, and Dick picked up the phone. "Hello?" he said in his most lackluster voice, which was his habit.

"Hi Dick, can I please speak to Meadow and Jeremy?"

"…No."

"No? Why not?"

"They don't want to talk to you."

"What?"

"They want to stay here. They don't want to live in Chicago." I got a scramble of bees in my stomach and grabbed the phone like it was my lifeline.

"Please, Dick, let me talk to them."

"No, you wanna talk to 'em? You come here." And he hung up. I screamed at the phone.

"No! Dick, no!" I burst into tears. Then I stopped, pulled myself together, packed my things, and wrote Lois a note. Before I left, I called Bruno and told him what happened.

Most of that six-hour trip back to Louisville, I spent stewing, thinking about the unthinkable. What if Dick wouldn't let me have Meadow and Jeremy back? What if he made good on his promise from long ago and disappeared with them?

The minute I got to Mom's house, I called Dick. No answer. I continued calling until Dick finally picked up.

"Hello?" My heart pounded.

"Hi, Dick," I said. "I'm in Louisville, and I want to see Meadow and Jeremy." Silence. "I could come out there, or we could meet someplace."

Silence. "OK." My blood started to boil. I fought back tears. "I've got some things to do in town tomorrow." Of course, everything had to suit his schedule. "I'll meet you at Hogan's Fountain in the park at noon." I thanked him, and we hung up. I immediately called my lawyer.

"Phil, Dick said the kids don't want to talk to me, and that they don't want to live in Chicago. I know it's a bunch of bullshit, but I don't know what to do! I've called at least once a day to talk to the kids, and most of the time, I haven't been able to. I'm going crazy!"

"OK, what exactly did he say?" Phil's mellow voice calmed my nerves for a second.

"He said Meadow and Jeremy want to live out there with them."

"I see, hmm. It sounds like Dick might be preparing to contest the custody agreement."

"Oh, my God! Can he do that?"

Phil told me it was possible and that I needed to prepare while he set up a court date. Which meant I had to rent an apartment in Chicago, enroll the children in school, and look for a job.

"OK. Thank you, Phil. I'll take care of it as soon as I get back!"

I got to Hogan's Fountain ten minutes early to meet Dick and the kids. I was nervous and fidgety, and had a full set of living knots twisting in my stomach. It was a gorgeous fall day. Big, billowy clouds floated through the bright blue sky, and a warm breeze blew through my hair.

I noticed there were surprisingly few children around, then remembered that some schools had already started, and that lots of the little guys must be in classrooms. But the park was alive with squirrels and chipmunks, and cardinals and jays filled the air with song.

Dick was ten nerve-wracking minutes late—typical passive-aggressive move. Finally, I saw his truck pull up, and the door swing open. Meadow and Jeremy came barreling toward me.

"Mommy!" they yelled. I struggled to keep my tears inside, to keep up a happy front for their sake. The three of us hugged and danced around. Then we played on the swings and the jungle gym while we talked about what they'd been doing with their stepbrothers and sisters. Dick just leaned against his truck and glared at us like a hawk eyeing its prey.

"Why didn't you call us, Mommy?" Meadow asked.

"Yeah," Jeremy said. "You were posta call evwy day."

"I did, sweethearts. I called you every day, but you all must've been playing because nobody answered the phone."

"Oh, OK," Jeremy said. "Let's play monstow!" And the games began. I chased them around the swings, and seesaws, and all over the grassy park.

About twenty minutes later, Dick called out, "Hey, guys, it's time to go." I was crushed, but didn't want to stir up any animosity in front of the kids, or that close to the custody hearing, so I forced myself to remain cheerful.

Meadow and Jeremy stopped chasing and looked at me, disappointed and confused. I rounded them up in my arms, and we hugged each other tight. "Listen," I whispered. "I'm going to see you all soon, OK? Your dad and I love you very much. We just have to figure some things out. Don't be sad, OK? Have fun and I'll see you real soon!" They looked at me with sad eyes. My heart broke.

"Guys, come on, let's get going." Patience was never one of his virtues.

The kids looked scared. "It's OK, sweethearts. I promise I'll see you real soon. I love you so much." We hugged even tighter, and I walked them to their dad's truck.

The next day, I drove back to Chicago faster than I should have. As soon as I got there, I devoted all my time to looking for an apartment. I found one a couple of days later in a nice working-class neighborhood. It had only two bedrooms, but it also had a big living room, and a family room. So, Jeremy and Meadow could each have their own rooms, and I could turn the family room into my bedroom. The place had lots of windows and was conveniently located over a small market on the northwest side of Chicago. I rented it. The bonus was a public elementary school only three blocks away. I also looked for waitressing jobs and got some interest, but nothing definite.

I called Phil and told him about renting the apartment and enrolling the kids in a nearby school. He was very pleased and told me our court date was scheduled for the following Friday.

Bruno was a huge help through all of it, not to mention the perfect distraction during those stressful days of driving back and forth from Louisville to Chicago. "It sounds like Phil knows his stuff," he'd say when I became overwhelmed with fear about losing the kids. He seemed to know the right thing to say to quell my fears.

Before I made what I hoped would be my last trip to Louisville for a while, I drove to Bruno's apartment to say goodbye. He took me in his big, strong arms, and whispered, "Go get 'em!"

I nodded, and with his words echoing in my head, I got in my car and headed out.

That drive back to Louisville was exhausting. First of all, I was sleep-deprived. I hadn't slept well since the whole nightmare began. And I was crazy anxious trying to gear up for the battle of my lifetime.

When I got to Mom and Dad's house, Mom had prepared my favorite comfort food for supper: pork ribs boiled in sauerkraut. I loved being with my folks. We discussed everything, even talked about the remote possibility of me moving back to Louisville if I had to—they liked that idea best. I did not. Then I tried to sleep, which went better than expected, probably because my belly was stuffed with ribs and sauerkraut.

The big day arrived, and I was ready. I wore my new lavender skirt and matching suit jacket, styled my hair, and put on minimal makeup. I looked very prim and proper, like the poster child for the perfect working single mother. The courtroom was small, but intimidating. It sucked the air right out of me. Phil and I sat in the gallery and waited our turn. I glanced at the door often, my stomach tied up in knots.

Eventually, Dick, Penny, Meadow, and Jeremy entered the courtroom. Tears came to my eyes and my heart choked. I took a deep breath. They looked like they had just stepped off the set of *Little House on the Prairie*. Meadow and Penny wore long countrified dresses, and Jeremy and Dick were in farmhand clothes. They were a sight to behold. I smiled. I knew what Dick was going for. He was hoping their old-fashioned, poor farmer look would engender sympathy from the judge. But Phil had already informed me that the judge who was trying our case was very straitlaced and conservative. He also favored the mother maintaining custody of the children.

Then, who I assumed was Dick's lawyer, came through the door. A tall cowboy-hatted, cowboy-booted, plaid-shirted dude, wearing none other than a bolo tie. He removed his hat the minute he entered the courtroom, exposing his greased-back 'do. I relaxed some after seeing the likes of Dick's lawyer. The second I saw Meadow and Jeremy, my heart leaped, and tears filled my eyes. I gave a small wave to them. They looked up at their dad. Then, without smiling, they surreptitiously waved back.

The judge was an older gentleman with salt-and-pepper hair cut short. He maintained a serious expression, but when he smiled, a kindness shone through. Or maybe it was just my wishful thinking.

Our case came up, and the judge read a document silently to himself. Then he looked at both lawyers and addressed them. "Why is the court being asked to consider a change in the custody arrangement?"

Dick's lawyer stood, and said something about me moving to Chicago, and how it wasn't fair because the children's father wouldn't get to have his rightful visitations. He also mentioned that Dick had remarried a wonderful woman, a mother of seven children, like the fact that Meadow and Jeremy would now have seven stepsiblings to contend with was a good thing. It didn't seem like the smartest move to me.

Then it was Phil's turn to speak. "Your honor, my client went to Chicago to look for work, and she has already secured an apartment with a good elementary school within walking distance." It was short and simple. He may have said something about my bringing the kids to Dick's place for summer vacations. I was so out of my mind with worry I didn't remember.

The judge looked at me, then at the cast of *Little House on the Prairie*, and shook his head. "I see no reason to change the custody arrangement. Motion denied. Case dismissed." He banged his gavel. I gasped, and tears filled my eyes.

I turned and hugged Phil. "Thank you, Phil. Thank you so much!" I ran to the kids, didn't even glance at Dick, just scooped Meadow and Jeremy up in my arms, and held on for dear life.

Everything else disappeared.

CHAPTER FORTY-ONE

1982

Sweet Home Chicago

THE KIDS AND I WENT TO MOM AND DAD'S HOUSE AFTER THE CUSTODY hearing and had a wonderful celebratory supper of leftover ribs and sauerkraut—they were even more delicious the day after Momma made them. After gobbling down too much dinner, Mom presented us with a special surprise—pineapple upside-down cake, one of our favorites.

Once we polished off most of the cake, we left the dishes and cleanup for whenever, so we could continue the party by playing our version of charades. Meadow and Jeremy huddled in a corner of the living room and whispered about what to act out—movies they'd seen, books they loved, people we knew, or animals. While they figured things out, they'd shoot threatening, accusatory glances our way to make sure we weren't listening in.

We adults made ourselves comfortable and waited to be entertained. When the kids were ready, they launched into big, elaborate pantomimes. Jeremy went first; he wiggled his nose, contorted his little face, and held his hands up like puppy-dog paws.

"A pig!" Dad yelled. Jeremy fell on the floor in hysterics, and the rest of us burst out in guffaws. There was always lots of laughter. My heart was so full being with my little guys again.

Watching them emote and dance around brought tears of joy to my eyes and much-needed nourishment to my soul.

We played and talked until way past the kids' bedtime. Finally, when we were exhausted and laughed out, we got ready for bed. I fell asleep with the kids curled up next to me on the hide-a-bed in Dad's office/art room. An hour or so later, I woke up and gently untangled myself from their small arms and legs, kissed them on their precious heads, and moved to my own bed where I got the best night's sleep I'd had in weeks.

Late next morning, I opened my eyes to sunshine filtering through the sheers. We had all slept in, and not a creature was stirring but me.

Mom and Dad's current house was the modern, plain-Jane place they'd bought across the street from Reverend Slider. It was meant to be the home that Packy would come back to. But shortly before the house sale was final, Packy committed suicide. The house was small and simple, boring really, and ordinary, as was the neighborhood. However, it was free of the dark, chaotic, mysterious energy the old house had taken on after our family lived in it for too long.

I lay there, in the small guest bedroom, looking around at Dad's artwork. His ceramic birds were perched on every surface, and his paintings hung on the walls depicting his beloved hunting trips: doves, quail, and pheasant flying over marshy lakes in dim predawn light. Every one was evocative of the wilderness at that intensely quiet time before the sun comes up when the silence is broken only by birdsong. Each painting was different, yet similar, all representing Daddy's love of his old hunting days before his hips gave out. I remembered, as a little girl, watching him clean the birds he'd shot or the fish he'd caught. He would set himself up at the kitchen sink in his ratty, old, stinky hunting gear with pockets. He'd be up to his elbows in feathers, blood, or fish guts. It was so gross, but it never bothered him in the least.

Freshly killed doves were everybody's favorite. Momma would sauté the naked little birds in bacon grease or butter, and salt and pepper, and the whole house would fill with the mouthwatering smell.

There was hardly any meat on the tiny things, but the taste of each morsel was so rich and delicate you wanted to crunch on the bones as well. I'd ask for a second, but there were usually only enough for each of us to have one.

I stretched, so relieved that the hearing was over, and I still had custody of Meadow and Jeremy. And it was all thanks to Phil, my hero. I closed my eyes, appreciating whatever benevolent universal forces had been at work the day before, and dozed off into a sweet dream.

I was floating on a large, oddly shaped, pastel-pink raft in the middle of a crystal-clear, blue lake. It was a gorgeous day, and I hadn't a care in the world. I looked around at the beautiful, budding forest surrounding the lake. Then I heard giggling and whispers. I glanced over my shoulder and saw Meadow and Jeremy waving at me from the shore.

Suddenly, out of nowhere, I heard a loud voice. "G'mornin', Mommy!" I was ripped from my dream as both kids pounced on me. I laughed and mused, *what a perfect way to wake up.*

"When did you leave our bed, Momma?" asked Meadow.

"I didn't." I looked around the room. "Wait a minute, where am I?" The kids laughed, and I lifted the covers. "Get in here!" They scampered in next to me, and we cuddled a while.

Then Mom leaned in the doorway. "Who's ready for some special banana, clown-face pancakes?" The kids exploded with excitement, scrambled out of my arms, and followed Mom out to the kitchen.

"I get to put on the waisins!" Jeremy screamed. And the day was off.

After the yummy breakfast, we packed up our clothes, smothered Mom with goodbye kisses and hugs, and hit the road. It was a perfect travel day, bright and cool, one of those nostalgic fall days that brought back memories of all the Halloweens from the past. We had lots of catching up to do, and the time flew by. I told them about meeting odd people called agents, and about my auditions, and described our new apartment. I even told them I met a sweet man named Bruno.

"Like the dog?" Jeremy asked. "Is yow new boyfwend a dog, Momma?" We laughed. "Hey, I wanna be Spidowman for Halloween," he declared. "Can you make me a costume?"

"Oh, yes! What a great idea!" Then they told me about living at their dad's house with their huge, new stepfamily.

"Sometimes Becky is kinda mean to us, though," Meadow said. She was nine by then and told me Becky was fifteen.

"Yeah," Jeremy said. "And we don't even do anything bad."

"Oh, dear, tell me what happened?"

"Is Daddy gonna be OK, Momma?" Jeremy blurted out.

"Yeah, he was really sad when we left."

"I know, but, honey, your daddy is very busy with work, and Penny, and all her kids. He'll be fine. Besides, I'm going to take you guys back to his place in a few weeks, and you'll get to spend a couple of days with him." That seemed to satisfy their concerns.

We arrived in Chicago and drove to our new address. I parked on a side street, and the kids and I got out of the car and walked along the tree-lined street to the corner where our new place was on the second floor. The weather was sunny and chilly.

"Is that a grocery store?" Meadow asked.

Jeremy ran and looked in the window. "Yeah! And look, they got toys too!"

Then Meadow pulled me down to her level and whispered in my ear. "Momma, there's a man watching us." She pointed to him.

I looked up, and there stood Bruno quietly spying on us.

I smiled, and so did he. "Hi. Guys, this is Bruno." He smiled, stuck his hands in his pockets, and edged a step or two closer. "This is Meadow and Jeremy."

"Hi," Bruno said. "Have you seen your new apartment yet?"

They shook their heads.

"Hey, guys, what do you think?" I said. "Shall we all go up?"

Jeremy looked at me, then at Bruno, and walked over, took Bruno's hand, and looked up at him. "Hi, Bwuno. Yeah, let's all go up. I thought you wu a dog."

The kids loved our bright, new, roomy apartment home. They especially loved having their own rooms. I made pretty, ruffly curtains for Meadow's room and bought cowboy sheets for Jeremy's. Bruno fit right in with our little family. He was a natural with kids. Meadow and Jeremy took to him immediately. So, by January, I asked him to move in with us.

Stone Academy was your typical public grammar school—not great, but not horrible—and was only a three-block walk from our apartment. A month or so later, the kids informed me that some of the teachers were too old, mean, and rigid to still be alive, let alone teaching. But both kids excelled in the beginning because they had been attending the small, excellent Montessori school in Louisville, and were ahead of the game academically.

Every so often, Dick would call to talk to Meadow and Jeremy. And sometimes, I'd pretend to be doing something in the kitchen, so I could eavesdrop on the kids' side of their conversation. I could easily fill in Dick's side of the call by the kids' reaction. Meadow and Jeremy would go from happily playing, to being deflated and sad, often to the point of tears. "I miss you so much," he had probably said, in his most "poor me" voice steeped in self-pity. He always preyed on their sympathies, when really, according to the kids, he hardly spent any time with them when they were at his house.

Other than the occasional, deadly, depressing calls from their dad, things were good. The kids developed friendships at school and started going to birthday parties and school functions. I'd walk them to school every morning, then go on auditions. We got a nice routine going, and I landed a few commercials, and some industrial films, as well. Bruno was always there to stay with the kids when I had acting work.

After getting settled in Chicago, sometimes, the kids had trouble sleeping. In the middle of the night, I'd hear little footsteps creep into my room. I'd look up, and there one of them would be, staring at me with tears in their eyes.

One morning, while they were snuggled close to me, I asked what it was that had frightened them. They'd say "scary dreams" but wouldn't remember them, so that would be the end of it. Then I noticed the nightmares seemed to happen more frequently after the kids spent a few days at their dad's house.

One Saturday afternoon, while Jeremy was playing ball in the park with a friend, I poked my head into Meadow's room. She was busily organizing her doll's clothes and jewels.

"Meadow, sweetheart, is Becky still being mean to you and Jeremy when you go to your dad's?"

"Yeah," she said matter-of-factly.

"Oh, dear." I went and sat on her bed. "Can you tell me what she does? I mean, does she hit you or—"

"No… it's weird, Mom." Meadow continued futzing with her dolls while she talked. "She plays these weird games. And when it gets dark out, she always talks about *The Tailor*, this monster, sorta like an old man who lives in mirrors and only comes out late at night to hurt and stab people…"

Shit! I was shocked and enraged at the same time. I had to fight my maternal instincts, and stop myself from driving to Dick's house right then and there, and torching the place with every one of them inside.

I took a breath. "Oh, honey, doesn't your dad do anything about it?"

"No, he doesn't even know anything. He's too busy."

"Huh, well… how about Penny?" Meadow shook her head. "Do you tell her about what Becky does?"

Meadow stopped what she was doing and turned to me. "Mom, it's different when we're there. Nobody listens to me and Jeremy. Nobody cares about us." I winced. It felt like I'd been punched in the gut. Blood rushed to my head, and I fell silent. Then a wave of anger bubbled up, so ferocious I could taste it. I went to Meadow and hugged her.

"I'm so sorry, honey." She hugged me back for a second.

"I know, Mom." Then she pushed me away and went back to her doll clothes.

"I'll talk to your dad—"

"No." She turned to me. "Don't. He won't listen anyway. And it'll only make it weirder when we're there."

I left her to her organizing and went to the kitchen—the farthest room from her bedroom. I didn't want her to hear me cry. I was heartbroken and furious. I folded myself over the kitchen counter and sobbed.

After that day, things changed. I didn't want to make the kids' trips to their dad's more uncomfortable by tattling on Penny's teenagers. So, I made up any excuse I could think of why their visitations were shorter. I told Dick they had school functions, meetings with their teachers, extracurricular classes, or plans with friends. And when he objected, I reminded him that he hadn't paid child support in months. That shut him up for a while.

But shortening the time Meadow and Jeremy spent at their dad's didn't seem to help the nightmares. And when I'd pick them up from his house, they were different for a day or two, quieter than usual, out of sorts, and moody.

So, while the kids were at school, I called Phil and told him that Dick hadn't paid any child support since we moved to Chicago and that his stepkids were bullying and terrorizing Meadow and Jeremy, and that we had to do something.

"Oh, dear. What would you like to do?"

"What can we do?"

"Well, if you report him, and he doesn't pay the back child support, he could go to jail."

"Oh my God, no! That would crush the kids."

"OK, how do you feel about bargaining with him? Would you accept a lump sum of a lesser amount as a back child support settlement in exchange for limiting his visitation rights?"

"Yes, that would be great, Phil. Meadow and Jeremy don't want to go there very much anyway. I mean, they'd like to see their dad, but..."

"Hmm," he said. "Would you like to stop the mandatory visitations altogether?"

"Can we do that?"

"We can offer Dick a deal. I'll tell his attorney that if Dick pays a reduced amount of his delinquent child support, and he gives up his visitation rights, he will no longer be required to pay any child support. How does that sound?"

"That sounds amazing! Thank you, Phil!"

"Let's hope it works."

"Knowing Dick, it will."

I was thrilled. I had gotten used to not receiving any money from Dick anyway, and since Bruno was paying half the rent, and I had a few residuals coming in from TV commercials, I knew we'd be alright.

Dick accepted the deal as I had predicted he would, and after that, the kids went to Dick's now and then for short periods of time only when *they* wanted to. Eventually, the nightmares stopped, and we settled into a nice routine in our little northwest Chicago apartment.

CHAPTER FORTY-TWO

1982

Meeting the Family

Living with Bruno in our new Chicago home was lovely. He was a natural. Watching him play with the kids and help them with their homework made me love him even more.

The Christmas before Bruno moved in with us, we all drove back to Louisville to spend the holidays with my folks, and any siblings that decided to show up. Before we made it to Mom and Dad's, we stopped at Dick's house to deliver Meadow and Jeremy, so they could spend a day or two with their dad and stepfamily.

I gave both kids plenty of hugs and kisses. "Now, you guys call me if you want me to come for you sooner. Otherwise, I'll be here to pick you up around noon, day after tomorrow, OK?"

"Yeah, Mom," Meadow said.

"K," Jeremy said. Then they jumped out of the car, opened the front door, and giggled while they dragged Bruno out. They were excited to introduce Bruno to their *other* family. They had told him everything about their dad and stepmom and her kids. I had told him in private, my version of the whole mess. So, Bruno was curious to see what all the fuss was about. I waited in the car. (There had been far too much water under the bridge for me to face Dick and the rest of them.)

Bruno came back to the car a good twenty minutes later.

"Jeez, you think you could've stayed any longer?" He looked at me with a mischievous smile on his face. "So, what'd you think?" I asked and started the car.

Bruno nodded his head and shrugged. "Dick was nice."

"Wow, lucky you. Must've caught him in a good mood."

"Yeah, I think he was making an effort. Penny and her kids were nice too. They made a big to-do over Meadow and Jeremy." On the hour-long drive to Mom and Dad's house, Bruno gave me a blow-by-blow account of his first meeting with Dick and family.

My folks hadn't met Bruno yet, and I thought Christmas would be the perfect time to 'present' him to the family, and let him see for himself why I was the way I was.

Bruno was charming, as always, and was a huge hit. Most of my siblings, their kids, and spouses were there, as well as a few cousins, and lots of family friends. It was our usual wild, fly-by-the-seat-of-our-pants kind of boisterous holiday. Bruno learned a lot, and made the best of all the nonsense.

When Mom got on her Christianity soapbox or questioned Bruno about being raised Catholic—she was always searching for more dirt on the old religion—Bruno told her the good and bad aspects of the church as he saw it. He never shied away from getting to the heart of the matter in any discussion. He told her about his immigrant parents' harsh, as he considered it, misconceptions about the Catholic teachings, and how his mother, in particular, hammered them into his brain. He mentioned a few vindictive, misguided priests and sadistic nuns he'd had the misfortune to have as teachers in his Catholic grammar school days. But also about his uplifting, enlightened religious teachers who believed in their students, and who took him under their wings, inspired him, and taught the purest form of Catholicism. Mom was impressed. She liked Bruno. Nothing made her happier than a good, honest, sharing of opinions.

After Christmas break was over, we all drove back home to Chicago, and Meadow and Jeremy went back to school. Soon after, I introduced the kids to Harrise, who had become my favorite agent. Harrise was great, easy to talk to, kind, and possibly the closest thing to a real person a talent agent could get.

We walked into her office, and Harrise was sitting behind her desk. She was a natural beauty and, as far as I could tell, seldom wore any makeup. Harrise was in her forties and had black, naturally curly, shoulder-length hair with occasional strands of silver running through it.

Behind her were large windows spanning almost the entire wall overlooking Michigan Avenue and the Magnificent Mile. The view was awe-inspiring. The classical architecture, top-of-the-line department stores, and restaurants with a sliver of Lake Michigan in sight. It was spectacular.

"Hi, Harrise. Hey, guys, this is Harrise."

"Hi," they said.

"Well, hello." Harrise gave them a big smile. "Your mom has told me so much about you." She stood up and reached a hand across her desk.

"Hi," Meadow and Jeremy said again, almost in unison. They giggled and shook her hand.

Harrise's office was very welcoming. A healthy-looking Ficus tree was in a corner, and some kind of leafy plant sat next to the clutter of papers on her desk. Headshots of the actors she represented covered one wall, and several framed pictures of her smiling kids and family were on her desk. Her office always smelled of freshly cut daisies.

Harrise leaned her head to one side, stared at the kids for a moment, and said, "I think I may have something..." She shuffled through a stack of papers, pulled one out, and looked at it.

"Here it is... I'm holding a casting session tomorrow for a local TV commercial, and you two are just the right ages. Would you like to audition for it?"

They both looked at me. "Can we, Mom?" Meadow asked.

"Yeah, Mom, can we?" And that was the beginning of a whole new adventure.

Soon, we were all auditioning for plays, films, TV shows, commercials, and industrial films. Chicago was just a booming actor's paradise full of opportunities and possibilities.

One day, I auditioned for a commercial and met Jenna, a fellow auditioner. We really hit it off, and since we had to wait for a good hour to audition, we spent the time getting to know each other. It turned out that her boyfriend, John, had gone to Goodman Theatre School at the same time as Bruno, and they probably knew each other. So, we thought it would be fun for us to have dinner together. Jenna and I exchanged phone numbers and set a time for the four of us to meet on the following Friday at a popular restaurant.

As soon as I got back to the apartment, I told Bruno about meeting Jenna and that her boyfriend, John, had gone to Goodman also.

"Do you remember him, honey?" Bruno was making himself a sandwich in the kitchen. I headed back to our bedroom to change out of my 'nice casual' audition clothes.

"Oh yeah."

"Yeah? Great, because we're meeting them for dinner on Friday."

"Oh God, no! Why?"

I was used to this response. For all the things I loved about Bruno, he could be fairly antisocial. He found small talk unbearable and a big waste of time. Ironically, though, he was often the life of any party, but afterwards, he would insist that he did not have a good time. What he loved most was a good, in-depth conversation, sharing ideas one-on-one, or with a few close friends.

I came out to the kitchen and found he'd stopped what he'd been doing, mid-sandwich, and was glaring at me.

"Oh, come on, honey, it'll be fun. We don't have many friends and hardly ever go out. We can get Ruth and Ben to babysit." Ruth and Ben were an older Jewish couple who lived in the apartment next to us. They had been married forever and were real characters.

"No." Bruno turned to me and threw his hands in the air. "John and I were never friends. In school he'd copy everything I did; the same monologues and scenes, whatever. He was always super competitive with me." He exhaled deeply.

"Oh. I'm sorry, honey… well… I have Jenna's phone number; I'll call and cancel. Tell her we have, um… tell her I forgot that we already had plans on Friday. Or maybe I'll just go."

Bruno crossed his arms and glared at me.

"Sorry."

"Fine." He rolled his eyes. "I'll go, damn it… but please check with me next time, *before* you make plans for us, OK?"

I agreed. We did go to dinner on Friday with John and Jenna, and I had a great time. But apparently, and you would never have guessed it, my other half did not. We double-dated one more time, thanks to much whining on my part, but after that Bruno put his foot down and refused to go anywhere with them. I'd always been more social than Bruno. It was like pulling teeth to get him to go to parties or any place where he might have to speak to other humans he didn't already know.

Several months later, Harrise called about a possible audition for the kids. Apparently, Goodman Theatre was going to produce Tennessee Williams's play, *A House Not Meant to Stand,* and the kids were eight and ten, just the right ages for two small roles.

As soon as they got home from school and took off their rain coats and galoshes, I hollered, "Hey, guys, you want to audition for a play at Goodman?"

"Yeah!" Jeremy said. "What play?" He came bounding into the living room, caked galoshes and all.

"Hey, mister!" I pointed down at his feet. Big blobs of dirty snow and ice were shedding everywhere. "Jeremy! Look what you're doing!" He looked down.

"Oops… sowwy." He galloped out of the room, and I grabbed a dirty towel and started mopping up the mess. Seconds later, he reappeared, sans galoshes. "What's the play about, Momma?"

"Don't know, honey. But it was written by a famous playwright."

"When?" Meadow called from her room. "Would I have to miss any school?"

"Don't think so, honey."

"Are there a lot of lines?"

"No," I said. "That's the good part. You'd be auditioning for the roles of two little ghosts."

Jeremy laughed. "Is the play scawwy?"

"Sounds like it might be. You'll probably have to make ghost sounds."

"Yeah, yeah, yeah!" Jeremy screamed and danced around the room making faces and spooky sounds. "Wooooo! I wanna be a ghost! Come on, Meadow." He danced around her. "Come on, Meadow, be a ghost with me!"

She laughed and finally agreed. I set up their auditions.

A couple of snowy days later, I picked the kids up from school and drove as fast as I could over the slushy streets. I parked the car in the theater parking lot, and we ran through the ferocious wind and cold and got through the huge doors of Goodman Theatre just in time. The kids said the audition people just asked them a bunch of questions and laughed when Jeremy made ghost noises. It was fun, they said, and they thought the people really liked them.

Turned out they were right because they got the roles!

There was a third little ghost played by Jamie, who became a good friend of the kids, and the three of them had a blast. (Sometimes they had too much fun and had to be reprimanded.)

The play got mixed reviews, but was well received with almost sold-out houses. Mom and Dad made a special trip up from Louisville to see the show and celebrate with us. Then the production got into a new play festival, and the kids and I got to enjoy a vacation in Florida while they performed for a week in the festival.

CHAPTER FORTY-THREE

1983

Loss of Heart

When the play ended, Meadow, Jeremy and I flew home with lots of stories to share with Bruno. We settled back into our routine while the kids finished up the last few days of the school year.

One afternoon while we were happily chatting about what to do for summer vacation, the phone rang, and I picked up. "Hello?"

"Reedy." It was my brother Jud.

"Hi, Jud, how're you doing?" I was surprised to hear from him; we weren't exactly close. I couldn't remember the last time he called me.

"I've got some sad news. Mom had a heart attack, and the paramedics couldn't save her."

I gasped, "Oh my God!"

"Yeah, she didn't make it."

I started sobbing when Meadow came in from the other room and looked at me with concern.

"What, Momma?" I looked up at the innocent, frightened face of my daughter and stopped myself. I don't remember what I did with the phone, but I think I just laid it down on the couch.

Then Jeremy came up beside his sister. "What wong, Momma?" he said, tears already on their way.

So, I tightened my grip, slowed the tears down as best I could, and took them both on my lap. "Oh, sweethearts, it's gonna be OK. That was your Uncle Jud." I stroked their hair. "Muddy had a heart attack, and, sweethearts, I'm afraid the medical people couldn't make her better." They both started crying. "But listen, now she's up in heaven with Jesus," I managed to say through sobs. "You remember how much Muddy loves Jesus?" We piled onto the couch in one sad lump.

Bruno had been making a dinner of smoked pork butt with cabbage, potatoes, and carrots. He stood by the kitchen door holding the big wooden spoon. The whole apartment smelled delicious. He came and sat on the coffee table close by. Then he reached out and grabbed my hand. I pulled him into our huddle, and he held us while the kids and I had ourselves a good, long cry.

Finally, I said, "Guys, let's call Papaw, OK?" We continued to cry, and I dialed the phone.

"Hello?" I could tell Dad had been crying and was trying to hold it together.

"Oh, Daddy, are you OK?"

"Hi, sweetheart… not really."

"Were you with Momma when it happened?"

"Yes, honey, your mom and I made love for two hours. Then I went out to the kitchen while she used the bathroom." He broke down in sobs, and so did I. "Sorry, honey. I called out to her, and when she didn't answer, I got scared."

Ten years earlier, Dad had to have both of his hip joints replaced. That was in the early 1970s, and they didn't have the procedure perfected back then. So, his legs didn't work so well anymore. He was only able to walk very slowly with two canes. He said that by the time he got back to check on Mom and call for an ambulance, it was too late. He was heartbroken. The kids both talked to Dad, and he comforted them, and we all cried some more.

I took the phone back. "We'll drive down tomorrow, Daddy. Are you gonna be alright tonight?"

"I'll be fine, honey. That'll be nice. Don't hurry. Just be careful." Then Bruno, the kids, and I shared our favorite stories about Mom while we cried and ate some of the delicious dinner Bruno had made.

After supper, I cuddled with Meadow and Jeremy in the big bed while Bruno did the dishes. Once they were sound asleep, I moved them to their beds. Then, I quietly grieved for hours while Bruno listened patiently and comforted me until the wee small hours of the morning when I could no longer keep my eyes open.

We drove to Dad's the next day and stayed with him for a week. There was no one like my mother; she was one of a kind. She believed in every one of her children furiously, with every fiber of her being. She'd always try her darndest to straighten us out when she thought we were headed in the wrong direction, but would never abandon us, no matter how misdirected or pigheaded we were.

Family and friends joined us at Dad's house bearing gifts, flowers, and delicious delicacies all week long. We celebrated Mom's life in royal fashion. She was stubborn and opinionated, but would have sacrificed her life in a heartbeat to save any one of us. I missed her more than I ever thought I would miss anybody. She was my rock. I missed her every day.

CHAPTER FORTY-FOUR

1984

Moving On

A year later, Bruno's funds were diminishing due to lack of well-paying commercial acting jobs. He and I had been studying improv at Second City where he continually caught the eye of, and got the highest praise in class from, our teacher, the renowned acting coach Del Close. Bruno also got excellent reviews in the stage productions he was in, but the money wasn't cutting it. So, he started doing odd jobs. He advertised in various laundromats and grocery stores and was soon working many hours a week as a handyman. He hated it. He didn't want to fix toilets. He wanted to make a living doing what he loved. He became more and more discouraged. (And less and less enjoyable to live with.) Until finally, he decided to follow his dream and move to Los Angeles.

He wanted us to come along, but we didn't have enough money for all of us to move across country. I was already well established within the Chicago acting community and was bringing in enough money to keep us going.

Also, Meadow had just gotten into Francis Parker, an excellent private school with exceptional arts and theater departments, as well as a reputation for being progressive by nurturing the best in each student. (The school wasn't cheap, but had a low-income sliding scale, which helped.) Meadow and Jeremy had both been on a long waiting list, and once she got a placement, there was no way we were moving anywhere.

So, we said our long, tearful goodbyes to Bruno, and he left. A few weeks later, we went to visit him. It was a long flight, but Los Angeles was awesome. It was beautiful and hot, but dry and cool at night. We loved it. The kids and I were used to the soul-sucking humidity of Chicago, so it felt like we'd landed in heaven.

Bruno was staying temporarily with an old Chicago friend in a not-so-great area while he looked for an apartment of his own. He was the perfect host and took us to beautiful downtown Burbank and to the studios where TV shows were shot, and to Hollywood, and Grauman's Chinese Theater with the footprints of all the big, famous movie stars, and to Disneyland. "Best vacation ever!" according to Meadow and Jeremy. After our visit, the kids and I talked to him on the phone often.

Then a month later, when he called, he sounded different. "How's it going, honey?"

"Good… good, I got a job at Disney Studios playing a clown."

"Oh wow! Perfect!"

"Yeah, it's only a couple hours a week, and doesn't pay much, but it's fun, and I'm making some good contacts. How're you guys doing?"

"We're doing OK. Jeremy's playing his guitar. Can you hear him?" I held the phone out. "He's getting good, can play three whole songs now. We miss you."

"Um, yeah," he said. "About that… um, I've met someone." My heart sank. Even though I was already dating a couple of guys, I still loved Bruno. Then he said, "And, um…we're only seeing each other."

"Oh."

"Yeah, I wanted to let you know…"

"OK."

"Look, I hope—"

"I don't want to talk anymore." I hung up. After that, there were no more phone calls for a while, no contact whatsoever. The kids and I talked about it a lot—I explained the situation as best as I could, and I think they kind of understood. The three of us cuddled a lot and consoled ourselves and talked shit about Bruno.

Gradually, Meadow, Jeremy, and I got used to a Bruno-less life. Meadow loved the school and made new friends. We were doing OK. We got busier with auditions, acting classes, and other extracurricular activities like sports, dance lessons, and plays.

Soon, I started dating someone new, and Meadow, who was fast approaching puberty, was not happy. He was not to her liking at all— at least, that's what she expressed incessantly. I couldn't tell if *he* was the problem, or if it was just Meadow's raging hormones expressing themselves.

Except that Jeremy didn't like him either, Jeremy however, was much less vocal with his objections. I liked my new guy, though. John was no Bruno—oh, yeah, that's right. It was the same John that was Jenna's boyfriend, the one Bruno absolutely did not care for. And I understood their opinion, John was no Bruno; he wasn't funny at all. But he did like parties. And people. And me and the kids. And he was interesting.

And he wasn't about to run off to LA and get involved with some new woman.

About the time Bruno left for Los Angeles, Jenna broke up with John (after turning down his elaborate sky-written marriage proposal at a Cubs game, no less!) and moved to Colorado.

Meanwhile, our careers were going great. Both kids were auditioning for local theaters and landing roles in some great plays.

Jeremy got a role in the play *The Accrington Pals* at The Absolute Theater Company, a small but excellent nonunion theater. The play was a World War I drama that had a large cast, and Jeremy was the only kid. He loved being part of the production. During the run of the play, his tenth birthday rolled around, but he wouldn't let me throw him a party because he claimed he had no friends at school. So, on his big day, Jeremy was super bummed.

The plan was that John was going to pick Jeremy up from school and take him to a big toy store so Jeremy could pick out something special for his birthday. Then Meadow and I were going to meet them at John's apartment before John took us all out for a fabulous birthday dinner.

When they opened the door of John's apartment, everything exploded. "Surprise!" Meadow and I yelled.

"Woohoo!"

"Happy birthday, Little Buddy!" hollered the entire cast of the play as they fought their way through balloons and streamers, jumping out from behind furniture, and out of doorways. Some ran in from the kitchen, and we all grabbed Jeremy and danced him around the apartment singing loud songs. "Today is your birthday!" The cast belted out rock tunes at the top of their lungs. "BADABADABA! Here's to birthday buddy boy!"

Jeremy was absolutely stunned at first, but as soon as he figured out what was happening, he got the biggest smile on his face. The whole apartment smelled like his favorite homemade chocolate cake that Meadow and I had baked while he was shopping with John. The dining room table was covered with Jeremy's favorite Mexican food on top of a bright blue happy birthday tablecloth.

We marched him back into John's living room chanting, "Jere-ME! Jere-ME! Jere-ME!" while blowing on kazoos and banging tiny drums and cymbals. Then we dumped him on the couch, everyone dropped to the floor, and the room dissolved into laughter.

Jeremy bounced on the couch. "I thought you all had other plans today."

"That's right, mister!" Elaine hollered over the racket. "You looked so sad yesterday." She wrapped him in a big bear hug. "Now, can you guess what our plans were?"

"Hey, Jer," Derrick said and sat on Jeremy's lap. "Open my present!"

Jeremy giggled, pushed him off, and Derrick handed him a toaster-sized box. The gift was wrapped partially in Christmas wrapping paper, and the rest in paper towels with a little toilet paper thrown in for good measure.

"No!" Greg screamed. He jumped up and wiggled his way between the two until Derrick fell off the couch. "Open mine first." Then Derrick attacked Greg, wrestled him to the floor while the others joined in. Then Jeremy piled on top, and the fun never stopped. The party turned out better than I could've imagined. John and I just got out of the way and watched it happen. The best part was that Jeremy realized he did have friends, good friends, and that age difference meant nothing.

It was the best surprise party ever. (Yay, Mom!)

Over the next two years, Jeremy and Meadow did plays at their school as well as others with small nonunion theaters. Then Jeremy landed a good-sized role in the play *Galileo*. It was a big Equity production at Goodman Theater. The play was to be performed in their grand main-stage theater, and Brian Dennehy had the title role.

Jeremy loved working with the big-time actors, and even though he was only twelve at the time, he took it very seriously and always behaved professionally. The play was a hit and got excellent reviews.

When Meadow was in her middle teens, she got an audition for a new TV pilot called *Married with Children*. She said she did a great audition and even got a callback, after which the producers immediately wanted to fly her out to Los Angeles for a screen test. Problem was I had too much going on and couldn't go with her.

So, as soon as I found out, I called Bruno. Although our relationship was still strained, he'd kept in contact by calling us a couple times a year, and I really needed a friend out there to make Meadow feel safe and loved.

"Hi!" he said as soon as he heard my voice.

"Hey, I was wondering if you could do me a favor. Day after tomorrow, Meadow's flying out to LA to screen test for a new pilot."

"She is? Wow! Good for her."

"Yeah, she's really psyched. Problem is I've got auditions tomorrow and a bunch of other shit to do, and Jeremy's got this thing… anyway, they wanna see her, like, now, and I know they're going to have a car waiting for her at the airport, but could you—"

"Absolutely!"

I laughed. "Pick her up at the—"

"Absolutely!"

I laughed again. "And take her to—"

"Yes!"

"Thanks, Bruno, I really appreciate it. Meadow says I'm being overprotective, that she'll be fine, but I want her to feel safe, and she'd love to see you anyway."

So, I gave him all her flight information, and he promised to take good care of her. "Fantastic, thanks so much. So, how're you doing?"

"OK."

"OK? Only OK? That's it?" In our occasional, long-distance conversations, we had avoided any topics regarding our personal lives. "What's going on?"

"…Well, um," he stammered.

"Come on, out with it," I demanded.

"Well, I… I kinda sorta had a kid…"

"What? You kinda sorta had a what?"

"A kid…"

"Really? You had a kid. Oh, my God! Boy? Girl? Did you get married?"

"Well… yeah… but it's not what you think. It's not going well." Then he told me the rest of the story about how his girlfriend had gotten pregnant by accident, and how the relationship was already on the rocks before it happened, and that they'd married only days before the birth—his Catholic roots showing again. (He did not want to bring a bastard into the world.)

He said when his son Christopher was born, though, it was the happiest moment of his life.

Then I told *him* I'd been dating John, his old classmate—the man he couldn't stand—for a whole year. In other words, Bruno and I spilled some important, juicy beans to each other. It was tit for tat.

CHAPTER FORTY-FIVE

1988

The Breaks

Bruno picked up Meadow from the Los Angeles airport, and she told me they talked all the way to the hotel the production company had booked for her. He carried her bag up to the room and helped her get settled. She got to see pictures of Christopher, Bruno's baby boy, and they chatted about the pilot she was going to screen test for.

Meadow called me after Bruno left. "Mom, Bruno read my audition scene with me and said I did great."

"Yeah? I'm not surprised, sweetie."

"He said he was really impressed by how prepared I was." She giggled and said how nice the hotel was, and about how unbelievably adorable Baby Christopher was in all his pictures.

The screen test was scheduled first thing the next morning, and her flight back to Chicago was a couple hours later, so her time in LA was short, and she wasn't able to see Bruno again.

When she got home, she said she felt good about her screen test and then forgot about it. A few months later, we watched the pilot of *Married with Children* on TV. Meadow wasn't upset that she didn't get the part because she wasn't a fan of the show.

"I'll tell you this," she said. "It would be a very different show if I had gotten the part." She was right about that. Meadow refused to get sucked into the vapid superficiality of Hollywood. She saw right through all the BS and knew exactly who she wasn't. She had zero interest in adapting to Hollywood's version of an overly developed, precocious, seductively dressed teenage girl. Meadow seldom wore makeup and never dressed provocatively. She was more of a "punk feminist in camo and combat boots" type.

After that, Bruno's phone calls were more frequent. He wouldn't stop talking about young Christopher, and the adorable things his son did, like smile, eat, and gurgle. He talked about his troubled marriage and said he had contacted a lawyer.

Bruno also asked about my current boyfriend John—his old fellow Goodman student that he didn't like. "We're doing just fine. Thank you for asking."

"Hmm, don't you find him the least bit annoying?" then he made a few more wisecracks. "What about that weird nose of his?"

I didn't respond. He was jealous. I was glad. Eventually, Bruno's calls dwindled down to once a month or so.

A couple of years later, he called. "Hey, I'm coming to Chicago."
"You are?"
"Yeah, I've got to take care of a couple of things and see my sister. I was wondering if I could stay at your place?"
"Oh… well, the apartment is pretty small… um, I guess I could sleep over at Eddie's, and you could have my bed." Eddie was my boyfriend at the time. He was a law student ten years my junior whom I'd met while teaching ballroom dance lessons. Eddie was a nice, mild-mannered guy that the kids liked, sort of. By then, Meadow and Jeremy were teenagers and didn't have much interest in Mom and her shenanigans anyway.

The year before, I had found a great, albeit tiny, three-bedroom, one-bath apartment a couple of blocks from Francis Parker, the private school that both kids were then attending.

Bruno was happy with the idea of staying at our apartment. In fact, he was a little too happy.

Months later, he told me that having stayed in my bed was a sign that he was going to literally *get back in my bed.* A 'sign' he called it. The obvious obstacles of us living thousands of miles apart, him being married, and my having a boyfriend didn't seem to matter.

I had already invited some friends over for a little dinner party before I knew Bruno was coming. And the moment he walked through the door, mid-party, I realized I still loved him, like we'd never been apart. There he was, my best friend, the love of my life.

The kids rushed to him. "Bruno!" they yelled. I joined the group hug, then introduced him to my friends and my boyfriend, Eddie. Bruno was once again the life of the party. He was only going to be in town for a few days, so the kids and I monopolized as much of his time as we could. Eddie was very understanding, as he was wont to be.

The morning before Bruno flew back to California, he had to pick up a couple of items from Kmart. So, I joined him. I got in the checkout line, and he came up behind me, enveloped me in one of his special bear hugs, and said, "Ahh, this feels like home…"

A few months later, Jeremy auditioned for the film *Grand Canyon.* Apparently, they were doing a national search for a fifteen-year-old boy to play the role of Roberto, Mary McDonald and Kevin Kline's son. It wasn't the first film Jeremy had auditioned for, but it was the biggest and a good-sized role to boot. He studied his lines by himself. Then he and I worked on the scenes together.

I picked Jeremy up from school the next day and drove him to the audition. He had basketball practice afterwards, so to save time,

I waited in the car. When he came down from Harrise's office, he opened the car door, plopped himself on the seat, and slammed it shut. He looked bummed.

"How'd it go, Jer?"

He shook his head. "Terrible. I don't know why. I knew the lines, but…"

I started the car. "Oh, well, don't worry about it, honey." That didn't help one bit. He was really disappointed in himself. Then, for all the good it did—which wasn't much—I tried to remind him not to fall into the 'actor's trap.'

"Listen, honey, don't stew about what you did or didn't do at the audition. It doesn't help. Maybe you did better than you think."

For an actor, it's almost impossible not to beat yourself up after what you considered a bad audition. You just can't help but run the thing over and over in your head, focusing only on your screwups for days.

Every actor knows what stage fright is. It can sneak up on you unexpectedly once you're in the hot seat, no matter how well prepared you are. You could be in your agent's office, and the moment of truth comes when the video camera light turns on. Or your brain suddenly scrambles when you're staring down the faces of too many distracted, unsympathetic producers—who usually haven't a clue what they're looking for in the first place. In reality, what they want is the actor to bring them some hidden magic, complete the creative process, and make the lines come to life in a unique and memorable way. But to be cool, calm, collected, and creative, and bring your best, most authentic self to the table under that amount of pressure is not easy.

Actors are often treated like trained monkeys. There you are, jittery with nerves and anxiously waiting to perform your best primate tricks. Then, often, the powers that be will quickly judge you, get you the hell out of their office, and move on to the next batch of small apes. This business is not for the faint of heart.

I understood, and sympathized with Jeremy. I had been in his place hundreds of times. So, I changed the subject—the old bait-and-switch. "What time's your basketball practice, honey?"

"Oh, yeah." He sat up a little straighter. "We gotta hurry, or I'm gonna be late." Then we talked about his friends that were going to be there, and about the band he was forming, and about a school project that was due soon. My bait-and-switch plan worked perfectly.

A day or two later, about the time Jeremy had stopped obsessing about what he considered his failed big break, Harrise called.

"Hi, Reedy, is Jeremy around?"

"Hi, Harrise, yeah, hang on." I put the phone down. "Jer, phone's for you." He'd been searching his mess of a room for his baseball mitt and came out to get the call.

"Hello?...I did?" He looked puzzled, but happy. He'd gotten a callback for the movie!

I was only a little surprised because that kind of thing happened a lot. You'd think your audition sucked, that you'd really screwed it up. Then somehow, you'd get a callback, or even the job. There was no way to predict anything in the business.

Jeremy thanked Harrise and handed me back the phone.

The callback was on Friday of the following week, and Jeremy and I were going to be flown to Lawrence Kasdan's Midwest country house! That was writer/producer/director Lawrence Kasdan! *His* Midwest country house! We had never heard of that kind of callback, ever!

Jeremy was shocked, amazed, and determined to be ultra-prepared. Still, every actor knows not to get too excited about the possibility of landing the part—never count your chickens, and all that.

The year before, Jeremy had come extremely close to landing the lead in a children's feature film, but at the last minute, another boy was cast in the role. Harrise said that the producer told her the reason was because Jeremy was too good-looking. It didn't matter if that was a lie or what the real reason was. Jeremy was devastated. He went into his room and cried. I felt like the worst mother ever. I cursed myself for getting the kids involved in this terrible, soul-crushing business.

Heartbroken, I knocked on his door and went in. "I'm so sorry, Jer. You know, maybe it's just not worth it. Maybe you should just stop auditioning and--"

"No, Mom," he barked through his sobs. "I'll get over it. I'm just disappointed."

I was blown away. *Wait a minute, who's the parent here?*

The week before going to the callback, Jeremy studied the script every day. I helped him learn his lines until we both knew them backwards and forwards. Then one of Harrise's agents coached him for a few days. Tara was wonderful. She was gentle and thorough, helping Jeremy to get focused until he felt truly prepared. Tara was an angel.

Jeremy and I were a bit nervous when we knocked on Mr. Kasdan's door. But he graciously welcomed us in, and soon we felt completely at ease.

He led us into his family room—a bright open space with two good-sized brown leather sectional couches, a large mounted TV on the wall, and glass doors looking out into his huge, woodsy backyard.

"Please sit," Mr. Kasdan said. "How was your flight?"

"Good," Jeremy said.

I looked at Jeremy and said, "Except before we even got to the airport."

"Oh, yeah," Jeremy said, and we laughed. "Mom couldn't find me, so she started yelling my name right there in the street."

Mr. Kasdan smiled and asked, "What happened? Did you run off somewhere?"

"No, I just went in this store where they had old clothes and stuff for a minute."

"For a minute? Yeah, right," I said. "I looked all over for you, honey. It freaked me out. I thought we were gonna miss our flight. Or that somebody snatched you!"

"Oh, Mom…"

Mr. Kasdan seemed to enjoy our little banter. We chatted for a while longer about everything from Jeremy's favorite subject in school, to the sports he was into.

"And he's starting a band!"

"You are?" Mr. Kasdan asked. "What instrument do you play?"

"Guitar."

"He writes songs, too," I chimed in. "And sings."

"Wow," Mr. Kasdan said. "Very good. Well, how about you read the scenes for me?" Then he turned to me. "Would you read the mom's part?" I hadn't expected to be Jeremy's scene partner, but I had the lines down, so would I like to read for Mr. Lawrence Kasdan? Oh, hell yes!

We read the scenes a few times, and Mr. Kasdan looked pleased. "Nice, thank you, we'll be in touch."

Then Jeremy and I left for the airport. "That went well. Great job, honey. See? Remember how bad you thought you did on the first audition?" Jeremy nodded. "In this business, ya just never know."

Less than a week later, while the kids were still at school, the phone rang. "Hello?" I said.

"Hi, Reedy," Harrise said.

"Hi, Harrise."

"Are you sitting down?"

"No, should I be?"

"Well, congratulations are in order. Jeremy got the job; he's going to play Roberto in the film *Grand Canyon*."

At that point, I kind of lost it. I've no idea what words came out of my mouth except: "What? Oh, My God!" and "Holy shit, are you kidding me?" and "Thank you, thank you, thank you!" I was about to explode, felt like we'd won the lottery.

After she finished laughing, Harrise said, "They told me Jeremy nailed it. Said they were very impressed when you and he read the scenes together because they could still feel the love underneath the anger when he fought with his mom."

"Oh, Harrise, my God, thank you!" I could hardly contain my excitement.

"Of course. I'll call you next week with your travel information and the shooting schedule. But tonight, why don't you take Jeremy and Meadow out to dinner somewhere nice to celebrate?" I thanked her many more times, and we hung up. I didn't know what to do, where to go, who to tell. I wanted to scream from the top of a mountain! I had to tell somebody. So I called Bruno, and thank God he was home.

"Hello," he said.

"You are not going to believe this… Jeremy got the part in *Grand Canyon*!"

"Oh my God!" He was almost as excited as I was. Then I called my boyfriend, Eddie, and Dad, a few close friends, and even an old boyfriend who lived in New York City.

When Jeremy walked through the door of our apartment, I blurted out, "Jeremy, you got the movie!" We jumped around the apartment for a while, whooping it up. When Meadow got home, we shared his news with her. She hugged him and joined in our celebratory dance. Meadow had graduated from Francis Parker the previous year and was then working at Potbelly's, a local submarine sandwich shop.

We three got all dressed up that evening, just as Harrise had suggested, and splurged by celebrating with a delicious dinner at a nearby, upscale restaurant that was usually well beyond our budget. Jeremy got the filet mignon with garlic-Romano mashed potatoes—the most expensive thing on the menu—and we talked about everything we had to do before flying off into the wild blue yonder. Meadow had been thinking about moving to Hollywood anyway, and this was the perfect opportunity.

CHAPTER FORTY-SIX

1990

Hollywood

Before we left for Los Angeles, I coordinated Jeremy's schoolwork with the production company for his onsite teacher during the shoot and arranged for a friend of Meadow's to house-sit our apartment and take care of Binky, our cat.

Days later, as our trip to California was approaching, I realized I could no longer procrastinate about talking to Eddie. I had some important stuff rolling around my brain.

We got back to his place after a nice cheap dinner at a local Mexican restaurant—he was on a budget because he was putting himself through law school. His apartment was a sparsely furnished one-bedroom in a nice residential neighborhood on the north side of Chicago. It always smelled fresh and clean.

"Eddie, you know, I've been thinking about… well, the kids and I are going to be out in LA for almost three months."

"I know." He took my hand. "I'm really gonna miss you."

"Yeah, I'll miss you too," I was about to embark on one of those dreaded "where is this relationship going?" conversations, and I didn't even know what *I* wanted. Eddie and I had been seeing each other for two years, so I wasn't being unreasonable by looking ahead.

But Eddie was sweet and trusting. In fact, he was a bit of an innocent, and rather fragile. I didn't want to hurt him. "See, we need to talk about… what we're doing here." I waved my hands between us, indicating our relationship.

He cocked his head like a puzzled puppy dog. "What we're doing here?"

"Yeah, you know, like when you finish law school, I mean. Any idea what you want to do then?"

Eddie had been working feverishly on his law courses while at the same time struggling to make ends meet. His self-imposed survival protocol was austere. He had relegated himself to only a small amount of pasta and a vegetable every night for dinner, when he was alone. And he didn't have an ounce of fat on his slender frame.

"Oh." He still looked a bit confused. "Well, I don't know what's going to happen over the next couple of years. I can't commit to anything because I have nothing to offer."

I nodded. "I understand." I was touched. Eddie was a love, but he was in his early thirties, and I was in my forties, a decade older. He had a lot of possibilities ahead of him: a law practice, marriage, children. We had never discussed having a family together, which was out of the question for me. I would soon be facing an empty nest and didn't want to go it alone. I wanted somebody to party with. I continued, "Eddie, I think I need to be open to seeing other people while we're apart."

"Oh." He looked deflated, like a balloon that someone had just punctured, and the air was slowly escaping. I fought with myself not to give in and retract my decision. He said he understood, and even though it was a little awkward after that, we had a few happy dates together before the kids and I left.

We landed at LAX, and as soon as we exited the plane, an official-looking man in a driver's uniform and hat appeared holding a large sign with Jeremy's full name written on it in bold type.

The man's name tag read 'Pete,' and he helped us collect our luggage, and when we walked out of the terminal into the beautiful California sunshine, the kids jumped for joy. It was a spectacular LA day, and Pete was super nice. On the drive to where we would live for the next three months, Pete answered all our questions and laughed while we babbled on about our big adventure.

Pete drove us to the Oakwood Apartments in Culver City, a temporary housing condominium sort of place where production companies often put up the actors that were in town for roles on TV shows or films. Pete carried our luggage in and gave us the shooting schedule. Our two-bedroom apartment had a large living room and a good-sized kitchen. It looked like it had been decorated by Motel 6. But it was perfect. Our suite overlooked the pool and hot tub area, and there was even a workout room inside the building. The production company also supplied us with a car. We had everything we needed.

As soon as Pete left, Meadow and Jeremy rooted through their luggage, flinging clothes everywhere, and found their bathing suits. "We're going for a swim, Mom!" Jeremy said as they both giggled and raced out the door.

"Wait, guys," but it was too late. I was hoping to figure out a plan for dinner, but they were too excited to deal with the mundane, so I called Bruno.

Jeremy's shooting schedule was relatively demanding, and since he was a minor, I was required to be with him. But Bruno and I still managed to squeeze in time to hang out together.

A week later, Bruno took me to the dumpy little house in Tujunga that he and Kitty, his soon-to-be ex-wife, bought before their relationship tanked. Bruno was living in a small, cluttered trailer in the backyard. I got to meet Kitty—which was awkward—and their little toddler, Chris.

One night when Meadow and Jeremy were off with some new friends who also lived in the complex, Bruno came over to the apartment.

We chatted for a while. The sexual tension grew by the minute. Then he said, "So, how's it going with Eddie?"

"OK. He's a little crazy right now. His computer ate a thirty-page paper he was writing for extra credit, and he's trying desperately to recreate it. He's got exams coming up too."

"Uh-huh." Bruno smiled, nodded his head, and made an exasperated 'what the fuck' face. "I mean, are you all… ya know, going steady or what?"

"Oh, no," I said and chuckled. "No." Then Bruno stood up. So did I. He pulled me into his arms and kissed me. I felt chills down to my toes and an overwhelming desire to eat him alive. I pulled away, took him by the hand, led him into my bedroom, and closed the door. I left it open a crack so I could hear when Meadow and Jeremy got back.

I had no idea when they'd be home, so I tried to keep it down. (I could be very *enthusiastic* under such amorous circumstances.) Unfortunately, while Bruno and I were involved in 'extracurricular' activities, Jeremy did come back, and we didn't hear him.

Apparently, he saw my partially closed bedroom door, even peeped into my darkened room, heard *things* going on, turned around, and left. Well, the next morning, I had some 'splainin' to do.

"What is wrong with you, Mom?" Jeremy ranted. "What about Eddie?"

"I'm sorry, honey. Look, Eddie and I had a talk before we left and—"

"God, Mom! Can't you control yourself?" He turned and stormed out the door.

I felt terrible and guilty and like a bad, slutty mother. It remained pretty chilly for a few days between my man-child and myself. But eventually, he cooled off, and I was able to argue my case.

I went into Jeremy's messy room. He was sitting on the bed studying the script. "Honey, can we talk for a minute?" He glared at me. "Look, Jer, I love Bruno. It's not like I had sex with some random dude—"

Jeremy covered his ears. "Mom!"

"Honey, Eddie and I agreed to see other people."

"Does he know? Does Eddie know, Mom?" Jeremy stood up, arms akimbo.

He was only sixteen years old, never had a girlfriend, or even dated really. How could he possibly understand? I was fighting a losing battle, so I gave up.

Soon after our little talk, Jeremy met Julie, a gorgeous young French girl about his age, who had just moved into the complex with her family. About the same time, his shooting schedule got more demanding, and he had to focus on work. Soon, either Jeremy forgot about the incident with Bruno, or he forgave me, or he got too busy to worry about old Mom and her love life. Also, I began to suspect that perhaps he was learning a bit more about love and sex thanks to his new, more worldly "friend." He was growing up!

Meanwhile, Bruno and I were falling back in love—it was so easy. But we had to be discreet around Jeremy and Bruno's soon-to-be ex-wife Kitty as well. So, he and I would sneak in clandestine meetings, and intimate moments, whenever and wherever we could. (Once in the bushes at the arboretum. It was risky, but very romantic.) It seemed Meadow couldn't have cared less. She was too busy bonding with her new friends, finding an agent, and work, and a place to live, so that when Jeremy and I went back to Chicago a few months later, she'd have her own place.

I talked to Eddie once a week or so. Then midway through the shoot, he called when Jeremy and I were about to head out the door for the shooting location. I only picked up the call because I thought it might be the producer with a schedule change.

"Hello?"

"Hi," Eddie said. "I'm coming out to see you next week."

"Oh." *Oh, shit!* "Hi, Eddie. You're what?"

"I booked a flight to come out there." He sounded so happy. I panicked.

"Oh, but… I'm really busy with Jeremy's schedule and everything, and, um, it's just not a good time right now."

"That's OK. I'll rent a car, and when you're busy, I'm sure I can find plenty to do."

Jeremy came from his room, script in hand, and went to the door. "Come on, Mom."

I turned away from him and lowered my voice. "Look, Eddie, I can't talk now, but… I'm seeing Bruno when I can and… I'm sorry, I've got to take Jeremy to work. Can I call you later?"

"Sure. I've been thinking a lot about what I want when I finish law school, and I want to talk—"

"Mom, come on, we gotta go!" Jeremy yelled. He stood by the door and glared at me.

"Yeah, OK, honey. Eddie, I've got to go. I'll call you later."

"OK, bye. Say hi to Meadow and Jeremy for me." It was a very busy day with multiple shooting locations, and I couldn't get back to Eddie until the evening. Fortunately, the kids went for a swim, so I was alone in the apartment when I called.

"Hello?" Eddie said.

"Hi, sorry it's so late. You busy?"

"Oh, hi, yeah, but thanks for giving me a break from this Goddamn paper I have to write."

"Long day, huh?" We talked for a while, and I broke the news to him gently about Bruno and me. I told him that it was not a good time for him to come out.

"I see." He sounded heartbroken. I felt like shit. "OK, I'll cancel my trip. But can we talk about things when you get back? Please don't decide anything until we can talk, OK?"

"OK." I was lying. I'd already thought seriously about moving to LA after Jeremy finished his last year of high school at Francis Parker. But I promised to call Eddie when I got back.

Meanwhile, several talent agents wanted to represent Jeremy—he was on his way! And Meadow took care of business, got herself an agent, and started auditioning soon after. By the time Jeremy and I flew back to Chicago, she had found an apartment, and friends to share it with in Hollywood.

The day after Jeremy and I got back home, I called Eddie. "Hi, we're home."

"How was your flight?" Eddie and I had continued to talk every week or so while the kids and I were in LA. "Can I see you tonight?"

"Sure, but only for a little while because I'm exhausted." So, we agreed to meet at a small park on the beach near Lake Michigan.

It was a warm, muggy, late July evening when I saw Eddie sitting on a bench. As soon as he saw me, he jumped up, gave me a big hug, and then we sat down. He clung tightly to my hand.

"You look great," he said. "I guess California agreed with you."

"I think it did."

"God, I missed you."

"Missed you, too."

"Did Meadow find an apartment?"

"She did, got an agent too, and even had a few auditions."

"Good, that's really good. How is it being home?"

"Well, that's a whole other story. Meadow's friend who was house-sitting our apartment did one hell of a lousy job."

"Uh-oh."

"Oh yeah. When we walked into the apartment, the smell alone was enough to make you hurl, and the place was a wreck. It was filthy, disgusting. I swear, the cat box hadn't been cleaned in… Jesus, I don't know how long, and some of my plants looked like they'd been brutally murdered!"

He chuckled. "Oh no."

"Yep, and except for emptying and scouring that nasty cat box, I was too exhausted to give a damn." Eddie and I chatted for a while. Then there was a pause in the conversation.

I looked out at the horizon and over beautiful Lake Michigan, and noticed that my eyes were stinging. I was jetlagged and hadn't slept well since we left LA.

Finally, Eddie said, "You know, Reedy, while you were away, I thought a lot about everything and realized that… I *am* ready to commit. I want to have a future with you."

"Oh, Eddie, I… Bruno and I got close while I was in LA and—"

"Wait, please." He turned to me and put his arm around my shoulder. "Please don't give up on us yet."

Tears dripped down his face, and soon he was sobbing. "I'm sorry I wasn't able to give you the answer you wanted before. I just needed a little time, you see. Needed to get my head straight."

His nose started running, and having nothing else to wipe it on, he used his sleeve.

"Eddie, honey, please don't blame yourself."

"No, it is my fault. I love you, Reedy, and… and I keep thinking about—see, I have a plan now… when I finish with law school, we'll buy a house and—"

"Eddie, stop, I can't… it's too late." He broke down and cried harder.

"Oh, please, please, it's not too late. Please, not yet. I've got this scene in my mind. You and I are painting the walls of our house… and a drop of paint falls and drips down your shoulder. I wipe it off, and we start playing around, and then we make love right there on the tarp and—"

The sun was setting behind us, painting the billowy clouds, sky, and lake with pinks and deep purples. There had been a rainstorm the day before, and the air smelled amazing. The light slowly diminished, and twilight took over. Such a brilliant, sad sunset. My head throbbed, and I could barely keep my eyes open. I was punchy with exhaustion.

After listening to Eddie's pleading and promises for what seemed like forever, I put my hand on his and said, "Honey, I need to think. I'm sorry. I'm just too out of it. My brain won't function anymore. Let me call you in a few days, OK?"

"OK, I'm sorry. You're tired, I know. You should go. But please keep an open mind. Just think about it."

I stood up. "I will. I promise. I'll call you in a couple of days." He stood, embraced me for a long time. I felt my heart break for Eddie.

It was a melancholy walk back to the apartment. I cried. For him, for me, but mainly from exhaustion. When I got home, Jeremy was out with friends and I went to bed.

A few days later, I made the call—didn't want to, had clusters of knots in my stomach, but made it anyway. "Hello?"

"Hi."

"Hi! How are you? Ya over jet lag yet?"

"Almost. Over the hump anyway. But I've been doing a lot of thinking and… and the truth is…" I so didn't want to hurt Eddie. He was such a sweet guy, and we'd had a fun two years together. But I explained as best I could, feeling horrible and guilty, that after Jeremy finished his last year of high school, he was going to move to LA, and I had decided to move out with him.

At first all he said was, "…I see." It seemed he'd used the few days since we'd met in the park to think about our talk and was ready to accept my decision. It was a short conversation, emotional, gut-wrenching, but short. We both said some kind words to each other and then a final goodbye.

On another front, Meadow and I talked whenever we could reach each other. She was very busy with her new life. She enjoyed living in California, for the most part, and was auditioning a lot. Every now and then, though, she'd complain about the heat, or her roommates, or how she wished she didn't have to work at her "shitty" restaurant job.

Then, a few months later when she called, she sounded different. "Hey, Mom." I thought I detected tears in her voice.

"Hi, honey, is everything OK?"

"Yeah," she whimpered. "You remember that movie I auditioned for?"

"You mean the one about the boat?"

"Uh-huh."

"The one with Kurt Russell?"

"Uh-huh."

"What happened, sweetie?" I feared the worst, negative feedback from the casting director, and/or a total rejection.

"I got it." She started crying.

"Oh, my God!"

"Yeah, and guess where it's gonna shoot? San Juan, Puerto Rico."

"Holy shit! Honey, that's incredible... and you're crying. Why?"

"I don't know." She burst into sobs. "What if I can't..." Turned out she had been hired to play Mary Kay Place and Martin Short's daughter in the movie *Captain Ron*. It was her first big role, and it was in a huge feature film.

"Meadow, of course you can, my darling! Don't you remember all the plays you've done and how hard you worked? You are such a wonderful actress. You're going to be amazing!"

And she was!

CHAPTER FORTY-SEVEN

1994

Old Bad News

CHRISTMAS WAS OVER, AND ANOTHER JOLLY HOLIDAY WAS WINDING down in Louisville at Dad's house. Actually, the family was celebrating that after-Christmas relief—all the build-up, the gift giving, who got what from whom, who said what to whom, what somebody thought they should've gotten from somebody and didn't. The whole ridiculous mess was over and done with.

It was all in the past, and there was nothing anybody could do to change it. Those exciting, but anxious moments were just fodder for shameless teasing.

This was our final celebration of the year before we all dispersed, running off to different corners of the world to resume our real lives. There was lots of yucking it up while Brud, my sister Sharon's nutty husband, did his absolute best to render everyone unable to catch their breath due to laughing at his cornball humor. Brud was smart as a whip, but he was born and raised in Hazard, Kentucky, so he sounded like an ignorant hick, and he'd exaggerate his drawl even more when he was entertaining us. The more we laughed, the more outrageous he got.

Bruno and I had gotten married a couple of years before by a minister friend of his in the small park next to our apartment complex. I was barefoot. It was a simple ceremony with only a few friends, some of Bruno's cousins, Dad, and my brother Jud, and his wife.

Bruno and I managed to get away from our busy life in Burbank to come to Dad's for the holidays. Meadow and Jeremy were both way too busy with friends, important industry holiday parties, and pursuing their acting careers to make it. But the rest of the family was there but for a few exceptions: my sister Sally, and her husband Ackie, lived on their own little compound in the hills of North Carolina and were usually too busy with their thriving vitamin business to join Dad and the rest of us for Christmas. They didn't celebrate any of the traditional holidays anyway.

My brother Scott, and his wife Barbara, were successful artists living in Atlanta. I believe Scott was the most emotionally fragile of all us siblings, at least those of us who were still alive. It seemed to me that Barbara thought our family was detrimental to Scott's mental health. She was probably right, so they rarely came to Dad's house for Christmas, or any other time for that matter. Through the years, though, Scott would occasionally show up unannounced at Mom and Dad's for a few days when the rest of the family was nowhere to be found. But even those visits were few and far between.

But there was never a shortage of bodies during the holidays at Dad's house. Several old family friends had joined us, and Sharon and Brud, and their brood of four, who were all grown up, most of them married and/or had several little ones of their own. That clan lived in Lexington, Kentucky or thereabouts, an hour and a half's drive from Dad's house. They wouldn't dream of missing out on the unpredictable, wild holiday fun with the family.

Then there was my brother Jud, his wife Bobbi, and their four kids, who also had lots of children of their own. They all lived not far from Dad in Louisville and would straggle over whenever it pleased them because they knew it was always a loosey-goosey, disorganized, chaotic mess of a celebration at Dad's place. A set schedule for just about anything was unfamiliar territory for most of my family.

By that time, Dad was soon to turn ninety, and his hearing had gotten pretty bad. Dad hated wearing hearing aids, though, so there was plenty of shouting going on. He was in excellent spirits, as always, and one of his favorite pastimes was having everyone, his kids, grandkids, in-laws, cousins, and friends gathered around his living room during the holidays, while he fell asleep in his favorite chair in the midst all the laughter and chaos. That made him a happy man.

After Mom died, Dad grieved deeply for months. But it wasn't long before several of their widow friends started buzzing around with invitations to dinners, parties, and church functions.

No surprise, really. My dad was sweet as pie, and nobody knew better how to woo a woman old school. Even at the ripe old age of ninety, he could charm the pants off anybody, and did so as often as he could.

Dad died a few years later, but not before plowing his car into his girlfriend Martha's house when he was returning her home after their date one night. No one was hurt in the accident, thank goodness, but Dad was plenty upset and embarrassed by the incident. He'd had both of his hip joints replaced when he was in his seventies, and I believe they didn't quite have the procedure figured out yet. Since the surgery had taken place twenty years earlier, his hips had become stiff, and he couldn't control his legs very well. The big gaping hole Dad's car left in Martha's living room got fixed fairly quickly, and he and Martha continued to date.

Dad met Martha at a church dinner, and he just loved to tell the story.

"Well…" he'd say with a big smile on his face. "When I went to the church, they usually have a big supper most Wednesday nights, you see. And by the time I got there, very few seats were left. A couple of them were next to this beautiful woman." He'd chuckle, and his face would light up every time he got to thinking about Martha and the first time they met.

"Her hair was fixed so pretty," he'd say. "It was dark with little bits of gray in it." He'd tell how he went right up to her. He wasn't too steady on his feet by then and had to walk with a cane in each hand. "So, I said, 'Excuse me, are you saving this seat for your husband?'"

Sometimes, he'd pause and look away, like he was remembering the moment. "She was so lovely dressed in pale pink. She looked like an angel, and smiled the most beautiful smile. 'No,' she said. 'Would you like me to save it for your wife?'" Then he'd laugh to himself. "I said, 'No. But if I may?' Then she said, 'Please, be my guest.' And I sat down next to her and looked into her sweet brown eyes." This was when Dad's voice would get shaky and his green eyes watery. "Then I said, 'I believe this is my lucky day.' And we laughed."

Dad would tell his story whenever anyone was willing to listen.

That was the beginning of my dad's last love affair. My almost ninety-year-old dad and his lovely sixty-five-year-old Martha. He used to say Martha was the best thing that had ever happened to him. I was just glad he was happy and didn't let myself think too much about "the best thing that's ever happened to me" part. Martha made his last few years a joy. In a way, she was an angel.

The after Christmas celebration was well underway. We were partying hard, toasting the upcoming new year, and celebrating the fact that the visit, thus far, had gone almost without a hitch, which was extremely rare. There was not one calamity. No one had to be rushed to the emergency room, or got bent out of shape at some innocent, or not-so-innocent, remark. There were no knock-down drag-outs, and no one even so much as caught a cold. We just behaved ourselves and got along. It was a Christmas miracle! So, we were imbibing perhaps a bit too much of Dad's special single-malt scotch—on the rocks, of course.

"Scotch is my only vice," Dad used to tell people. (He didn't count piling mountains of sugar, salt, and butter or puddles of cream on nearly every bite he put in his mouth.)

Not surprisingly, my sister Sharon's outfit stole the show again. She wore a bright, festive, albeit hideous, red-and-green sweater that had to be two sizes too small and would ride up, exposing her ample belly now and again. The sweater had tiny Christmas trees woven into it with different colored beads and sequins attached, many of which hung by a thread or had fallen off, decorating the carpet in her wake. One of the sleeves had a small hole at the seam that looked like it was only a matter of time before the whole thing unraveled. I figured she'd picked it up at some Goodwill store for fifty cents on her way into town. That was so like my sister. She kept the thrift stores in business.

The atmosphere in the house was electric. The whole place smelled of booze, sweat, and trouble. All of Dad's great-grandkids were flying high, matching the energy in the room. It was a genuine case of contact-buzz, sprinkled with loads of sugar. The little ones ran wildly from room to room in their pajamas or birthday suits squealing, and we adults weren't behaving much better. We were in rare form: booze before noon! Suddenly, there came a loud crash.

All the mothers stood up and screamed, "SHHHH!" Everything went quiet; then chaos ensued. People ran around, bumping into and falling over each other, searching for the scene of the crash. Seconds later came ear-splitting wails, and like a flock of birds, all the parental figures changed direction simultaneously and ran toward the source of the shrieks. Two children lay screaming and writhing on the floor in the back hallway between the bedrooms, and a third was out cold.

Everyone sprang into action, consoling, searching for bandages, cleaning wounds, kissing tears away, and listening to accounts of the accident. Fortunately, there were no concussions, knocked-out teeth, or black eyes. In fact, not one serious injury to speak of, and no one was even to blame. According to reports, little Bobbi was scurrying back from the bathroom, and young Ted was heading in the other direction, both running at top speed when they rounded a corner at the same time, and bam! Three little heads and bodies collided with full force. That was it. The unconscious child was Stevie, a neighbor's boy, who just happened to be in the wrong place at the right time, but he came back to consciousness seconds later with a big, blue knot forming on his forehead and a bellyache. There were plenty of other booboos, cuts to clean up, lumps to ice, and wounded egos. But much hysteria and many kisses later, after baby aspirin had been dispensed and band-aids applied, things died down, and the party resumed at a calmer pace. So much for that Christmas miracle business. The whole episode was a real buzzkill. Eventually, things picked back up, and the room exhaled. Then my niece Tisa, Sharon's oldest daughter and now the mother of three teenagers, came over and plopped down on the carpet next to me.

"Hey," she said. "You remember when Packy got kidnapped?"

"What?" I said with a slight laugh. The room had gotten really loud again with everyone shouting and showing off, so I thought maybe I'd misheard Tisa, or that she was trying to be funny. Not that she would typically begin a conversation like that in jest, disparaging her long- deceased uncle, but we were an out-of-control, rowdy bunch, throwing down Daddy's scotch pretty freely, not to mention it had been a good two-and-a-half decades since Packy's death. So, I thought perhaps Tisa was attempting to construct some sort of twisted joke. I'm just saying it wasn't out of the realm of possibility, knowing my family.

"You know," Tisa said. "I heard he was about nine when it—"

"What the hell are you talking about?" I asked with more anger than I realized.

She stared at me and cocked her head to one side. "Don't you remember? Maybe he was eight. I don't know. And then later, like the next day, Muddy found him tied to a tree." (Muddy was what all the grandchildren called Mom. She didn't want to be called "Grandma" or, God forbid, "Granny," so "Muddy" is what Teddy—her first grandchild—called her, and it stuck.)

"Wait, what?" I shook my head, my mind wrestling with her words. "Tied to a tree?"

Just then, the room broke out in laughter. "I don't know what you're talking about," I yelled over the racket. "Who told you that?" From the look on Tisa's face, I knew she was serious. My head filled with questions. It didn't help that I was sufficiently buzzed. Was it true? Had Packy been kidnapped? If he had, why did Tisa know about it and I didn't? Who else knew?

Terrifying drawings of Packy's popped into my head: evil, deformed faces peering from behind trees in dark shadowy woods. Desperate-looking figures, naked men in chains, struggling. Huge erect penises—I'd discovered the drawings when I was quite young and nobody else was around.

They scared the hell out of me. But I thought the drawings were just more evidence of his mental illness.

My brain stumbled. I hadn't thought much about Packy in decades, but now I pictured a boy bound to a tree, panic-stricken, crying, screaming, his little face drenched with tears and snot, struggling in fear for his life.

I stared at Tisa, my head spinning, stomach churning, afraid I was going to puke. Packy was dead and gone. I'd worked through as much of it as I could and had long since put it to rest. I had moved on despite the thousands of questions that had been left unanswered.

I always knew Packy had problems, but I didn't know much about his life before I entered the scene. A few months after I gave birth to Jeremy, Mom and I had a conversation about when she had Packy. The year was 1930. "I was barely twenty-one," she said. "I had no idea what to do with a newborn. So, I read this book by Dr. Spock. He was the expert back then." I could tell she was uneasy talking about it. She picked at her cuticle the whole time. "Dr. Spock advised new mothers to nurse their babies only three times a day, for breakfast, lunch, and dinner."

"From birth?" I was aghast.

"Yes, from the day they were born."

"Oh, my God, Mom. I nurse Jeremy whenever he wants. Sometimes it's every twenty minutes. That's what they recommend because you know it's not just for sustenance, but also to reassure the child that he is loved and will never be abandoned."

"Yes, I know," she said, looking down at her hands. "Dr. Spock recommended trying to appease the infant by rocking him, or whatever it took other than feeding him, to calm him down. And if he wouldn't stop crying, to just… let him cry it out."

"Oh no. What the hell was wrong with that man? Did Packy cry a lot?"

She nodded. "It broke my heart. Sometimes he'd scream for hours… until he could hardly breathe."

Had the kidnapping really happened? Was that long-buried trauma the catalyst for Packy's undoing? Could it be the missing piece to my brother's tragic story? Who else knew about it?

Packy was the oldest, and my sister Sharon had to have been no more than seven years old, if that, Jud about five, Scott only three, and Sally maybe one. I was sure Mom and Dad would never have traumatized any of them by revealing anything about it at the time.

I felt a hand on my arm. "Reedy?" Tisa said. "Hey, you OK?"

I turned to face her. "Huh? Yeah."

"You never heard about it? You didn't know?" I shook my head.

Just then, Kristen, Tisa's oldest daughter, ran up and said something to her mom that I couldn't hear over the noise. Tisa turned to me, rolled her eyes, made an "oh shit!" face, and off they went. Was that it? I thought. Stunned and confused, I watched them scurry away.

I was in a boozy daze. I looked around, compelled to find out more. Who could I ask? Sharon was Tisa's mom, so she probably knew. Sharon was also Packy's closest sibling.

But at the moment, she was busy being straight-man for her husband. I thought maybe my brother Jud knew about it, but he was in a corner with his family laughing at some inside joke—probably about the rest of us. And Dad was sleeping happily in his chair. This wasn't the time or place, and I was too hammered to get to the bottom of anything, much less a mystery that happened nearly a decade before I was born.

I forced myself to stop thinking about it, promising I'd ask questions later, or the next morning before we all took off. Then I went to the freezer, filled my glass with fresh ice cubes, poured myself another scotch, guzzled a sizable swig, and got reabsorbed in the family jumble.

Later that evening, all the little ones were sprawled out in small sleeping piles on the carpet or draped over laps, and Jud and his clan were getting ready to depart.

I took him aside. "Hey Jud, do you remember anything about when Packy was kidnapped?" He looked at me, puzzled.

"He was young, maybe nine or so?"

Jud shook his head. "What are you talking about?" We stared at each other for a long moment, and I realized it was news to him. Then, a few of the slumbering children started stirring. "Sorry, I've got to go." With that, he turned and grabbed a couple of his grandchildren off the floor, shook his head, and said, "I don't… call me some time."

"Of course. Happy new year!" I whispered.

"Yeah, you too," he said. Then, amid a few tears, grunts, and groans, their family left bearing many droopy children.

The following morning, Bruno and I woke up late. Dad always maintained that good scotch was the only alcoholic beverage that didn't cause him to feel like he'd been hit in the head with a sledgehammer the next morning. He was right, but I did feel a bit raw after all I'd consumed during the previous day. My brain was soggy. I vaguely recalled that I had questions to ask. Someone. About something. I could feel the relevant information bubbling up in my brain at a snail's pace while I made my way out to see who was up, and who had already left.

Dad was sitting at the dining room table finishing his pre-breakfast bowl of fruit: half an orange, a couple of almost-ripe strawberries, and a few chunks of cantaloupe. He firmly believed fruit before breakfast kept his body running like a well-oiled, ninety-something-year-old machine. I sat down at the table. "Morning, Dad," I said loud enough for him to hear me. I yawned. He reached over and squeezed my hand while he finished chewing his juicy bite.

"Good morning, sweetheart," he said.

"Where is everybody?"

He picked up a slice of orange and admired it. "You just missed the last of 'em, sweetie. Lee and her bunch left a few minutes ago. They made so much noise. I'm surprised y'all didn't wake up."

"Damn, I wish we had."

"Oh, I'm sorry, honey. The kids wanted to come into your room, but y'all seemed to be sleeping so soundly I told them not to."

"It's OK, Daddy. Listen, I know it was a long time ago, but do you remember if Packy was kidnapped when he was little?" As soon as the words left my mouth, I could've kicked myself. I felt horrible. What a thing to bring up while he was having his lovely plate of breakfast fruit. I wasn't thinking straight.

He cocked his head and looked at me while he chewed his strawberry. "What's that, honey?"

"I'm sorry. I heard… oh, never mind. You just enjoy your fruit, Daddy. We can talk later." I kissed him on the head. "How about I make you some nice bacon and eggs?"

"Why that would be lovely, honey." A smile lit up his sweet old face.

CHAPTER FORTY-EIGHT

1995

After the Party

IT WAS VERY EARLY ON A SATURDAY MORNING A COUPLE OF DAYS AFTER we flew back home to Burbank from Dad's house. I was still recovering from jetlag—and from Christmas with my family.

Our sweet, little Burbank house was just what the doctor ordered—peaceful, cozy, and devoid of all other humans.

I called Meadow and Jeremy when we returned and shared all the latest family gossip and holiday stories, including the very old news about Packy's kidnapping. Funny thing, Meadow knew about the abduction and was surprised I didn't. Both she and her brother had had a great holiday, and had lots to tell me. Turned out they were enjoying the after-Christmas quiet as well and were laying low to recuperate from too much partying.

In a few days, Bruno was going to pick up his son Christopher, who lived part of the time with his mom, and part of the time with us. Christopher was a dear little eight-year-old, towhead, with his father's good looks. All was well.

Bruno had just left to meet with a client who was planning to remodel his house. Bruno had shut off all the lights on his way out, leaving everything in total darkness. I pulled back the light-blocking curtains of our large bedroom window, leaving only the sheers closed, and stared out at the darkness. I watched the occasional car pass—headlights scanning the black wetness outside. I could hear the pitter-patter. It had been storming all night long, and every little thing was drenched and dripping.

I snuggled down under the covers and heard the heat kick on. My mind wandered back to our festive week in Louisville. Dad snoozing in his favorite chair while all hell broke loose around him. My family had an unusually raucous way of communicating. I remembered the silly banter and the arguments that usually ended with everyone talking at once, in an attempt to soothe hurt feelings. The memories warmed my heart, and I chuckled as I drifted in and out of sleep.

Next thing I knew, the sun woke me peeking through the giant California pepper tree in our front yard. Thankfully, I had nothing to do the entire day, so I just lay there and watched the wind wreak havoc on the huge, old tree—its heavy, water-laden branches swaying, shaking, and splashing everything underneath. It had been predicted to be an unseasonably cold, rainy winter for Los Angeles (meaning January and February), and I couldn't have been happier.

When the showers finally let up, I took a walk around our soggy, little town. I had to wear my waterproof boots, warm raincoat, and the maroon cap and matching scarf my cousin Donna knitted for me for Christmas.

Most years, more often than not, less than a month after the holidays—or springtime as we Angelinos called it—the sun would come out to stay, the temperature would rise, flowers would appear everywhere, and the heavenly scent of orange blossoms would fill the air. Not so this year. We were having real weather—an actual winter.

When I walked out into the chilly dampness, I caught my breath and pulled my hat down over my ears. I strolled out into the beautiful, dark day, as happy memories of our holiday trip ebbed and flowed through my mind.

I giggled to myself while I splashed through puddles and inhaled the sweet, clean air.

Then I remembered Tisa asking me what I knew about Packy's kidnapping. I wondered if I was the only one in the family who didn't know.

I had asked Jud if he knew about the abduction, while he was quietly leaving Dad's at the crack of dawn, laden with several sleeping grandchildren. And he said no. So, I decided I had some phone calls to make when I got home.

As soon as I walked in the door, I grabbed the phone and dialed Dad. He was ninety at the time, and I wondered what the odds were that he'd remember anything from that far back.

"Hello?"

"Hi, Daddy."

"Hi, sweetheart! How's my girl?" We chatted a while, caught up on how our flight home was, how the kids were doing and the weather and such. Then I asked him if it was a good time to talk. "Of course, honey, just finished my lunch. What ya wanna talk about?"

"You know, Daddy, the day before everybody left the house, Tisa asked me what I knew about when Packy got kidnapped when he was a kid. You remember that?"

"Hmm, gosh, honey… Packy was kidnapped?" He was quiet for a minute. "Can't say as I do. I forgot a lot of things…and that was a long time ago. Memory's not what it used to be. Hmm, I recall something major happened to one of you kids… can't remember which one or what it was, though."

So, I thanked him again for a wonderful Christmas, told him how much I loved him, and hung up. My next victim was Sharon. Sharon was fifteen years older than me and no spring chicken either.

After many rings, my sister picked up. "Hello?"

"Hi, Sharon, how're you doing?"

"Hey, baby sister, I'm doing just fine! Y'all make it back to California OK?"

"Yep, we did. Listen, Tisa told me something that happened a long time ago and I didn't get a chance to ask you about it when we were at Dad's. She said that Packy got kidnapped when he was about nine years old. Did you tell her—"

"What? Packy got kidnapped?"

"Yeah, that's what she said."

"Really? Tisa said Packy was kidnapped? Who told her that?"

"Don't know, thought maybe you did."

"Well, I never…"

"Yeah, then, supposedly, Mom found him tied to a tree."

"He was tied to a tree?"

"Supposedly."

"Who told you that?"

"Tisa… your daughter."

"Where'd she hear it?"

"I don't know. That's what I'm trying… oh, never mind. So, how's the weather in Lexington?" Clearly, Sharon hadn't heard, or didn't remember anything, and before our conversation turned into a "who's on first" comedy routine, I changed the subject. We chatted for a while longer. Then I said I had to go and that I'd call her back later.

Next, I called my brother Scott, but got his answering machine. So, I left a sweet "Hi, Scott, missed y'all at Christmas!" message and hung up.

Then I called my other sister, my last shot; I was running out of siblings.

Sally picked up. "Hello?"

"Hey, sweetie!"

"Hi! Are ya home?" Sally and I had become very close even though we lived a country apart. We talked on the phone often, and our calls usually lasted at least an hour, maybe two. But this time, the Packy kidnapping mystery had been gnawing at me. So, I jumped right to it.

"Yeah, we made it home. Hey, I wanted to ask you, do you know anything about Packy being kidnapped when he was a kid?"

"Um… yeah. I mean, it's not much, but…"

"Well, Tisa asked me about it in the middle of the craziness at Dad's, and I just talked to Sharon, and she never heard about it. And Jud hadn't either. What'd you hear?"

"Well, God, it was a long time ago. I was home from college for a few days and overheard Mom on the phone… she was pretty upset, must've been talking to Packy's psychiatrist at Central State because she said something like, 'a homosexual? Oh, God!' Then after a pause, she said, 'No, but he was kidnapped when he was just a boy, and I found him tied to a tree. Maybe that's why!' And that's all I heard."

We talked for a while longer, I told her about some of the holiday shenanigans that went on at Dad's and that she was missed, and we hung up. There it was. More than likely, that was all I was ever going to be able to find out about it. But somehow, it felt OK not knowing definitively if it really happened. It was going to have to remain another one of life's mysteries.

So, I rolled up some newspaper, put it in the fireplace with kindling and logs on top, lit a fire, and watched the flames slowly grow. I decided not to turn on any lights because the green fog that had enveloped the house created a dark gloom that suited my mood. I draped a cozy throw over my lap and listened to the rain pounding on the roof.

Looking back, I tried to bring up happy images of Packy when he still lived in our house. I remembered some of our fights, like the times he came in my room uninvited and wreaked havoc with my schoolwork, or teased me unmercifully until I was furious and fought back. Then I had a thought. Maybe those times made me strong, put fire in my belly.

I decided to let the shadowy images of my brother fade. Then I recalled my thirteenth birthday party when Packy thrilled my friends with his snake present and acted like he and I were in cahoots and had planned the whole show just for them. I pictured his smiling face and thought about the times we laughed together.

I chased away images of him falling from the water tower and stared into the fire. Suddenly, all those stories of people having near-death experiences popped into my mind. Maybe that's what really happens, I thought. Maybe Packy was met with a glowing white light when he hit the ground—no more pain, no more struggle, only beloved friends and family with welcoming outstretched arms. Or maybe he was born into a brand-new body. Those were possibilities I could live with. I pictured him happy. It warmed my heart.

I watched the flames dance in the fireplace and realized that I was no longer a pile of broken pieces—just a whole, happy woman.

THE END

ACKNOWLEDGEMENTS

Thank you to Meadow and Jeremy, my amazing children. Without you, I would've had—a lot more freedom, but very little depth. You both were, are and will always be the lights of my life.

Thanks to my family, every wacky one of you. Especially to Sally Moss, my dear sister, who died way too young—exposing once again her fierce courage. (My heart still hurts). Thank you for your wise guidance and showing me a way out of the toughest pickles I got myself into.

A big thank you to Bruno, my husband, without your love, support, and encouragement, not to mention tolerance, I'm not sure if I would have had it in me to complete this book.

Another huge Thank You to Jack Grapes, my brilliant teacher and mentor, whose wild techniques released the writer in me. Thanks to you I discovered my voice!

Also, many thanks to Adrian Bloom, my excellent editor, to my good friend Anna Ruuska, who proofread my manuscript just because she wanted to! And to my dear friends who suffered through chapter after chapter, providing me with 'fresh eyes,' so I could have valuable feedback; Susan Foster, (an amazing writer!), Jocelyn Coblenz, and Dalia Acalinas, just to name a few.

And thanks to my wonderful team at Paper Raven Books for their hard work and for taking care of all the technical aspects of freeing my life stories, sending them out into the world, and for guiding me through the 'social media' stuff—which was all Greek to me.